a sense of regard

a sense of regard

Essays on Poetry and Race

EDITED BY LAURA McCULLOUGH

The University of Georgia Press ⌣ Athens and London

© 2015 by the University of Georgia Press
Athens, Georgia 30602
www.ugapress.org
All rights reserved
Designed by Melissa Bugbee Buchanan
Set in Adobe Garamond Pro by Graphic Composition, Inc., Bogart, Georgia.
Printed and bound by Sheridan Books, Inc.

The paper in this book meets the guidelines for
permanence and durability of the Committee on
Production Guidelines for Book Longevity of the
Council on Library Resources.

Most University of Georgia Press titles are
available from popular e-book vendors.

Printed in the United States of America
19 18 17 16 15 P 5 4 3 2 1

Library of Congress Cataloging-in-Publication Data
A sense of regard : essays on poetry and race / edited by Laura McCullough.
    pages cm
    Summary: "McCullough has collected the voices of living poets and scholars in
thoughtful and considered exfoliation of the confluence of poetry and race in our time:
the difficulties, the nuances, the unexamined, the feared, the questions, and the quarrels
across aesthetic camps and biases. The book brings together essays by a range of writers and
academics whose work varies in style from personal accounts and lyrical essays to challenging
criticisms. McCullough believes this approach allows for more avenues and angles of
exploration on this complex topic. She has also strived to be as inclusive as possible, to reach
past the black/white perception of race and offer essays from numerous racial backgrounds.
The anthology covers many issues that cross racial and ethnic borders and is divided into
sections based on these issues: Americanism, the experience of unsilencing and crossing
borders, interrogating whiteness, and language itself"— Provided by publisher.
    Includes bibliographical references.
    ISBN 978-0-8203-4732-5 (hardback) — ISBN 978-0-8203-4761-5 (paperback)
    1. American poetry—History and criticism. 2. Poetry—Social aspects—United States.
3. Race relations in literature. 4. Race in literature. I. McCullough, Laura, 1960– editor.
PS310.R34S46 2015
811.009'355—dc23

                                                                        2014019831

British Library Cataloging-in-Publication Data available

contents

acknowledgments

I would like to thank the poets R. Dwayne Betts and Leslie McGrath for their many hours of discussion and e-mailing during the early stages of this project. Their thinking affected mine enormously. Thank you to Michael Broek for his unflagging support.

A number of essays in this volume were first published, in slightly different form, in the following journals and magazines:

Garrett Hongo's "America Singing: An Address to the Newly Arrived Peoples" first appeared in *Parnassus* and was reprinted in *Fourteen Hills*.

Ken Chen's "Walt and I: What's American about American Poetry?" first appeared at *Poetry Society of America*.

Jason Schneiderman's "Inaugural Poems and American Hope" is adapted from an essay that first appeared in *American Poetry Review*.

Camille T. Dungy's "I Am Not a Man" is adapted from an essay that first appeared in *Painted Bride Quarterly*.

Major Jackson's "A Mystifying Silence" appeared in *American Poetry Review*.

Martha Collins's "Writing White" appeared in *American Poetry Review*.

Jaswinder Bolina's "Writing like a White Guy" appeared at *Poetry Foundation*.

Kazim Ali's "What's American about American Poetry" first appeared at *Poetry Society of America*.

Rafael Campo's "What It Means to Be an American Poet" first appeared at *Poetry Society of America*.

Tony Hoagland's "No Laughing Matter: Race, Poetry, and Humor" appeared in *American Poetry Review*.

a sense of regard

introduction

LAURA MCCULLOUGH

A poet once said to me that what she wanted from a good poem was that it move her *from one sense of regard to another*. In these essays about poetry and race, while some are more heavily about one or the other and some bring in complicating factors and concerns, it seems to me that they are all about *regard*, and that the denotations and connotations of that word—to observe, give attention to, think about, have feelings for, hold in esteem, be moved by—speak to the multiplicities of this project. Certainly I was looking to embrace mystery as opposed to mystification. I was also looking to be inclusive of both working poets and scholars, of writers with differing aesthetics as well as differing racial and ethnic identities and ideas about race and ethnicity, while according consideration to other identity markers with normative or marginalizing potential, such as gender, sexuality, religion, age, and bodily status.

This anthology is an effort to collect the voices of living poets and scholars in thoughtful and considered exfoliation of the current confluence of poetry and race, the difficulties, the nuances, the unexamined, the feared, the questions, and the quarrels across aesthetic camps and biases, and with a broad scope regarding the idea of race itself. While not all of the aspects of intersectionality are germane here, the idea that constructed categories of the human condition intersect, bleed and feed into each other, shift in dominance, and are differently privileged (even within groups) is at the core, and this project is in itself an intersectional and hybrid document in that it attempts to bring together contrasting views by people within and across many categories without judging the primacy of their categories. Rather, this project seeks to honor the complexities, especially when borders seem to be permeable, porous, crossed and recrossed, of each contributor's lived experience alongside the intellectual exfoliations of other contributors. Somewhere in the nexus of what we live and what we think, this project took hold, the idea being to query, to quarrel, and to consider.

Edward W. Said, cultural critic and literary theorist noted for his work in postcolonial thought, wrote:

> No one today is purely one thing. Labels like Indian, or woman, or Muslim, or American are not more than starting-points, which if followed into actual experience for only a moment are quickly left behind. Imperialism consolidated the mixture of cultures and identities on a global scale. But its worst and most paradoxical gift was to allow people to believe that they were only, mainly, exclusively, white, or Black, or Western, or Oriental. Yet just as human beings make their own history, they also make their cultures and ethnic identities. No one can deny the persisting continuities of long traditions, sustained habitations, national languages, and cultural geographies, but there seems no reason except fear and prejudice to keep insisting on their separation and distinctiveness, as if that was all human life was about. Survival in fact is about the connections between things. (1994, 406)

Said's sensitivity to Otherness, the multiplicity of its origins and shifting mutabilities as imperialism as a concept changes and can be applied in different ways, indeed the way it might even be applied to the arts, is useful in finding a way to enter the essays that make up this anthology. He wrote that

> hybrid counter-energies, at work in many fields, individuals, and moments provide a community or collective made up of numerous anti-systemics [that offers] hints and practices for collective human existence (and neither doctrines nor complete theories) that is not based on coercion or domination . . . [leading to] mixed genres, unexpected combinations of tradition and novelty, political experiences based on communities of effort and interpretation . . . rather than classes or corporations of possession, appropriation, and power. (406)

The essays collected here illustrate Said's words in that they are often hybrid in form, and certainly hybrid in representing individual thinking, often trying to refract something out of the personal, historical, and aesthetic condition, oppression, or legacies of the writer. In confluence, this anthology is a hybrid of lyric and scholarly approaches to rendering the query, the quarrel, and the consideration in efforts toward making what these writers discovered become a *knowing* and in their curation and arrangement a larger body of *knowing* that could be entered into and engaged by many kinds of readers.

The act of writing these essays, by poets, poet-scholars, and scholars, necessitated a close examination process, but they are not meant to be definitive. In fact, Said is again helpful in preparing to read them. He wrote that "it is more rewarding—and more difficult—to think concretely and sympathetically, contrapuntally, about others than only about 'us'" (407). His intent here is a contrapuntal strategy for reading literature by holding more than one idea in the mind, very much as intersectionality might suggest, so that we read with multiple perspectives being, again, queried, quarreled with, and considered. Said's original concern was regarding the colonized and the colonizer, but this is a foundational concept upon which to consider the multiple aspects of identity that will be explored in these essays, as well as their limitations, the possibility that they can be used as another kind of oppressive and alienating factor, and, too, the ways in which, taken together, they help to shape a view of the human condition that may not be fully apprehended through any one lens.

Authenticity and respect are two of the foundational components of this project. This does not mean that difficult subject matter is avoided, but it does mean that I challenged contributors to examine their own biases and to quarrel, first, with themselves, digging deeply into what they have experienced and know. Poets were asked to write essays the way they would write poems, to know something afterward that they themselves didn't know going in. Scholars were asked to write not only for academics but for a broader audience of readers and writers of poetry.

The contents range from lyric essays by poets who mine their own experience to serious analysis of poets who perhaps have not yet received the critical attention that they warrant. Other essays take on matters of debate and political concerns, while others focus more on aesthetics or try to locate race in a web of complexities, and this enriches a larger, but controlled and composed, dialogue about the moment in time and poetics we are in with respect to both poetry and race.

Given that both of these lenses, poetry and race, are mutable and hard to define, the collusion of the two creates a kind of *terra nullius*—a term that is Latin for "land belonging to no one" and has come to mean, in international law, land that is not specifically governed by any one nation, though it may sometimes be "occupied." And given the often incendiary nature of debates about poetics and race, the Balkanization of aesthetic camps as well as identity-based groups, this project was not about "occupation" so much as about trying to create a neutral territory wherein writers of varying class, race, ethnicity, sometimes origin outside of the United States, but certainly often ancestral lineage of many cultures and countries, and from different aesthetic training or schools of critical thought, could give voice to thoughtful and mindful and sometimes soulful concerns.

This anthology seeks to move into this unowned territory with a sense, not of the dignity of the parts, but of a respect for the hybrid and intersecting nature of the project. Many of the writers take risks here as they attempt a new kind of engagement with the core concerns of the project and the many questions it sparks: How does one tease out race? Deal with real and perceived issues of trauma? Exfoliate the overlapping borders of multiple identities (of race and also of aesthetics)? Explore and embrace hyphenation (of artistic, biological, cultural, political identities)?

This is not meant to be exhaustive, but a new engagement that embraces multiple perspectives and, hybrid in itself, will be a powerful and provocative artifact that allows the nuances of those artistic, biological, cultural, political identities and experiences, the roots of both thinking and creating within the contributors to come into relief. These are complicated concerns taken on with great delicacy, vulnerability, and considerable intellectual power, but neither singly nor in the aggregate do they become definitive. Rather, they raise questions. This is a primer, a safe starting place for discussions that are rarely had and, when they are, have often led to breakdown in communication. The truth is that it is both hard to *be* the Other and hard to *hear* the Other, and confronting this paradox leads to another one: *we are all the Other*, an idea Said's work suggests is a key not only to the future of literary theory but to the future of humanity.

With that in mind, I did not set out to gather a manifesto, but to allow for an Introduction to Otherness, in the layered and fraught zones of poetry and race, and to ask questions. Does poetry need to reflect to us something of ourselves? What about when it doesn't? Does it engender empathy? Is empathy the same as compassion? Do we see ourselves in the eyes of the Other, and can we establish the value of Otherness by the Other, and examine our relationship to the very concept of the Other? Does a poet need to represent an identity group, and what happens when the poet confounds expectations about that group or, even more interestingly, *of* that group? These questions and more are not so much answered as they are articulated across these essays and in the organization of them into four units.

The anthology is divided into four sections. The first, "Racialization & Reimagination: Whitman & the New Americans," includes essays that address either directly or slantwise issues about Americanism. Race, racialization, poetic as well as political legacies are unpacked, and this opening section speaks to and manifests both hybridity and intersectionality. These contributors raise questions. They consider. They risk. They even confess. All of them include a sense of wonder and, whether directly or indirectly, evoke perhaps the most important legacy of the American poetic icon Walt Whitman.

In the essays in the second section, "The Unsayable & the Subversive," the poets and scholars write about the experience of *unsilencing* or about writers or concerns that seem to cross borders, those categories that intersectionality tries to illumine while recognizing the critical nature of the intersections themselves. What happens in the interstices? Why is one category more valued than another, and indeed what occurs when someone does something outside an applied category? What are the risks? What are, possibly, the rewards of crossing or confounding borders?

The third section circles around or in some cases directly interrogates the racial category of *whiteness*. What it means, what it excludes, what the borders are, the legacies, the privileges, the limitations and oppressions of and by. So, too, does it enter the peculiarly American tension between black and white histories and aesthetics. "Imperialism & Experiments: Comedy, Confession, Collage, Conscience" includes essays that all pry open doors that seem closed, and the hinges are creaky indeed.

The final section, "Self as Center: Sonics, Code Switching, Culture, Clarity," most directly confronts language in the intersection of poetry and race, and the ways in which language is both a part of identity categories and the tool with which we render poetics. The essays in this section are very concerned with architectures of sound and culture, of race and the literary community, of poetry and being a poet in a racialized world.

The groupings in the anthology are meant to generate topics for discussion, to raise questions, to decenter and destabilize, to provoke, and maybe *to move*. By its nature, civil discourse requires participants willing to speak in good faith, but it also requires participant listeners who can hear positions that they may disagree with, to, as Said exhorts, read contrapuntally. To know what it means to be human requires not only perceiving the Other but confronting the nature of our own Otherness as revealed through "them." Who is, intersectionality suggests, *us* and *them* when so many categories of being intersect, cross, and connect?

The contributors to *A Sense of Regard: Essays on Poetry and Race* invite us to listen in as they try to speak what they know, discover what they didn't, and in the process often find something out about themselves. They invite us to be moved from one sense of regard to another. What that might be will depend on each of us. They invite us to be provoked and to linger in that state, to see what it reveals to us, to talk to others about it, to ask questions of each other. To query, quarrel, and consider. The larger story lies in the interstices.

BIBLIOGRAPHY

Said, Edward W. 1993. *Culture and Imperialism*. New York: Knopf.

I. RACIALIZATION & REIMAGINATION

Whitman & the New Americans

The essays in this opening section illustrate the contrapuntal in that they embrace hybridity, of thought, of race, of aesthetics in the forms within and the perspectives out of which they are written, and, to, in confluence with each other. Garrett Hongo's "America Singing: An Address to the Newly Arrived Peoples" evokes Walt Whitman and imagines a new polyphony out of the American optimism. Following and complicating the Hongo essay, Sara Marie Ortiz in "Song" explores difficulties and mutabilities in First People's poetics and bravely queries herself within those discussions. In "Finding Family with Native American Women Poets," race and gender collide as Ravi Shankar explores the intersections of what seem to be separate worlds, beginning with the question "You a red or a brown?" Ken Chen's performance piece/essay "Walt and I: What's American about American Poetry?" begins and ends with the speaker "hanging out" with Whitman and "dreams" its way though an exploration of multiple identity issues. Jason Schneiderman in "Inaugural Poems and American Hope" examines a number of ceremonial poems written for and/or performed at American presidential inaugurations and considers their implications about race. In "Refusal of the Mask in Claudia Rankine's Post-9/11 Poetics," Joanna Penn Cooper "unmasks" stylistic and racial confluences in the Jamaican American poet. This section closes with the ways gender, race, and poetry sidle next to each other in Camille T. Dungy's introspective "I Am Not a Man."

I ∼ america singing

An Address to the Newly Arrived Peoples

GARRETT HONGO

Maybe you've seen the sign
On old Sepulveda. *Tai Song,*
Cantonese Cuisine, on your way
to or from the L.A. airport.
 Greg Pape

I've never been in Peking, or in the Summer Palace,
nor stood on the Great Stone Boat to watch
the rain begin on Kuen Ming Lake, the picnickers
running away in the grass.

But I love to hear it sung.
 Li-Young Lee

I hear America singing, the varied carols I hear.
 Walt Whitman

I am fascinated and thrilled that there has been such a surge of new immigration from across the Pacific these past few years. That, as a country, we are again in the process of being renewed and reformed by the new Americans from Asia and elsewhere. These newly arrived peoples, I know, come not so much from Japan and Okinawa and Guangdong, as did the ancestors of us third- and fourth-generation Asian Americans, but rather they are now coming, in increasing numbers, from Taiwan, Hong Kong, Korea, Southeast Asia, Tonga, Fiji, Samoa, the Caribbean, Central America, and the Philippines. Their presence has charged our society with energy and change.

When I visit California now and walk about in the resurgent downtowns of San Jose and Santa Ana, I pass Vietnamese markets, Korean grocery stores, and restaurants for every kind of Pacific/Asian cuisine. When I was teaching at the University of Houston in 1988, I did most of my shopping in a huge supermarket run by Chinese for almost every Asian ethnicity. There was a Korean section, a section for Japanese foods (napa cabbage, daikon, kamaboko fish cakes, and Kal-pis in the coolers), and racks and racks of Chinese condiments like chili oil and oyster and plum sauces. I saw what I've always loved seeing—bins full of bean threads, bags of sesame seeds in various grades, cellophaned flats of dried seaweed, cans of black beans and bamboo shoots, fifty-pound bags of rice. The smells were gorgeous. The market was in its own little complex of shops, a big parking lot ringed with little storefronts for a travel agency, an optometrist, a records and tapes store, a bookstore, a coffee and dim sum shop, a casual restaurant, and a movie theater that showed chop-sockie Saturday matinees, mildly lurid cheongsam romances on weekend nights, and serials all week long.

I was taken there by one of my master's students, Edmund Chang, a graduate of Tufts in Boston, who was born in Taiwan, had grown up in Malta and Libya, went to high school in New Jersey, and had just become an American citizen the year before. He wanted to show me where to buy rice. We went with my small sons, themselves half Asian, who loved the sweet rice candies but wrinkled their noses at the carded yellow circles of sliced, seal-wrapped octopus hanging on hooks near the check stand. And me, I loved the goddamn place. I loved the feeling of the throng of new peoples swirling around me. I loved the feeling that I was in a vortex of cultures, a new republic of exchange—the thrilled New Americans around me. I heard a new chorus. It was America singing.

Before leaving Houston in 1989, I decided to get my car detailed. I didn't know if I was going to sell it or drive it to the West Coast where I was to take a new job. I took it to a detail shop I'd noticed while driving by one day. The guy there was a young hotshot, a sassy white dude who could do everything—I knew it and he knew I knew it. I liked him. He had Benzes, Beamers, even a Maserati in his shop. There was a Volvo being vacuumed and shined up when I drove in. He gave me a guarantee and a good price. This was the place to get the job done right, I thought.

We made the deal and I handed him my keys. He leaned out of the little waiting room and yelled over to one of his employees inside the garage, who was busy shammying down a slick black Riviera. "Juan-o!" he said, an inside joke between the two of them. Juan was a handsome Native American–looking guy with thick black hair who was to drive me home in the shop car. He and I climbed into a Jeep Cherokee, freshly shined and, inside, its plastic wiped down with Armor All. We rode together in silence for a while. Then, when I'd stood about as much of it as I could, I struck up a conversation.

"Where are you from?" I asked. His hair was jet black, his skin rich and brown like stained Hawaiian koa wood. He held himself stiffly and shifted gears with precision. He had the posture and build of a Navajo, I thought.

"El Salvador," he said, and turned his face to show me his grin.

"Oh," I said, surprised. In an instant I felt annoyed with myself for being nosy. But I was curious, too. "Are you here to save your life?" I said.

He told me, "Yes, mine and my mother's, my wife's, my children's. We all come." There was a silence again as we moved through traffic into the little university village near where I lived. I wanted to give him something.

"Do you know the phrase," I said, "*el pueblo unído, jamás será vencido*?" I learned it from my Chilean friends who had fled the murders after the coup of General Pinochet. It means "The people, united, will never be defeated" and was a slogan used to rally the various splinter groups of the Latin American left into a unified coalition. Hundreds of thousands chanted this as they marched in demonstrations through the streets of Santiago in support of the democracy of Salvador Allende, the doctor and socialist who was the elected president of Chile and who was deposed and murdered by his own military and, it is frequently said, with some assistance from our CIA.

This Salvadoran man next to me turned and grinned again. "Yes, sir. I know this saying. It is full of heart. We in El Salvador say it too, though we die for it."

What unsettled me was his modesty, his resolve. Riding through Houston in that car, we were both humbled by the histories we carried and invoked.

Some folks—a lot of white Americans who fear people like us, who fear the oncoming change as weak, inner-reef swimmers fear the largest swells at sea beyond the reef—look to our renewed cities with anger and pessimism, consider them now terra incognita, lands where monsters dwell and where they are no longer safe or welcome. Many of the people I talk with in so-called educated circles feel that the inner cities, the ghettos, are a demilitarized zone, an unknown, an X or Mysterious Island where others belong but not them, not the real Americans.

I remember a time—it was some years ago, in '82 or so—I invited another poet out to lunch. He was older than me by perhaps a generation, a teacher of mine in a way, one who was part of the 1960s shift away from formal verse toward freer, more popularly accessible forms. I revered him a little and wanted to be his friend. He'd just moved to the suburbs east of Los Angeles, had a new job teaching at a private college there, and, as one who had grown up very eastern in Philadelphia, was missing cities and their splendors. I called him up and offered to show him L.A.'s Chinatown, take him for dim sum at the Jade Gardens, my current favorite, and then to an afternoon movie downtown. We made the date and met at some designated corner of the city that weekend.

Dim sum started out fine. He marveled at the variety, at the tastes, at the throng of Asians all around us at round tables, the dozen or so carts like street vendors making their way around the huge upstairs hall of the restaurant. He said, "Oh, this is wonderful. Oh, this is better than Philly. Oh, how has the world kept this secret from me?" He went on to tell me about how he had met Ezra Pound, the great and politically strange poet of high modernism. He told me about the revolution against formal metrics during the sixties and the wave of interest in open forms, primitive and international poetries, and social justice. He might have joined the black and white Freedom Riders who rode together on the buses to integrate the South, but he was too young then, he said.

Yet there were things about him that were enormously troubling. At the same time as I enjoyed his stories of his apprenticeship in the afterglow of modernism, the generous accounts of his time scuffling up the literary ladder and finding his rung on it, I was disturbed by his other anecdotes, his ample score for other poets of his generation, and his complaints. He talked incessantly about a rival, another poet he'd once been close to but with whom he'd had a severe falling-out. He spent an entire course of dim sum bashing the other man's reputation and debunking his political theories, ridiculing his rival's lack of skill at "true" poetry—that which was metric and lovely and free of politics. As an ephebe in the art, it was hard for me to listen; both men were genuine heroes to me. He then recanted much of his own work at midcareer, work done during the sixties when the two poets had been friends, calling his own poetry of that time—the poetry that I admired so much and that had inspired me to seek him out—"sentimental, misguided and stupid—another man's poems." I poured tea for him in a small porcelain cup decorated with dragons, and he leaned toward me and said, "I didn't know what I was doing.

I was on dope all the time and chasing girls and nirvana. I thought life was a circus, and I wasn't serious."

After lunch we rode a bus to a downtown theater: the old Orpheum, a once-lavish Fox palace gone the route of decay and semi-abandonment. Yet it was open, showing a Richard Pryor comedy for the four o'clock matinee. We went. My friend marveled at the ornate appointments and plush chairs inside. He reminisced about his childhood in Philly. He laughed uproariously at the jokes, the sight gags, the crazy, convoluted plot that ended in a long chase scene. I relaxed and hoped the bitterness in him had been dispersed by our good time. We left the place euphoric and, junior that I was, I was pleased I'd pleased him.

Outside, the city had turned dark. The sidewalks, moderately trafficked when we entered, were now thronged with Friday-night cruisers, crowds of the poor and hustling. Buses and dirty cars jammed the streets. We heard rap music from a huge stereo boombox a passerby shouldered like a cargo sack as he sauntered before us. Like the calliope music of a carousel that thrashes tide-like together with a Ferris wheel's countersongs and squeals from its riders, we heard disco pouring from the electronics store next door mingling with the car horns of traffic noise and hubbub from the passing crowd. A hawker in a red tuxedo and frilly dress shirt announced in Spanish that a ticket dance was fixing to start in the basement room below the movie theater. The New Americans surrounded us—Jamaicans in shiny polyester disco shirts, Cubanos and Puerto Ricans, Salvadorans, blacks from Watts and Compton and Inglewood, Chicanos from Whittier and East L.A. They were a processional of penitentes. The feeling was grand and powerful and strong. I felt the beat and wanted to dance.

My friend was terified. He panicked, running out to the street and hailing down a bus, making it stop, banging on the pneumatic door until the driver hissed it open to let him in. He stared blankly for a moment and then recoiled at all the Asian, black, and Hispanic passengers' faces. He fell backward from the bus and fled back to me, shouting. He pushed past me and ran for the street corner, where he may have seen a taxi cruise by.

I let him go. He had refuted all that I had loved about him. I recognized, finally, that he suffered from that Lethe-like, irrational wish—in poetry and in his concept of civilization—for an unblemished purity that can only be accomplished in death, that lavish extinguishment of desire and differences. There was in him a tremendous fear that may have begun, innocently, as mild cultural disdain, a kind of antipathy-budding-into-intolerance, which had eventually metastasized into a powerful Kurtz-like horror of those of us who come from struggle in the Heart of Darkness and want to help shape and belong to the New America. The general term is racism. And it grows strangely.

I remember one of my professors in graduate school—a place I still refer to as Apartheid Tech—sidling up to me at an afternoon reception and jostling me in a friendly way. I turned and he was beaming a little, clearly drunk from sampling the ample supply of chardonnay (though we were a state school, there was always money for such things). "Hey, Hahngo," he said, punching my shoulder, chummily macho. The happy people in the room around were oblivious, abuzz with their own excited chatter, our mentors in sensible shoes and tweeds mixing with graduate students. I overheard someone pontificating on the lyrics to John Lennon's tunes, comparing them to Spenser's *Amoretti*.

"Hey, Hahngo," the professor said again. "I hear you've got an interest in gook lit." I felt the skin on my face freeze. I was stunned. I couldn't tell what he meant. "You know, that minority stuff," he continued. "I'm glad there's finally someone around here to cover it"—he gestured with his plastic wineglass to the universe—"to fend off the Mongol hordes." He clapped me on the shoulder, turned away, and ambled over to the tray of cheeses and grapes. The room with its plate glass windows opening to a view of California eucalyptus and blooming jacarandas gyred around me as if my place in it were the mirrors of a circus carousel. I was fixed to the earth, speechless. And sickened.

I look upon the newly arrived peoples—Hispanics, Caribs, Asians and Pacific Islanders, refugees and refuseniks from Europe, our new inhabitants of the inner cities, a new middle class renovating and swelling the suburban satellites around our cities, our new workers in the farm belts—with great hope and expectation. I know they are what my father was when he arrived in Los Angeles from Hawai'i thirty years ago. I know they are what my great-grandfathers were when they arrived, tanned and thinned by seasickness and lousy food, crossing over the long gangplank of the Immigration Station at Honolulu Bay more than a hundred years ago. My grandfathers were the immigrant poor who were rich in hope and expectation. They would give their bodies and their spirits to make a place for their children in this new land. They would give us their singing, a small legacy of pain and sacrifice, and they would give us some of their courage.

I rode from the Upper East Side of Manhattan once, leaving early for a plane back to Hawai'i or Houston or Missouri or wherever it was I was teaching or fleeing from teaching that year. My driver, a guy I simply hailed down as I stood on the street corner in front of my hotel that morning, turned out to be an elderly man from Greece. Other times the man was from Russia or Jamaica or Korea or Romania. They each had a story. I glanced at the identification shield hanging from the visor over the passenger's seat in front, and I noticed his was a long, lavish name like Popoladopolous. "Mr. Popoladopolous," I began, "I am guessing you are Greek. Can you guess where I am from?" It is one of my favorite games when I travel. The night clerk from Poland stationed at the front desk of my hotel guessed Singapore. The Egyptian cardiac surgeon who wanted to buy my freshly detailed car in Houston guessed China or Taiwan.

"You are right," my Greek driver said. "But you have the advantage over me—you know my name."

"I am Hohngo," I said, giving it the Japanese pronunciation, as I would back home in Hawai'i. On the mainland, in "America," I give in and pronounce it "Hahngo," attuning myself to the dominant accent that calls my senator Daniel Inouye, officially, "Inui."

"Oh," Popoladopolous said, "you are a complicated man. You are an American from California or Los Angeles, and you are Oriental. Your father maybe came from Japan?"

"Very good," I said. "You are almost perfectly right. I am from Hawai'i, and yes, my great-grandfather came from Japan."

The traffic was intense. We ran into the infamous Manhattan gridlock as we headed toward the East River and one of the bridges. I asked what he was doing in America. He told me he had been an attorney in Greece, a prominent man of his city, with a family—a wife and several daughters. Then the Colonels took over. "Do you know the Colonels?" he asked me.

I knew that there had been the terrible conflict between the different factions in Greece. The Costa-Gavras film *Z* is about that. The books *When a Tree Sings* and *Eleni* by my friends Stratis Haviaras and Nicholas Gage tell both sides of a tough story. I remembered the headlines about Greece when I was a teenager in Los Angeles, the exile of the king, the military dictatorship, and the protest of the oppression by film star Melina Mercouri. I thought of the poet Yannis Ritsos and how he had lived so long in exile. "Yes," I said, "I know the Colonels."

"I was an attorney in Greece, in Athens—a dirty but beautiful city. I was a leader and supported the wrong side. I came to America. I brought my family.

My daughter, she is grown now, and she is next week taking the New York bar examination. She will be a lawyer as well. Here, let me show you. Come with me."

Popoladopolous jumped out of the taxi and motioned for me to do the same. The traffic was still locked around us. He went to the back and lifted the battered trunk lid. There were clothes, books, a loose-leaf binder. He grabbed a small parcel. Inside were photographs and a certificate.

"See?" he said, pointing and holding up a snapshot. "Here is my daughter in red and my nieces and myself in back." I saw buxom young women in party dresses and heavy makeup and Mr. Popoladopolous in a gray suit standing behind them. "This is her graduation from Hofstra School of Law. We take her to the restaurant of my son-in-law." He flipped through more photographs— his house in Queens, his old house in Athens, snaps of an island holiday on Evvoia many years ago—and finally he held up the certificate I'd noticed, wrapped in yellowing plastic.

"To be an attorney," he said, "this is my diploma from Greece." For an instant he held it up over our heads like a chalice, and then he handed it to me. "So, you see," he said, "I am telling truth to you." I saw it was smallish, only about five by seven inches, but there were seals and signatures on it. I nodded yes, I believed him. "But why do you not practice here?" I asked, though I knew the answer. It was ritual. "This is not possible," he said brusquely. He could not return to law school, study for the bar, begin again as a clerk, then associate, and so on. "I must work for my family, feed them, send my daughter to school. Give them my future. I drive cab, make money. The house in Queens. We are Americans now. Greece is the past. I am lonely for it, but here I live."

The traffic loosened around us. We got back in his cab and sped away to La Guardia, feeling our common resolve.

Some years ago, on leave from Missouri, I went to Los Angeles to do some poetry readings. It was winter, January in Southern California, and the great beauty of the place was in the snow-lined ridges of the Angeles Crest and the San Gabriel Mountains, a stunning natural backdrop to the city that swarmed around us in its infinite patterns of distraction. You could be driving from the south up the Harbor Freeway and the mountains would be constantly before you, blue behemoths splashed and lichened with snow. This time of year, the air was clear as summer in the Arctic, and visibility stretched from the pier at Long Beach to the Hale Telescope at the Cal Tech Observatory on the ridge-line above the city.

One morning I gave a reading to a teenage audience at Alhambra High School, a place just east of Pasadena tucked in one of the canyon valleys against the San Gabriels. I drove up from the south where I was staying and parked my rented car under an enormous palm tree next to a warehouse a few blocks from the school. I liked Alhambra. It was an older section of the metropolis, built up during the forties and fifties and the aircraft boom; the scale and vintage of the streets and buildings seemed to come straight out of a Raymond Chandler novel. I noticed small custom garages, a coin shop, bakeries, a few restaurants and diners, and one place with that classic extravagance of neon, stainless steel, asphalt, and glass that could only mean a drive-in.

The day's event was sponsored by California State University Los Angeles, an idea thought up by Carl Selkin, director of their Poetry Center and my host. This was to be part of an outreach program by the university to the communities nearby, gone largely "ethnic." It was an experiment run as part of the celebration commemorating Dr. Martin Luther King's birthday. At Cal State the day before, Selkin had explained that the poet on their faculty had not been interested in doing this, had found it impossible to reach an audience he deemed "largely illiterate." But the high school English teachers—many of them graduates of CSU's excellent education program—were thrilled with the idea. Two of them had studied with Zbigniew Herbert, the great Polish poet who had once taught at CSU in the sixties. They wanted me to come, so I agreed.

I was put in a large science classroom where I sat in front of a huge desk with a sink on one end and a kind of projector that looked like a clunky, off-scale microscope on the other. The teachers told me I would read to an assembly made up largely of Asians and whites—about a hundred students, most of them juniors and seniors. The Asians were a mixture of Chinese and Southeast Asians, they told me, some of them Vietnamese, some Cambodians, a lot of them from Hong Kong as well. Some four or five English classes were put together to make up the audience, and the students trooped in and took their seats, the whites giggling and self-conscious, the Asians largely silent.

I read my poems about the inner city and my poems about Hawai'i, about my leaving there as a child, returning to it many years later as an adult, a poet, and seeking out the old places—the plantation lands, the sugar mills, the cane field and graveyard where I might have played as a child, the rough seashore which was like kin. I read a long poem about walking through the old Japanese cemetery in Kahuku on the plantation, told them how it was placed on a promontory overlooking the sea on a sandy point jutting into the ocean. I told them how we Japanese and Filipinos and Chinese put our cemeteries there because it was the land given to us by the growers who needed the good land, the land that was arable, for growing the sugarcane and the pineapple. But what we didn't know, what the growers didn't know, was that the sea would come and take our dead from us then, in the periodic raids of rips and tidal waves from a swelling ocean. The Hawaiians knew this. They took the bones of their dead to the high ground, up to the caves on the cliffs and the rock mounds on the rainy plateau above the shelves of land, between the sea and windward mountains. But we immigrants, we newly arrived laborers, placed generation after generation in the sand by the sea.

A tsunami came in 1946 and took more than half of our dead in one night. "Bones and tombstones / up and down the beach," my poem said. I told them of walking over the patchy carpeting of temple moss "yellowing in the saline earth," the stinging sand clouds kicked up by the tough onshore wind. I recalled a story of a murder committed out of outrage and shame—it was an act of victimage committed within the community—and paid homage to it as part of my past. It was to the journey I paid homage, the quest and travail of it from an Asian past to our American present. And it was to its remembrance, as shame and pride, that the poem was dedicated.

When I was finished, I looked up. In the back row was a Chinese girl, or maybe she was Vietnamese, dressed in a plain white school shirt and dark woolen skirt. Her hair was long and hung in two thick braids against her ears and jaw. Her eyes were shining. She wept, staring at me as if I were a statue. I averted my eyes, glancing quickly across the row and throughout the assembly, and saw others weeping too, wiping their faces. Some were embarrassed and gazed down at the floor or at their shoes. A few teachers nodded. I don't remember anyone smiling. Nothing like it had ever happened to me before. There was a heaviness in the room, a momentary silence. I was surprised and a little unsettled by it.

The assembly broke up, a teacher standing and thanking everyone, gesturing toward me and calling for more applause. Then the classes began filing out, and an Asian girl came up to me and asked me to sign her Pee-Chee. Another had me sign a napkin. A few more had xeroxes of my poems. I signed them all. A boy with acne and hair cut close to his temples but thick with pomade at the top—it was a style then coming into fashion with urban rappers—asked if I'd be reading for "adults" anytime that week. He wanted his parents to hear me too. I phlumphered something about the Pacific-Asian Museum that Saturday.

I had lunch with the teachers. They took me to the cafeteria, and we sat at the long bench tables I remembered from my public school days. Over the fish sticks and tapioca pudding, we talked poetry and the new Asian students. A youngish man dressed in brown tweeds then spoke. He had a light brown beard, neatly trimmed.

"I've never seen them respond like that," he said. "Never seen them act so open, show emotion like that before. You really connected."

I was learning something, something new and strong. These children with so much passion, so much raw affection, were teaching me that I had an audience, that my experience and sensibility spoke for their experiences, that I could address a world of others like myself, of Asians newly arrived, of peoples wanting to make America their place too. Up until then, I'd pretty much felt embattled as an artist and taken it as part of my identity. I saw myself as an individual presence up against cultural ignorance or mild hostility, particularly because my subject—the history of the Japanese in America—was something I thought few cared to hear about. Apart from some wonderful exceptions, and most of these among my fellow poets, I'd felt that, even if I were allowed a place in academe or the literary world, it would be on sufferance; no one was intrinsically interested in my obsessions, my passions. I thought of America as an establishment apart from me. But after that assembly beside the Los Angeles mountains, signing the Pee-Chees and the napkins and the xeroxes those teenage students had of my poems, I sensed that I was beginning to belong to something, to join a throng of voices in need of their own signing.

When Walt Whitman, the great America poet of the nineteenth century, wrote his poems of robust American optimism, full of the democratic spirit and lust for challenges and union jobs, he shouted, "I Hear America Singing!" and announced a theme that characterized more than a century of our history. Well, I look upon all of us here, now, us, the New Americans, among the newly arrived peoples with their boat trails of memories from across the oceans, and, I think, I Hear America Singing too.

2 ～ song

SARA MARIE ORTIZ

Part I. Starting

Signifier and signified

I have never written about race. I figured a great way to start would be to start with a great title, so I wrote *Creation and Reimagining Race: Self-Actualization in Contemporary Indigenous Poetics*, and then I realized that I had never written about race before. Not really. And then, after beginning to dig a bit deeper, I realized that *every single thing I'd ever written*, said, done, sung, danced, loathed, dismissed, raged quietly at, and forgotten entirely . . . was, in fact, about race.

I started, stopped, started, then stopped again.

Part II. Asking

I knew there were some important questions that I needed to try and answer if I was going to come even close to speaking to my "topic." None of it was topical. It was all a sticky matted fabric of memory and experience. I had lied to myself about race and my "okay-ness" with it all, I realized.

A lot.

Questions:

What do you really want to say about race and indigenous poetics?

Why should anyone care?

What have you read or written or experienced in working as a Native writer, and among them, that has given you an explicit indication of how contemporary Native poets, particularly younger, feel about race?

Why is the conversation among contemporary Native American poets about race ever complicated by classism, assumptions (or non-assumptions) of (white and every-colored) privilege, the mirage of inclusivity, re- or self-assigned marginalization, and indigenous self-actualization versus decolonization in and through poetry?

What indications or implications lie in the fact that my favorite poets are Whitman and white women poets like Louise Glück and Mary Oliver and not Native poets?

Why am I so mad at Native poets for all they have and have not said—way madder at them, in fact, than at white poets for their omissions?

Part III. Contraindicators

I knew there were some very important nodes, points in process, "factors" that signified my whole life, that precluded my delving, and deeply, into a real, bloody, and courageous exploration of race and the way it was or was not functioning in my creative work, and in the work of my contemporaries.

My lens seemed to be a little off. Did I really want people knowing how off my lens was?

Onward.

Factors or plot points that complicate my conversation about race, poetry, and the unmasking taking place in the realm of contemporary indigenous poetics:

1. I used to think I was Mexican. I grew up in New Mexico, surrounded by Hispanic/Chicano people. My white mother was one of the only white people in our neighborhood. My Native father was nowhere in sight. Everyone I knew was Mexican. And thus I became.

   I attended ceremony at the Acoma Pueblo from birth. I was given my Acoma name at birth. And I still didn't fully realize my Native-ness until my teens, and not until I myself was the mother of a Mexican/Acoma/Anglo daughter. I named her Monique. I loved the French language. I gave Monique her Chicano father's last name: La Riva.

2. I began my college studies at a tribal college, a fine arts college in Santa Fe dedicated entirely to the preservation and development of Alaska Native and American Indian arts and cultures. I ended up attending

this tribal college after a failed attempt to study where my grandmother lived, in an all-white college town in eastern New Mexico.

My bubble of experience studying creative writing at the Institute of American Indian Arts (IAIA), among other privileged Native artists like me, actually began to serve as a conflated reality, a mirror-mask of sorts, where I was both mirroring a particular and more comfortable reflective identity back to my peers and also masking my realest identity, reality, and selfhood. When I left the comfortable confines of this IAIA *asylum*, I got a very rude awakening and entered into a very different reality—in academia, in the professional sphere, and elsewhere—and I realized this alter-reality of IAIA had actually disserved me in many, many ways.

3. My white grandmother and mother raised me, it wasn't until I was eighteen and studying at the IAIA that I began to self-identify fully and readily as my father's daughter, as an indigenous/Native/Acoma Pueblo writer.

4. So many of my earliest ideas about the power, possibility, and "specialness" of indigenous literature, and poetics specifically, now ring hollow to me, particularly some of the most dominant and blatant self-aggrandizing and self-righteous assumptions about racial hierarchy and privilege.

5. I am a woman. I am a progressive. I am a Native American. And I am a neo-racist.

6. More often than not I have failed to assume, or have negated entirely, my responsibility to examine my own preconceived notions about race, class, and privilege.

Part IV. Fragments

I have never written about race.

And yet, every single thing I've ever written has been about race. As has been said about Langston Hughes's work, every turn of phrase, the form I've chosen (or not chosen) in my writing, the language I employ to convey my experience as an urban contemporary Native Acoma Pueblo woman and poet cannot help being about race, cannot help but tell a complex, labyrinthine story about identity, memory, self-actualizing amid such complexity. It also tells a story about the ways in which I've encountered the language of other poets—indigenous and all—who also self-actualize amid what often seems a stream of unending dialogue about identity, race politics, fragmentation, othering, and what our poetry is *saying* about these things in light of it all. Hughes took specific issue with black poets of his day who didn't want to self-identify as "negro poets" but wanted to be known on the merit of their poetry alone, and I—like most of my contemporaries—have been asked this question over and over again. Who are we, if not "Indians"? If not "Native"? I began to ask: What of our self-inflicted, proudly conflated Otherness, and our self-assumed exoticization?

This infinitely complex and evolving architecture came into sharp focus when I had graduated with my MFA in creative writing, with a specialization in creative nonfiction, from Antioch University in the fall of 2009, following my BFA from the Institute of American Indian Arts in Santa Fe. My experience at IAIA was rife with rich complexity and contradiction at every turn.

While still a student at IAIA, I reveled in the richness, almost entirely, feeling as though I'd have plenty of time to enter into the stickier, more matted fabrics of race politics and what it meant to "write Indian" much later. It came on much quicker than I'd thought or hoped it would.

I allowed myself, and was allowed by my professors, among them Jon Davis, Evelina Lucero, and Arthur Sze, all longtime architects and faculty within the program, to explore and change and grow as needed, challenged but never forced to face identity politics and specific issues of race, gender, and class within my own work and the work of others. Form, content, and context of experience matter greatly. They are a language unto themselves. And my experience studying at the Institute of American Indian Arts was an evocative representation of that. The land on which the classrooms were situated, where we studied the work of Walcott and Allende and Li Po and Harjo and Momaday, it too was language. I thought I spoke that language while there. Sometimes I think I still do. But most days I'm not so sure.

We, majority indigenous writers of many nations and heritages, Pueblo, Inupiat, Navajo, Lakota, Comanche, Cherokee, Salish, became a confluence of indigenous voice and aesthetic and experience and memory, and we existed as both the fertilizer and the fertile soil itself when self-actualizing with poetic license, creative agency, and developing our creative-intellectual ethos amid the great complexity that was the very educational structure and strata in which we were studying and also being allowed to shape each other.

My colleagues have almost all gone on to complete their MFAS or other graduate programs, some taking up prestigious fellowships at universities like

Brown, Cornell, NYU, Syracuse, Stanford, and Columbia, and several have published highly praised poetry collections.

I have never written about race.

And yet, everything I've ever written, done, spoken about, dreamed about, screamed silently about, raged about, or been indifferent to . . . has been about race and/or my privilege and my assumptive, and often dismissive, attitudes with regard to race.

My mother is white. My father is brown. My mother is of Dutch, Irish, and Scottish heritage and was born in eastern New Mexico on the Texas border. My father is a "full blood" Native American son of the Haaku'meh Hanoh, the Acoma Pueblo people of central New Mexico.

I grew up in Albuquerque, fully my mother and father's daughter in every sense of that turn of phrase. But I thought I was Mexican until I was a teenager. I'd been told my whole life that I was a daughter of the Acoma people, given and told my Acoma name in the Keres tongue, at and since birth. I attended ceremony at the pueblo regularly and I knew (at least cursorily) who my father was, and what his name meant in the realm of indigenous arts and letters. I am born of the eagle clan, but not for them. When my name is called out at ceremony, I know myself as an eagle child, but mostly only in that context. I cannot serve within pueblo government because I am a woman. And I am not a fully functioning member of Acoma society because my mother is not Acoma.

I have never written about race.
And I'm not sure that I'll ever really be able to.

Seattle, March 2013

3 ～ finding family with native american women poets

RAVI SHANKAR

You a red or a brown? That was a question I would get growing up in Manassas, Virginia, in one of the few South Asian families around—the essentialist query from the booger-chewer on the school bus who wanted to know specifically what I was. An Indian. A brown Indian American, a TamBram to be specific, a Tamilian Brahmin whose parents came from Tamil Nadu in South India to settle in northern Virginia. I didn't know much about the First Peoples back then, and it was never clear to me, back then and even now, whether I would rise or diminish in someone's appreciation by revealing that I did not live on the rez but rather ate rice with my hands.

Over the years, fragments of the rich, vexed history of Native Americans in Virginia were revealed to me, through what was implied but never fully articulated in my civics textbook, or from the visit to the Blue Ridge Mountains I took with my parents. As a detour, we went to the Native American Village at Natural Bridge, and I remember sitting cross-legged (Indian style, but red or brown?) on a dirt floor while an interpreter showed us how to tan hides and weave rope mats. I was struck by the note of nobility and dignity in the stories I heard of the native way of life, pre European settlers. Only much later would I realize that this entire endeavor was pure simulacrum, a re-creation of what an operational Indian village might have looked like based on archeological conjecture. Still that note of unity across tribes, technological innovation, and dignified forbearance, elements I had never learned about in my middle school classroom, remained with me.

Therefore it came as something of a revelation to me (though it perhaps should not have been surprising, given what I know of the provincialism of ethnicity), when we put together *Drunken Boat #15* and more specifically a folio on Native American women's poetry, to find out that even within the Native community of writers there were rifts and discords, the privileging of certain stories and the suppression of others, all of this happening within—and without—an already subjugated community. As Gloria Bird wrote in her introduction to the 1998 Norton anthology *Reinventing the Enemy's Language: Contemporary Native Women's Writings of North America*, "the very nature of the politics of publishing for native women from the beginning has remained hidden beneath the more obvious issues that all native people face. . . . There are many interlocking dynamics that come into play. The lack of female editorships, which are few and far between, says more about control of the publishing end, and privileging of the native male voice. Though there certainly have been, and continue to be, many non-native editors as well, the concerns about the control of native literary production impact not only upon native women but upon all native writers" (22). I was floored when I first read that and therefore much obliged to our contributing editor Layli Long Soldier for her superb work in bringing to our journal and our international readership the voices of contemporary Native American women writers, working now.

The intrepid Layli Long Soldier is Oglala Lakota, with family in Pine Ridge, South Dakota, and northwestern Idaho, and I think of her as an exemplar of the diversity and richness of Native American women's poetry today. Her work is a synthesis of her culture mediated through the lens of millennial America. Take a prose poem like "Tokahan," the title derived from a Lakota word that is defined in the epigraph of the poem as a verb, "to lose, to suffer loss, to be gone, lost." The poem begins:

> Used in reply to, *what has become of it?* Found in the answer: it is light and those bubbles blown from a plastic wand to spring air into a hundred silent bursts. Or the large tree shadow, the trunk of it, with finger and limb tips across the lawn to my toe. It is the talk we engage and the unnoticed way this shadow rears back, with black arms and twig teeth it engulfs me, your love, whole.

That word, the poem's title, is in all likelihood headed the way of the dodo bird, a cultural relic with too few mouths to speak it, and accordingly the poem proceeds with a frequently elided subject, the verbs standing in for the noun lost in time. Like the lost childhood in which a wand could produce ephemeral bubbles, or the much more substantial but no less fleeting tree trunk, in shadow, personified to commune with the speaker, to bleed into the speaker's body, already absent, nearly gone.

The poem goes on to encompass the world of modern technology. The speaker of the poem wields the word *tokahan* in response to an e-mail received from a friend she hasn't seen in years, with an attachment of photos of his face swollen with wounds. Why has this long-lost friend sent this disturbing image, prefaced by so little explanation? The speaker doesn't know and can't bring herself to reply except with this Lakota word for loss, which assumes a kind of incantatory, anaphoric effect in the last part of the poem:

> So I return to this: Tokahan, this shell and husk, this outer word. Tokahan, I say, in the shaking he gave me, my friend, his face, the world. Tokahan, for why I never did hit *reply*. Tokahan, my fingernails—dirt lined, digging. Tokahan, in guttural silence under a swing and *whump*. Tokahan, this tire-iron to the eye.

In spite of the insistent repetition, the word for loss here is literally lost, as is the friend whose face has been met with confusing violence, like the barbarism performed on a culture and on specific individual languages and bodies in time. The hollow of the word that appears in no English dictionary is like the Buddhist void, a place of nothingness that is nonetheless visceral, full of eyes and fingernails, and embodied in sound, in the onomatopoeia of "swing and *whump*," in the rhyme between "reply" and "tire-iron to the eye," and in the oxymoron of the guttural silence, a welling up of sound that gurgles at the back of the throat but produces no sound. This Lakota word is the only equivalence the speaker can find to describe her lost friend and her receding mother tongue.

Long Soldier is a deeply lyrical and yet compellingly political poet who is as influenced by Joy Harjo as she is by Gertrude Stein and bpNichol, as invested in identity politics as she is in the polysemous play of language. In an interview in 2013 she says,

> I am not a spokesperson for all Native American Peoples and their experiences. Even within my own family, my cousins or sisters or aunties have had vastly different experiences from mine. . . . the other thing I want to mention is that I have avoided the term "White" and working directly with the subject of White America. This is for several reasons, but maybe the most important is that mainstream American society (as in non-Indigenous) is not all White. America is diverse, many peoples of different colors and heritages. Yet, whatever background Americans come from, many stumble over the fix or conundrum of what language/terms to use to refer to the Native Peoples of this country. Indian? Red Indian? American Indian? Even I, as you may have noticed, interchange Native with Native American with Indigenous.

It's a mess. But in all fairness, as you point out, the heart of the problem lies in the language we are working with: English. And yes, therein is the power structure. Because, in my opinion, if we were really fair and just, Americans would refer to Native Peoples with the terms we use for ourselves, in our own languages.

Here Long Soldier highlights the very plurality that is reduced by the generalization of the language we have to describe our rich profusion of cultures, the same feeling I often have when I'm forced to explain that Hinduism is not a monolithic religion but rather a catchall term meant to describe thousands of different ritual practices and forms of worship, just as India itself is vastly diverse culturally, geographically, linguistically, gastronomically, and spiritually, a fact clearly evident to anyone who has traveled the subcontinent. Similarly, Native cultures are polyglot and multiple, overlapping and discrete, and our insistence on generalizing between them might make some sense in terms of political mobilization but very little in terms of poetics.

Indeed, as Long Soldier tells us later in the same interview, the gap in our understanding of each other is often due to "languageness." As she describes it,

In my experience, when I am with Native Americans, the terms Native, Native American, Indian, Indigenous, in many cases, become obsolete. If I were to meet a Hopi woman, for example, we'd introduce ourselves with who we are, where we come from. If I were to say to her, in general terms, "I'm a Native American," without a specific tribal affiliation, she'd likely think, "But who are you?" If I say, "I am Oglala Lakota," this establishes geography, history, community and family for both of us. My inner compass shifts, I feel centered, I feel acknowledged. She and I are not the same; we remain an "other" to each other in some manner; but acknowledging our differences is a gesture of respect. Between us, there's a refusal to accept the generality; we ask for and expect the specific. Immediately, this particular way of relating to one another engenders a degree of intimacy.

And what is a poem if not a heightened degree of intimacy?

Drunken Boat's folio on Native American women's poetry, curated by Layli Long Soldier, gives us some sense of the rich possibilities, and perusing the poems she's chosen points to the vast array of Derridean *différance* that exists between these various women poets.

Take Mojave and Pima poet Natalie Diaz's "Reservation Grass," which is a mash-up of her own words and Walt Whitman's. Beginning with an epigraph from *Leaves of Grass*, "I keep no account of lamentation," the poem creates an adversarial relationship between the grandfather of American poetry and the speaker from its very first line: "We smoke more grass than we ever promise to plant." That line resonates on a number of levels. First, the stereotypical and racist notion of life on the reservation consisting of alcoholism and drug use is confronted head-on with a kind of disdainful bravura in the firm declarative sentence. This is not the world of harmonious interconnectedness espoused by Cree proverbs and Sun Bear of the Chippewa Tribe, the wisdom of sustainable living co-opted by environmentalists to further their own legislative imperatives, but the raw and ready world of reality as experienced by this speaker. A world where federally subsidized meals come in the form of canned corned beef on the first of the month and where the men, likely unemployed, linger to drink in the dirt. The juxtaposition of Whitman's words from *Leaves of Grass* is particularly poignant here, his famous "multitudes" placed next to "shards of glass [that] grow men bunched together," and the poem radiates the irony that comes from lifting a phrase—"dance with the dancers and drink with the drinkers"—out of an excerpt from a section of Whitman titled "Native Moments" and placing it next to the image of these men "leaning against the sides of houses."

Whitman's poem is considered the epitome of inclusivity, and grass itself becomes a microcosm of this feeling, of the earth we share with one another. As Desirée Henderson has written on the section referenced by Diaz, "One of the most memorable moments in Walt Whitman's 'Song of Myself' is the section known as 'What is the grass?' Named after the question that initiates the poet's musings, this part of Whitman's sprawling poem is considered by many to illustrate themes central to the entire text: the innocent inquisitiveness of the poetic mind, an emphasis upon the multiplicity and diversity of perception, the reunion of living and dead through a shared natural environment, and, above all, the symbolism of the grass as a democratic plant linking all people through and to nature" (89).

But for the speaker of Diaz's poem, there is no grass, just glass and dirt. This ubiquitous democratic plant and the promise it represents hold no sway on the reservation. By the time the poem gets to the red aborigines—again referencing Whitman, who, it must be admitted, romanticized and even abrogated the Native Americans in book II of *Leaves of Grass*:

> The red aborigines,
> Leaving natural breaths, sounds of rain and winds, calls as of birds
>   and animals in the woods, syllabled to us for names,

Okonee, Koosa, Ottawa, Monongahela, Sauk, Natchez,
  Chattahoochee, Kaqueta, Oronoco,
Wabash, Miami, Saginaw, Chippewa, Oshkosh, Walla-Walla,
  Leaving such to the States they melt, they depart, charging the
  water and the land with names

—all of a sudden I'm not quite comfortable with what Whitman, whom I adore and think of as a more profound humanist than even someone like Abraham Lincoln (as an interesting aside, in 1862, during the same week that Lincoln signed the Emancipation Proclamation, he also ordered the execution of thirty-eight Dakota men—the largest mass hanging in U.S. history), pronounces of what the air holds for the red aborigines. Grass, in Diaz's poem, becomes not the inheritance we all share but a suburban growth that demarcates lines of inequity and the mash-up of his words with her words both proposes and undermines the notion of unity. When the reader reaches that last line, "What have we—the red aborigines—out of hopeful green stuff woven?" we are all aborigines bereft of grass.

A very different kind of poem included in the folio is Tria Andrews's "On the Border." Andrews is a mixed-race Cherokee, Irish, and Filipina poet whose research examines culturally relevant forms of rehabilitation for Native American youth in juvenile detention centers on tribal grounds. This prose poem is much more straightforward, with little of the conflation and juxtaposition of Diaz's poem; right from the opening we are put in the liminal space between cultures and peoples, a space that the speaker of Andrews's poem seems to inhabit herself, since she "passes," is not seen to be Native, which allows the people she meets to speak freely with her about their ideas about Native Americans' life. In the poem, the speaker has stopped at a restaurant on the border, "looking for something local, but tired, hungry, lost." What the border separates is never revealed to us, but the notion of partition is ever present. She is headed, one infers, to the Rosebud Indian Reservation, and as the waitress says, "Rosebud is a whole 'nother world. You'll see. Stray dogs, trailers without windows." The polyvalence of that signifier "rosebud" not only points to the Lakota reservation in South Dakota but also conjures Citizen Kane, the magnate whose warehouse of immense fortune certainly is a world away from where the speaker is headed. When she reveals that she is working in Ethnic Studies, a bearded man joins the conversation to comment, "Ethnic Studies? No one studies U.S. history anymore."

There's little to read between the lines here; the poem with its spare dialogue, which interestingly is not set apart from the rest of the text, points to a world where there's a sense of boundary between us (the nonnative natives) and them (the native nonnatives); there's a prevalent sense of otherness, a gulf between those on the reservation and those outside, and yet their worlds overlap as well, as when the waitress explains laughingly to the speaker that her husband works for the local jail. "Because of Indians, he has a job," she says. There's little sense to these people that there might be something wrong with the disproportionate racial populations in American prisons or that U.S. history is only composed of ethnic studies, plural, that the sanctioned worldview that has continued to hold hegemony in American schools is only one of a number of parallel and concurrent stories, none of them illegitimate for not being widely known. The speaker is part Native American, but because she's not recognized as such, because her ethnicity is not written on her body in the expected way, she's taken to be distinct from the Native Americans with whom she is headed to live. The last line of the poem, ominously, refers to a grasshopper that has landed in the laughing man's beard: "As long as no one notices, maybe it won't be harmed." So it goes for the grasshopper and for the speaker; if you are not identified through your physical characteristics with a marginalized group, you too might stand a chance of remaining safe.

At the opening of Long Soldier's introduction to this folio, which includes the work of twenty-one contemporary Native American women poets representing tribes as various as the Inupiaq/Inuit and the Standing Rock Sioux (but still representing only a minuscule portion of the nearly three hundred indigenous languages of North America), Joy Harjo's anthology *Reinventing the Enemy's Language* is again evoked with this quote: "The literature of the aboriginal people of North America defines America. It is not exotic. The concerns are particular, yet often universal. Anyone of these lands shares in the making of this literature, this history, these connections, these songs. It is a connection taken in with our mother's blood and milk, constructed of the very earth on which we stand" (31). The performance of race and gender in the poems Long Soldier collects is deeply particular, taking on different forms and inflections, veering from the narrative to the lyrical, from the exophonic to plainspoken English, and for this brown Indian, himself a byproduct of a country with thousands of competing dialects and ritual traditions, himself in exile from his homeland, a displaced American living on land borrowed from the indigenous peoples, for me the poetry of Native American women speaks persuasively of what it means to lose everything and yet to persist in the face of this loss. I can think of nothing more prosaic than this fact and yet nothing more courageous and extraordinary.

If I contain multitudes, then the multitudes contain me; if I have suffered loss, it is only because we all do; if I am wandering the border, tired, lost and hungry, looking for something local, then these voices are the bed, compass, and cornbread for my aching bones, a precise and exacting articulation where I might stay—and savor—the night as an honored guest. No, as family.

BIBLIOGRAPHY

Andrews, Tria. "On the Border." *Drunken Boat* 15 (2012). drunkenboat.com/db15/tria-andrews.
Diaz, Natalie. "Reservation Grass." *Drunken Boat* 15 (2012). drunkenboat.com/db15/natalie -diaz.
Harjo, Joy, and Gloria Bird, eds. *Reinventing the Enemy's Language: Contemporary Native Women's Writing of North America.* New York: W. W. Norton, 1997.
Henderson, Desirée. "'What is the grass?': The Roots of Walt Whitman's Cemetery Meditation." *Walt Whitman Quarterly Review* 25 (Winter 2008): 89–106.
Long Soldier, Layli. "The Poetry of Layli Long Soldier." *Talking Stick* 13, no. 2 (April–June 2010). amerinda.org/newsletter/13-2/longsoldier.html.
———. "Profiles in Poetics: Layli Long Soldier." *Women's Quarterly Conversation*, March 6, 2013. womensquarterlyconversation.com/2013/03/06/profiles-in-poetics-layli-long-soldier/.
Whitman, Walt. *Leaves of Grass.* 1895. gutenberg.org/ebooks/1322.

4 ~ walt and i

What's American about American Poetry?

I. Friends of Walt

Walt Whitman and I were hanging out the other day. He had thick and dirty hands and a regal look in his eyes and was so friendly I would not have trusted him if he had not been so shy. But he seemed moved by something strange and deep. He wanted to tell me about all his friends, the whole gang of them. He told me about his secretary, the poet Sadakichi Hartmann, who wrote avant-garde cosmological rhapsodies. "I like them," I said. "It's like László Moholy-Nagy directs the Big Bang."

We walked to Angel Island, where so many lonely men carved their souls into the gray, unlit walls. One of the men was still there, all skeleton and tea-stained smiles. He said, "Did you know the Filipinos came here before the *Mayflower*? Barbers for the Spanish Armada. Did you know Idaho was once one-third Asian American?" He handed us a Styrofoam cup, the white surface of which appeared crenellated with small grooves and indentations. Walt Whitman saw me looking at the indentations. "I think it's Arabic," he said.

"I found the cup on the floor when I was walking through Gitmo," our host noted. "Those flecks are poems that the prisoners wrote with their fingernails."

Walt and I look at each other, not sure what to say. We offer to buy the man a drink, but he only smiles. "It's okay," he says. He lies down and waits for us to leave.

The author clears his throat and notes obvious problems, or as Bhanu Kapil asks, why do our "responsibilities to each other end at the border of our countries, or at our cities, or halfway across cities, or at our skins?" (33).

What's American about American poetry? You know already the first step in answering this question. Feel queasy. Make darting glances at your wristwatch. You must avoid the obvious traps of answering the question's *America* side or its *Poetry* side. You can answer by broadly defining American identity (Mongrel! Plain-talkin'! Democratic!) or by narrowing your inquiry to literary genealogy (the names Whitman and Dickinson as prefix to a yawn). If you answer on the *America* side, you feel like a caricaturist painting your bathroom mirror. If you answer on the *Poetry* side, you risk pedantry, the vain docenting of your own poetry mix tape. And there is a third, far worse problem: when you point this out, you sound like a prig.

Whether on the *America* side or the *Poetry* side, the question requires one to engage with the word "American" as it first appears in the question (normatively), rather than in its second appearance, where it is irrelevantly descriptive ("American poetry" no doubt defined as any poetry written by Americans). The question asks for the respondent to assume a firsthand acquaintance with the American essence. Here we can imagine a demotic visionary doing Walt Whitman impressions by the bar, part speaker of the soulful language of the black church and the glued-together English of immigrants, part slangy and savage maverick-hustler—in other words, the barbaric love child of Martin Luther King and Lady Gaga. While I'd love to hang out with such a poet, such essentializing would ignore actually most contemporary American poets, play into some sketchy American exceptionalism, and mischaracterize as daring our MFA finishing schools, lit mag slush piles, and ladies who lunch. And it would ignore the transnationally porous nature of American writers—the Transcendentalists cribbing from Hindu and Buddhist dialectic, the modernist project of parodying classical Chinese verse, and maybe our central contemporary poet, John Ashbery, who often reads to me as a Gallicized and privatized, rather than expansively "American," Whitman. In other words, a normative response to this question (e.g., "American poetry is democratic") could only be nondemocratic.

The author evinces skepticism at the folk understanding of nation whether defined via bloodline or citizenship or whatever and imbibes booze.

It's 4 p.m., Walt Whitman, and we're drinking! We're having a pint at one of those holy houses, a London pub. It's my friend Daewha's bachelor party. The gents we've met ask us where we're from. Daewha, the affable expostulator, says, "I was born in Oregon in the States, I live in London, and my ancestry is Korean." The man we've just met? He says, "I'm a Welshman. My boy, he's born in England but there's nothing that's going to make him not a Welsh-man." He actually makes a fist when he says this—not belligerently, but in a way that unambiguously communicates his status as a proud dad. "You know what they say. *You got a dog that's born in a barn, that don't make it a horse.*"

Two other guys in his wedding party are there. Job grew up in Denmark, spent his adolescence in America, and now lives in Albany. The Czecho—dude grew up in the Czech Republic, so we call him the Czecho—is a London-based architect who looks like a werewolf. He is proud to be a Werewolf American. Who knew that the most perfect model for pluralistic multinationalism was a drinking hall?

The author narrowly avoids conducting an inquest on the corpse that was called multiculturalism and bemoans how no one thinks Asian American literature is for them.

I left a career in law to become the executive director of the Asian American Writers' Workshop—a classic American story of transformation!—and part of my job description is being asked to interpret what we mean by "American" or "Asian American." Alongside my other vocations as grant-proposal writer and strategic planner, high cultural talk show host, and toilet seat installer, one of my roles at the workshop is what could be called a "therapist of nationalism." I have two constituencies. The first constituency consists of Asian Americans, many of whom do not consider themselves American and many of whom do not consider themselves Asian. Believe it or not, many Asian American writ-ers, the sometimes enthusiastic lapdogs of assimilation (myself being the most obvious example), find themselves breaking out in hives when encountering the label "Asian American." Writers, like nerds, a nonidentical but overlapping category, are often writers because they had no choice. Writing rescued them from their loneliness, their brains, their lovable ineptness—and so, having been loners all their lives, many writers of color find themselves startled to find that their identities have become a genre, their isolation a group. Many of the Asian American writers I've hosted realize that when the target of one's writing becomes an attempt to achieve something essentially "Asian American," then one has written kitsch—the same kitsch one commits when one's exclusive goal is to write as an American or a lyric poet or an avant-gardist, rather than hitting such adjectives accidentally while aiming to describe a true and not-conforming object. Many of the Asian American writers I know are eager to clamber out of what Amitava Kumar once called the ghetto of multicultural literature, which is assumed, with a type of unconscious racism, to be sentimental, extra-literary, possessing low literary merit, and (insert other ways of demarcating people you don't want to hear from). Speaking of myself, I always believed that I chose my own generally non–Asian American forebears, a motley clubhouse that included psychedelic comics writer Grant Morrison, faux-blue-collar modernist Henry Green, and Taoist stand-up comedian Lieh Tzu, none of whom I now realize is/was American. I did not, in fact, believe I was an Asian American writer until I noticed that much of my first book, *Juvenilia*, focused on assimilation, postcolonialism, and the other greatest hits of ethnic studies. (Silly me, I'd thought I'd been scribbling gossip about my parents' divorce!) I grew up in Silicon Valley, where I was often bored by everyone, including all the Asian Americans who wanted to become doctors or lawyers. I became a lawyer. Most of my life, in other words, I've been a self-hating Asian American. The funny irony—no, let's call it fate!—is that my job requires me to let other Asian Americans know that it is okay to be Asian American and themselves.

Oh, what's the second constituency I mentioned? This constituency consists of non–Asian Americans. Members of this constituency may not view themselves as prejudiced (a rather low bar to pass as egalitarian), but it would never occur to them to imagine themselves as being Asian American. This may seem like a strange request, but consider how the most innocuous blockbuster or TV miniseries requires the typical viewer to imagine herself as white or a man. My job is to talk these constituents into empathizing with writers who do not look like them. I try to show them that Asian American literature is not just a niche sliver or a tribe or a heritage knitting circle but a thrilling chapter of the American story. I try to imply that Asian American literature is tautologically American literature. I am not always successful.

II. Parable

> I used to pretend I was American.
> This was before I realized I was American.

The author discusses not being invited to parties and the ambivalence with which many writers identify themselves as American.

I was once on Chinese TV in college for being an outstanding nerd. I would answer questions in a Mandarin that was enthusiastic and dumbo and give up and finish in English. The other two guests spoke Chinese fluently. A man called up and said, "This question is only for Ken, not for the other guests.

Ken, if you saw a Chinese man and an American drowning, who would you leap into the waters and save?"

He hung up, and the host looked at me and said, "And we'll cut to a commercial break!" And after the show was over, I told the story to my Milton professor, who said, "You should have said, *I would save them both because they would be one man and that man would be Chinese American.*"

I looked at him, baffled and a little stupid. It had never occurred to me, at the age of twenty, that people actually believed in the mythology of America, all this democracy and inclusiveness stuff, which I'd assumed was something we kept around for good manners. I was naïve, not cynical. I grew up in a household where the word "American" meant white people. I think the word is commonly used this way in immigrant households. I think this is how the word is used by Americans themselves.

Speaking of myself, sometimes I want nothing more than to be American, for better or worse. I approach classical Chinese poetry, which I appropriate, like an American. I love Duke Ellington and Richard Rorty and Lincoln's Second Inaugural the way an American would. I am bemused by the wonderful myth of America, a myth that I too love. And I've spent my life being asked where I'm from, a question that could not possibly be answered by "America"—or by my standard comeback, "San Diego." Many of the writers I work with—let's call them Asian American—have also been asked to go home, a request many Americans have also submitted to more than a quarter of Arizona's population and to the president of the United States of America, who could not possibly be American. Maybe these writers have spent their lives being called Asian without the suffix "American," as in the sentence "His wife is Asian and he's American." And maybe the writers I'm thinking of could not be anything other than American and could not think of their home as other than America, that country that may very well have colonized, annexed, and invaded the countries of our grandparents. (In fact, what I think was hilarious about the Bush administration is that it could have been the first time many Americans felt the conflict that a typical second-generation immigrant might feel about her own American identity.) The point is not a poetics of banal moralizing ("Racism is bad!") but another ironic joke. The alienated and humorous lyrics of so-called ethnic writing, whether Frances Chung transcribing white men staring at her in a Chinese restaurant or Amiri Baraka's vehement post-9/11 poem that caused the termination of the poet laureateship of New Jersey, are so often interpreted as anti-American, these sad poems with one stanza starting "I'm leaving this party" and the next stanza rejoining,

"Well, you were never invited in the first place"—such writings could not be other than quintessentially American.

The author interprets the history of Walt Whitman criticism as a model for reimagining America.

Walt Whitman's made several walk-ons and cameo appearances in this essay as the laureate of American nationalism. This is not surprising—after all, is he not the eulogizer of Lincoln, the man who demanded a "genius in America" and who celebrated America as "a poem in our eyes"? It was against this inherited interpretation that June Jordan first discovered another Walt Whitman, the homosexual bohemian who nodded his head sadly at the slave market and called for an infinitely inclusive New World poetics. Jordan writes with an astonished and jokey affinity, surprised that the canonical American poet ended up being a poet of witness(!), the forebear not of the self-hating all-American anti-Americanism of T. S. Eliot, one of my favorite poets, but of ethnic studies:

> Listen to this white father; he is so weird! Here he is calling aloud for an American, a democratic spirit. An American, a democratic idea that could morally constrain and coordinate the material body of USA affluence and piratical outreach. . . . I too am a descendant of Walt Whitman. And I am not by myself struggling to tell the truth about this history of so much land and so much blood, of so much that should be sacred and so much that has been desecrated and annihilated boastfully. (249, 252)

(She observes, quite convincingly, that Whitman would never get published today.) Borges also noted what we may call Whitman's multiculturalism—his "ferocious tenderness" that allowed him to imagine himself as a "mother of old, condemn'd for a witch, burnt with dry wood" or a "hounded slave that flags in the race, leans by the fence, blowing, cover'd with sweat" (69–70). Yet Borges expanded Whitman further: "Whitman felt and was all of them, but fundamentally he was . . . a kosmos. . . . He was also the one who would be in the future, in our future nostalgia" (70). In other words, Whitman is not exclusively an American patriot or a multiculturalist but a writer so capacious that his empathy extends in all directions of space and time. We may then reason that if Whitman is a cosmic poet, he could not be a national poet. He is almost, you might say, the poet of our globalization.

At the Asian American Writers' Workshop, I am often asked what "Asian American" means—a question that differs from our American question only in scale. We have answered this question by presenting writers that a typical

American would not consider Asian or American: not just the usual Chinese or Indian writers, but writers from an Asia fatter and wider than the way we typically use the word "Asian" (Iran, Palestine, Afghanistan, Sri Lanka, Burma), adoptees who grew up in non–Asian American families, and transnational and émigré writers who would never think themselves American. When looking at Asian America and by extension America in this playing-around, hapless, inclusive way, startling combinations emerge. You can argue that an essential part of the American canon might be the American-obsessed literature written by the folks detained at Angel Island (by which I mean anonymous immigrants imprisoned for three decades without any criminal charges; one poem ends, ominously, "I have yet to be interrogated"), the internment of Japanese American citizens (consider the haiku of Shiho Okamoto, where the conventional landscape motifs are replaced by images of guards and sentries), and the holding pens at Guantánamo Bay (Sami al Haj writes: "America, you ride on backs of orphans / and terrorize them daily" (43)). You might see nothing wrong with a panel that brings together an academic studying Arab American youth, a Pakistani novelist writing a post-9/11 Huck Finn, and a band playing from the emerging genre of Pakistani punk rock. Or, for that matter, a symposium that explores the ethnic politics of what it means to be a nerd.

We've sought to look at our question, not as a chance to make a category cohere within a limited boundary, but as an adventure in dreaming. Like Whitman, we conceptualize Asian American identity as simultaneously an American project, a multicultural story of injustice, and an expanding story that noses sideways with transnationalism and invention. We sense that our identity, whether as "Asian Americans" or as "Americans," is necessarily incomplete, just like the always unfinished manuscripts of *Leaves of Grass*, because we are always open to what the future of these categories might hold for us. You will notice that this method of definition is happily problematic. We abhor the neatness of definition in favor of possibility, pragmatism, and the all-loving self-contradiction of Walt Whitman. And we also believe that if it's possible for Asian American literature to imagine so broadly, then it must be possible for American literature to do likewise. In fact, one of the central projects of American art—in Whitman, in Agnes de Mille, in Duke Ellington—has been to build a maximalist collage that can encompass a nation that believes itself beyond limits. We may ask *What is American poetry?* and dumbly answer, *Poetry written by Americans.* Okay, then, who are Americans? The Brookings Institution in 2010 reported: "Racial and ethnic minorities accounted for 83 percent of U.S. population growth from 2000 to 2008. The continued faster growth of Hispanic, Asian, and black populations put the country as a whole on track to reach 'majority minority' status by 2042, and for children to reach that milestone by 2023" (51).

The author channels Bobby Kennedy and asks American poetry for more demographic imagination.

Another microcosmic avatar of American poetry might be that goofy old crackpot Ezra Pound. Pound—the bigoted and multicultural poet who sought commerce with Walt Whitman and invented classical Chinese poetry—famously defined poetry as news that stays news. What one often forgets about this maxim is how it defines poetry as reportage. (Pound may have been familiar with the *Yueh fu*, the musical bureau of the antique Chinese government that'd send Confucian poets into the countryside—imagine Alan Lomax garbed in Han dynasty robes—to record folk ballads, specimens of the nation's moral mood.) And the obvious question one would ask any two-bit journalistic outfit is: How good is the coverage? The boring and obvious answer is that American poetry would make a lousy national news bulletin, one that only reported on the melancholia, gibberish, text messages, and stand-up comedy of well-educated elites. Reading American poetry, you would rarely encounter a poem by a prisoner or a postoperative transsexual or, for that matter, a Christian. You would not learn that one out of every eight Americans is an immigrant and that nearly half of all kids are second-generation immigrants in Los Angeles, Miami, San Francisco, and New York. Viewed in this way, it is easy to see the underlying affinity between the camps that Ron Silliman has simplistically labeled quietist or post-avant-garde. Both of these poetics are largely apathetic about the poet's role as a citizen, rarely curious about the subject matter of the world, and largely written by the same scholar class adjuncting at academic institutions. Forget whether or not anyone's racist. The question is whether, to borrow the jargon of wealth disparity, we want 96 percent of American poetry to be written by only 2 percent of the population (numbers I just made up).

III. What's American about American Poetry in *Blade Runner*?

Pragmatism is a future-oriented practice premised on hope. It asks us to solve our way toward the more idealized situation of our imagination. So I'd like to ask a rather serious question. Have you ever thought about the American poets in *Blade Runner*? How about the poets in *Star Trek: Deep Space Nine*—what do they write about? Would these dystopic bards care about our internecine poetry warfare, our contests and careerism? This is a cheeky way of saying that one answer to our instant question is to ask what American poetry can become, unshackled from kitsch. We can ask what it means to live within a poetics where the curious, unreliable hope we might feel as we mentally grope our way toward a future American poetics might resemble that of an immigrant first landing in America, an immigrant such as Ichiyo, who writes in the Japanese American National Museum's history of making his way to America, the sails on his ship overfilled, but with hope.

What strange lineage will these future poets cobble together from our instant moment, what wonderfully miscegenated narrative of their own they will lift from our present, like someone pulling up a colored thread that had been buried in the sand?

IV. Descriptionist Interlude

Walt and I strolled from the Bronx to Bowling Green and saw Bangladeshi cab drivers chatting on earpieces, an international arbitration panel about the legal rights of two imaginary giants, a hungry man burping a trombone in a subway basement, shops that sold cigarettes and dreams and coffee, a man and a woman ditching work together at the Frick (what nerds!), a Jamaican girl raising her hand in class even though she was not sure she knew the answer, an exhausted banker who went to a movie in the summer and fell asleep while it played and felt liberated. In fact, everyone was falling asleep. There were bodies snuggling the sidewalk. There were heads nestling on steering wheels. I thought they were dead at first. I felt the pulse of the woman who was now slumped against the unicorn tapestry at the Frick and her pulse was still beating. These men and women were not dead, they were dreaming together. They were snoring this silly behemoth into invention.

BIBLIOGRAPHY

Borges, Jorge Luis. *Other Inquisitions, 1937–1952*. Translated by Ruth L. C. Sims. Austin: University of Texas Press, 1964.

Brookings Institution, Metropolitan Policy Program. *The State of Metropolitan America: On the Front Lines of Demographic Transformation*. Compiled by William H. Frey and Audrey Singer. Washington, D.C.: Brookings Institution, 2010.

Japanese American National Museum. *Japanese American History: An A-to-Z Reference from 1868 to the Present.* Edited by Brian Niiya. New York: Facts on File, 1993.

Jordan, June. "For the Sake of People's Poetry." In *Some of Us Did Not Die: New and Selected Essays*, 242–54. New York: Basic Books, 2009.

Kapil, Bhanu. *The Vertical Interrogation of Strangers.* Berkeley, Calif.: Kelsey Street Press, 2001.

Lai, Him Mark, Genny Lim, and Judy Yung. *Island: Poetry and History of Chinese Immigrants on Angel Island, 1910–1940.* Seattle: University of Washington Press, 1991.

Sami al Haj. "Humiliated in the Shackles." In *Poems from Guantánamo: The Detainees Speak*, edited by Marc Falkoff, 41–43. Iowa City: University of Iowa Press, 2007.

5 ~ inaugural poems and american hope

I. Humiliation, 2009

When President Obama announced Elizabeth Alexander as his inaugural poet, I was thrilled. I loved *American Sublime*, and her publisher Graywolf is my dream press. I liked her personal connection to Obama. I saw in her the hope that somewhere at the colleges where I have worked, I might rub shoulders with someone who would turn out to be president. I *identify* with Alexander. Yes, this is an aspirational identification. She has tenure at an Ivy League school, a loyal and well-regarded press, and a significant readership—all things I do not see on the horizon for myself. But in the penumbra of the Obama flame, wasn't hope itself a form of aspirational identification?

When the day arrived, I eagerly sat in front of the TV. I couldn't wait to see what Michelle Obama was wearing. I loved her outfits throughout the campaign. I have an entirely unironic love for the first couple. I literally swooned over Barack Obama's description of their courtship in *The Audacity of Hope*. Their victory fist bump was the most genuine moment of affection I have ever seen between a politician and his partner. I wanted to bathe in the reflected glow of the Obamas' affection and triumph.

The day of the inauguration, I sat glued to my TV. I had no interest in braving the cold and actually going to Washington. John Roberts fumbled the oath. Obama's speech was wonderfully calibrated. Yo-Yo Ma and Itzhak Perlman gave a riveting performance. Aretha Franklin sang "My Country 'Tis of Thee" and I loved her hat. Then the finale: Elizabeth Alexander and the inaugural poem. I may never have anticipated a poem so much.

But the camera cut to the audience. These dedicated souls, who had braved freezing temperatures to see the president take the oath of office, were leaving.

They were getting up and leaving. En masse. Some stations actually stopped their coverage after Aretha had finished. We had worked so hard for this day. *I* had worked hard for this day. And there, at the end of it, were people walking away from the art form I love. There stood poetry where it always seems to stand. Ignored. Humiliated. Abandoned.

II. Robert Frost, 1961

I've never really been able to warm up to Robert Frost. Certainly, "Stopping by Woods on a Snowy Evening" has the amazing talent of memorizing itself into your brain, but I've always found "The Road Not Taken" about as endearing as head lice. My educational experience has always presented Frost in one of two lights. Either he is the charming New England curmudgeon—hardworking, honest, straightforward—or he is the sly parodist, playing at northeastern grit while winking at the careful reader.

Frost was the face of American poetry, and in many ways he still is. It may seem odd that Frost was the first poet to give an inaugural poem, but it was actually the removal of poetry from public life that motivated Kennedy to ask Frost. According to William Meredith, an inaugural poem "was a novel idea, and one that focused attention on Kennedy as a man of culture, as a man interested in culture" (Parini 412). It was precisely that movement of poetry out of the mainstream—a movement that had taken place a good six decades earlier—that set the stage for Kennedy to look cultured by appreciating poetry.

Kennedy did not ask Frost for an inaugural poem, but rather specified the poem that he wanted Frost to read. Frost, however, did write another poem to introduce that poem (after he had been firmly told that he could not give an unscripted introduction). The introductory poem proved impossible to read, as the cold was making Frost's eyes tear up, and "The Gift Outright" was read to the gathering from Frost's memory.

When I was beginning this essay, I looked up the "The Gift Outright" and read it to my husband. The poem begins, "The land was ours before we were the land's" (Parini 335) and explores the transition from colonization to belonging to the landscape. "Oh my god," I said, "did he just celebrate genocide?" My husband responded with a suggestion that I am prone to hyperbole.

Frost biographer Jay Parini points out that the poem might "seem horribly chauvinistic, even belligerent. . . . Frost's poem ignores the Native American angle altogether" (336), although Parini means that Frost ignored their perspective rather than their existence. The poem says, "The deed of gift was many deeds of war." I find it hard to believe that this is simply war with colonial powers.

As a military brat and a Jew, I was raised to believe in America as an ideal rather than a place. Because my homes were arbitrary and changing, I never developed a true attachment to place until well after college. There were lots of places, and they all had their charms and drawbacks. But the texts that formed my life seemed necessary and specific. The Old Testament and the Constitution are not replaceable.

Frost's poem ultimately serves as a powerful corrective to my deracinated idea of America. It insists on the violence of displacement and the violence—both physical and emotional—embedded in the achievement of statehood. The final couplet ultimately seems to me to speak of how we tell ourselves a story of sui generis emergence, even when we know it to be false: "But still unstoried, artless, unenhanced, / Such as she was, such as she would become." Certainly this suggests a blank slate for the colonials to start with—but it also suggests the violence of erasure. Not "storyless" but "unstoried." The stories are being removed, and carefully displaced to make room for us—or the *us* to whom we trace ourselves.

When I first started with Frost, I felt his poem was itself an erasure of America's violent past, but now I've come to feel it as a careful exploration of the perspective that condoned and embraced that violence.

II. Maya Angelou, 1993

One hesitates to say too loudly that one does not like Maya Angelou's poetry. In some circles it goes without saying—you simply walk into a faculty lounge and bemoan the fact that the only poem your students have ever heard is "Still I Rise." Harold Bloom wrote, "Her poetry has a large public, but very little critical esteem. It . . . makes no formal or cognitive demands upon the reader" (9). *Library Journal* assessed her first volume of poetry as "well done schlock poetry, not to be confused with poetry for people who read poetry" (Avant 13).

But in other circles, Maya Angelou is the quintessential role model. She embodies the major themes that preoccupied twentieth-century America: overcoming adversity, making victimhood a position of strength, and celebrating one's heritage. At a moment when many writers were focused on the impossibility of communication through language, Angelou was focused on making her own letters crystal clear—and it won her an audience that included President Clinton.

While I tend not to think of Frost and Angelou as having much in common, Angelou's inaugural poem "On the Pulse of Morning" contains multiple echoes of "The Gift Outright." Like Frost, Angelou gives the land a seductive agency, insisting that the inhabitants of America inhabit her. She opens with the landscape, but ultimately reveals that her poem is in the voice of that landscape: "I am that Tree planted by the River, / Which will not be moved. / I, the Rock, I, the River, I, the Tree, / I am yours—your passages have been paid" (272). Angelou does cast a wider net than Frost. She lists multiple peoples, making the country speak to a veritable laundry list of heritages, including sexual orientation and economic privilege in her list. While Frost began with the arrival of the colonists, Angelou goes all the way back to the Jurassic period, remembering even "the mastodon / The dinosaur, who left dried tokens / Of their sojourn here / On our planet floor" (270).

When Toni Morrison in 1998 called Bill Clinton "our first black President," perhaps she did not mean that he was somehow in tune with black culture, but that his body had become subject to the kind of hostile surveillance and judgment to which the black body has long been subjected. Maybe Angelou was the ideal poet to inaugurate Bill Clinton in that she had dedicated her life to pushing back against the racism that subjugated American blacks. In fact, Angelou had left America entirely, living in Ghana until Malcolm X inspired her to return.

I don't remember the poem from the inauguration, but I do read it every year. It's in the High Holidays prayerbook of the Reconstructionist Movement (that's a branch of Judaism, I should explain), and I always look forward to reading it. The ending is amazing:

> Here, on the pulse of this new day,
> You may have the grace to look up and out
> And into your sister's eyes,
> And into your brother's face,
> Your country,
> And say simply
> Very simply
> With hope—
> Good morning. (273)

I spend a lot of my time explaining why I love certain poems, but the best poems catch you off guard. The best art simply floors you, and that "Good morning" always floors me. The build to it seems so rhetorically inflated, and the poem includes the sort of lists that usually make me cringe. But the closing is almost like those Beach Boy harmonies that are so sweet they hurt like cacophony; the plainspoken turns into a quotation of itself, unmooring the simplicity of the simple.

IV. Elizabeth Alexander, 2009

Adding to the painful humiliation of America essentially walking away before the inaugural poem was read was that I wasn't inclined to stand up for the poem. My non-poet friends started calling me the day after the inauguration to ask the same question: Was Elizabeth Alexander's poem as bad as they thought? Unfortunately, I felt that I had to confirm that it was. The inaugural poem had broken one of the central tenets of good poems. It had too many things at stake. Instead of focusing on a single consciousness, it had spread itself too thin. The *New York Times* published a transcript of the poem that butchered the lines. When I spoke to other poets, there was almost no love for the poem. We all agreed that it was clumsy and diffuse—that it was trying to appeal to too wide an audience.

Still, I've come to love "Praise Song for the Day." With multiple returns, it feels wiser and wiser. The title is accurate, but the poem is about the difficulty of joy in the face of history's weight. It opens onto the conflict between community and isolation: "Each day we go about our business, / walking past each other, catching each other's / eyes or not, about to speak or something" (9). I did not realize how much this captured what I've come to feel about democracy—how we have to speak to each other, and yet we don't—for very good reasons. A later line says that we have "each / one of our ancestors on our tongues," recognizing that to actually start the conversation might be to fight or entrench. Our heritage is always with us, and our grievances are real. The poem is about effort, not achievement; the progressive tense, not the perfect. "Someone is trying to make music"—the music never arrives. People wait, people begin, but there is no conclusion, no triumph, no reward. "We need to find a place where we are safe" (13).

At the time, I thought this was placing the emphasis on America's promise rather than America's reality. But I think this was because I didn't want the inauguration to be a beginning—I wanted it to be the victory. I wanted to feel finished—to let Obama work his magic. Alexander's focus on process was ultimately prescient. The poem says, "we encounter each other in words" (13), and what felt truistic in 2009 feels more complicated in 2014.

The poem ultimately embraces love as the necessary mode for connection. "What if the mightiest word is love?" (19) the poem asks. This is an easy line to ridicule, and certainly I did. But this is the problem of all liberals. Conservatives can find consistency in their positions, as can radicals. The poem embraces the light of love and concludes "praise song for walking forward in that light" (23). I tend to prefer sentences rather than nominal phrases, but in the nostalgia for the hope I felt that morning, this seems like the right ending.

Alexander's poem, newly composed for the day, shows how poetry straddles the line between art and lecture. Perhaps an inaugural poem can only be evaluated from the other side of a presidency, and it's unfair to ask it to be evaluated too soon. "My Country 'Tis of Thee" has had more than two hundred years for us to warm up to it. Why should "Praise Song for the Day" not be given a couple of years?

V. To praise what America will be?

I began this essay not to praise inaugural poems but to damn some of them, yet living with these poems, I've found more and more to admire. We repeat to ourselves over and over that we live in highly polarized times, though it does seem odd that we have to keep repeating it. The repetition compulsion of the twenty-four-hour news cycle might be a sign of the death drive. To quote Langston Hughes, "America never was America to me." But all of these poems look at the America that's all of America—even when it fails to live up to the promises that we like to call "America," and especially when we remember the sheer expanse of violence on which our nation was built. As Langston Hughes writes later in that poem, "And yet I swear this oath—America will be!"

It's interesting that two of our inaugural poets have been black women—a constituency that has often found itself caught in the double jeopardy of a double oppression, but also an identity that has often represented comfort and authenticity in the larger social imagination (think Oprah; think *The Help*). And in thinking that I disliked these poems initially, I now sense I allowed the bad habits of our political climate to inform my listening practice. I rushed to judgment; I substituted personality for substance; I read superficially; I listened to gossip rather than returning to the source. I allowed myself to make polar decisions of for/against. When I listened closely, I found a great deal to love in what I heard.

Now if only the rest of America would sit in their chairs long enough to listen. Even on a really cold day.

VI. Coda

Since this essay was originally published in the *American Poetry Review*, Barack Obama has been inaugurated for a second term, and there has been another inaugural poem, this one by Richard Blanco. "One Today," Blanco's inaugural poem, took the same strategy as Elizabeth Alexander's poem but fleshed it out more narratively and personally. The PBS pundits loved Blanco's poem; the *Chronicle of Higher Education* called it a "frenetic mishmash." It's important to note, however, that our first black president chose the first gay and first Latino inaugural poet.

BIBLIOGRAPHY

Alexander, Elizabeth. *Praise Song for the Day*. Saint Paul, Minn.: Graywolf, 2009.

Angelou, Maya. *The Complete Collected Poems of Maya Angelou*. New York: Random House, 1994.

Avant, John Alfred A. Review of *Just Give Me a Cool Drink of Water 'Fore I Diiie*. In Bloom, *Maya Angelou*, 13.

Bloom, Harold, ed. *Maya Angelou*. Bloom's Major Poets. Broomall, Pa.: Chelsea House, 2001.

Brennan, Teresa. *The Transmission of Affect*. Ithaca, N.Y.: Cornell University Press, 2004.

Hughes, Langston. "Let America Be America Again." 1935. poets.org/viewmedia.php/prm-MID/15609.

Morrison, Toni. "Comment." *New Yorker*, October 5, 1998.

Parini, Jay. *Robert Frost: A Life*. New York: Henry Holt, 1999.

Schneiderman, Jason. "Oracular." In *Starting Today: 100 Poems for Obama's First 100 Days*, edited by Rachel Zucker and Arielle Greenberg, 139–40. Iowa City: University of Iowa Press, 2010.

Williams, Miller. "Of History and Hope." 1999. poetryfoundation.org/poem/176494.

6 ～ refusal of the mask in claudia rankine's post-9/11 poetics

JOANNA PENN COOPER

In *Don't Let Me Be Lonely: An American Lyric* (2004), Jamaican-American poet Claudia Rankine explores post-9/11 American existence through innovations in hybrid form, stylistically performing themes of disconnection, searching, and grieving. The text comprises, as the back cover indicates, something between prose poems and lyric essay, as well as photographs depicting images from mass media, many by her husband and collaborator John Lucas. Additionally, the text includes twenty-one pages of endnotes, forming a parallel text whose more "straightforward" knowing pulls against the main text's journey into grieving alienation. Ultimately the poems, images, and endnotes resonate, providing an innovative engagement with lived experience's mediation through film, television, journalism, the messages of government, and those of the medical and pharmaceutical industries. Despite the book's subtitle ("An American Lyric"), *Don't Let Me Be Lonely* resists lyrical gestures toward "wholeness" and "unity" that erase real trauma. Claiming neither the easy affirmations of some lyric poetry nor the subversive mask of much twentieth- and twenty-first-century ethnic American literature, Rankine instead offers fragmentary counter-gestures that resist closure, suggesting the power of genre experimentation to challenge received knowledge. Rankine's non-masked but politically and existentially searching speaker reawakens her reader to how artistic innovation helps resist the numbing discourses playing across contemporary Americans' minds and bodies.

The book's searching, numb tone is introduced in the first poem, one not accompanied by an image. Here the book's themes of loss—in the form of the illness or death of family and friends—emerge, as well as its engagement with the question of whether one can connect with another person's loss as more than an outside observer. The book begins, "There was a time I could say no one I knew well had died. This is not to suggest no one died" (5). The speaker describes a miscarriage suffered by her mother and the death of a grandfather. She comes home from school one day to see her father with "a look that was unfamiliar; it was flooded, so leaking. I climbed the steps as far away from him as I could get. He was breaking or broken" (5). He has learned of his own father's death, and he gains the look of "someone understanding his aloneness." After returning home from the funeral, we learn, her father speaks of it no further.

This piece illustrates the book's stylized flatness, and also introduces the way theme and style dovetail throughout the book. Rankine's use of parataxis creates the effect of numbness, but also of searching, a circling around death and aloneness, much as the speaker carefully circles around her father, witnessing his pain while remaining apart from it.

The piece also introduces a concern for how racial blackness and death are associated in the mass media: "The years went by and people only died on television—if they weren't Black, they were wearing black or were terminally ill" (5). What are the connections, the poem asks, among racism, perception, media, death, grief, and connection to others? How and when does communion fail? And how, the reader wonders, is this "an American lyric"?

We can imagine Rankine's poetics in *Don't Let Me Be Lonely* as a psychically exhausted, twenty-first-century response to Whitman's affirmative poetics in "Song of Myself." In 1855 Walt Whitman offered an ecstatic vision of the poet's body as conduit for national thought. As Whitman's preface to the first edition of *Leaves of Grass* explains, the American poet "incarnates [the nation's] geography and natural life and rivers and lakes" (7) and takes into himself [*sic*] the nation's history, character, and struggle. The great poet, for Whitman, contains contradiction, transmutes into song the national materials surrounding him—including natural beauty, social stratification, cultural trauma.

If, in the pre–Civil War nation, Whitman imagines the poet taking the nation into himself in all its multifarious complexity and singing it into a poem of transcendent (but perhaps ultimately colonizing?) unity, for Rankine in this text, the role of the poet is less to ecstatically dissolve boundaries than to work through grief toward witness. This speaker imagines the poet as one who fully examines how bodies and minds are marked by difference, how we become dissociated through the alienating effects of the media, continuing racially motivated violence, political manipulation, an out-of-control pharmaceutical industry, and personal and national traumas.

The poet's position here relates to African American poet Ross Gay's notion of the "anti-affirmative." In "Black Poetics and the Anti-Affirmative" Gay explains the concept as a poetic stance that makes room for discourse about debility and trauma. For Gay, "the affirmative first claims what is truth, then goes about proving how it is true." In his view, the *anti*-affirmative is a courageous and necessary corrective to our peculiarly American tendency to under-engage with the spiritual traumas underlying depression, for instance, and, in our cultural production, our desire to provide imaginary resolutions to historical schisms. The "anti-affirmative," for Gay, provides a necessary corrective to the false, hegemonic dynamic at work in our society that—in capitalism, in popular culture, in politics, sometimes in art—asks to deny injustice, pain, or historical trauma. Gay identifies the anti-affirmative as important in much contemporary African American poetry, pointing to Richard Pryor's monologues as a valuable model, as Pryor's broken, jarring vulnerability sometimes left early audiences in stunned silence rather than laughter. As demonstrated in Rankine's text, this mode resists aesthetic moves that easily suppress the ghosts.

Rankine's anti-affirmative differs from the school of Pryor, however, in her lack of engagement with what Houston A. Baker in *Modernism and the Harlem Renaissance* has called the African American artist's "mastery of the minstrel mask" (17). As Baker has observed, this canny redeployment of the minstrel mode has been a major strategy of much African American cultural production, and artists aiming to "engage in a masterful and empowering play within the minstrel spirit house needed the uncanny ability to manipulate bizarre phonic legacies" (24). Thus the "spirit of the mask" Baker identifies depends upon slippages of meaning and manipulation of cultural discourses. For Baker, modern African American cultural production was marked by "the black spokesperson's necessary task of employing audible extant forms in ways that move clearly up, masterfully and re-soundingly away from slavery" (101). Today poets such as Terrance Hayes demonstrate the power of redeploying "phonic legacies" to address the cultural horrors of the subjugation of the racial Other, as well as to keep alive a spirit of play, hope, and redemption. In *Don't Let Me Be Lonely*, Claudia Rankine does something different: she refuses the mask.

We can see Rankine's "refusal of the mask" in the relative flatness of the diction, the parataxis, the exposed vulnerability—these elements suggest a speaker that, while stylized, resists the subversive persona implied by Baker's discussion of the mask. Of course, Rankine's speaker is a crafted invention. In a 2009 interview conducted by the Academy of American Poets, she observes how transmuting lived experience into poetry differs from transmuting it into nonfiction. She explains that

> a lot of people assume that *Don't Let Me Be Lonely* was autobiographical because of the "I," the use of the first person. It's not—and it is. I feel that when I'm working on something, I will take from anywhere I know to get at the place that I'm going. . . . And I will use whatever I can to investigate whatever it is that I'm investigating. . . . But . . . [u]ntil I say I'm writing nonfiction, I'm not writing non-fiction. . . . feel like the making of the thing is the truth, will make its own truth. (2009)

While we must recognize this speaker as a crafted invention, the poems are not "persona poems" in the way we generally use that term. Instead there is a vulnerable commitment to witnessing one's pain and numbness, and that of others, to moving through alienation and back toward human connection.

This numbness and the concomitant attempt to reclaim the position of witness appear in a dialogue with the self in one piece that reads in part:

> I thought I was dead.
> You thought you were dead?
> I thought I was.
> Did you feel dead?
> I said, God rest me. (16)

In several other pieces the text connects American psychological depression, the political turmoil of the early 2000s, and the textual materials of the pharmaceutical industry. The speaker describes an evening with a depressed friend, a speechwriter who has had to take a "medical leave from his job." As they watch a Werner Herzog movie, the friend begins to cry:

> While watching the movie, tears rolled down his cheeks. Apart from their use in expressing emotion, tears have two other functions: they lubricate the eyes so that the lids can move over them smoothly as you blink; they wash away foreign bodies. It is difficult to feel much tear-worthy emotion about anything in *Fitzcarraldo*. . . . I decided that apparently my friend was expressing emotion and was not fine, not okay, no. (42–43)

The matter-of-factness here highlights the pathos, as does the inclusion of an image of the prescription label for, presumably, the friend's bottle of lithium.

Meaning accrues as the book proceeds. In another section the speaker is a writer who is working on a book on hepatotoxicity, or liver poisoning. Rankine writes, "Again and again there exists an 'I' who was institutionalized because 'I swallowed a bottle of Tylenol' and went into a coma" (53). Here the speaker and the hypothetical "I" blur into one another: "The nurse . . . informed me the day I was to check out that the first thing I'd asked when I first awoke was, Alive? She said she answered, Yes, love, you are alive. . . . Why are you smiling, my smiling nurse?" (53). On the next page the speaker continues to blur the boundaries between herself and her compatriots, and imagines meeting with her book editor, who asks her to tell her "exactly what the liver means to her." The image accompanying this piece shows the outline of a person with the esophagus, stomach, and liver indicated in gray and black, and another organ in the bowels, one shaped like the United States. In the text next to the image, the speaker explains that she "care[s] about the liver . . . because the word *live* hides within it." She goes on, "Or we might have been able to do something with the fact that the liver is the largest single internal organ next to the soul, which looms large though it is hidden" (54). Rankine here performs an anti-affirmative, yet strangely Whitmanesque, move. The poet imagines the relationship between the nation and the body but somehow, unlike Whitman, has difficulty locating the soul.

The inability to find hope, find the soul, is here a necessary first step in claiming the position of witness and moving toward human reconnection. In her piece about the death of James Byrd, the black man who was "dragg[ed] . . . to his death in . . . Texas," Rankine references Cornel West, who "makes the point that hope is different from American optimism" (21). West's "American optimism" compares to Ross Gay's American affirmative. In both there is a lack of engagement with the realities of injustice and violence in the national ethos. Both also suggest the need for radical engagement with reality and hope, rather than easy "optimism" or "affirmation." But after watching the election results in 2000, Rankine's speaker observes, "However Bush came to have won, he would still be winning ten days later and we would still be in the throes of American optimism"; she reflects that this is "the same Bush who can't remember if two or three people were convicted for dragging a black man to his death in his home state of Texas" (21). She finds that she is suffering from "a deepening personality flaw: IMH, the Inability to Maintain Hope," noting that "Cornel West says this is what is wrong with black people today—too nihilistic. Too scarred by hope to hope, too experienced to experience, too close to dead is what I think" (23).

How, then, does the text find any movement beyond nihilism and locate a position from which to reclaim hope, without providing an imaginary resolution to this very real despair? The last section of the book proposes a strategy of *presence* and artistic shaping of experience. The first poem in this section recounts a dream: "where I am going or what I want is behind a black curtain, but it is so dark the curtain becomes the night" (127). The speaker's husband suggests she feels her "voting won't make a difference." There is, however, a turn away from nihilism in the last two sentences of the poem: "Sometimes you read something and a thought that was floating around in your veins organizes itself into the sentence that reflects it. This might also be a form of dreaming." Two pages later Rankine writes, "Or, well, I tried to fit language into the shape of usefulness" (129). The last two pages of the text show us a way forward, indicating the integral role art plays in claiming the right to presence, even hope. Rankine cites Celan's line "I cannot see any basic difference between a handshake and a poem," and her piece then explains, "This conflation of the solidity of presence with the offering of this same presence perhaps has everything to do with being alive" (130). The book ends on these words: "In order for something to be handed over a hand must extend and a hand must receive. We must both be here in this world in this life in this place indicating the presence of" (131).

Even as Rankine's speaker rejects the subversive masked persona in favor of a cracked-open, searching one, the text ultimately gestures toward the role of artist-as-healer, its own archetypal performance. In his 1958 essay "Change the Joke and Slip the Yoke," Ralph Ellison explains, "From a proper distance *all* archetypes would appear to be tricksters and confidence men: part God, part man, no one seems to know he-she-its true name, because he-she-it is protean with changes of pace, location and identity" (102). Ultimately, despite her text's sharp deviation from Whitman's ecstatic mode, Rankine's work, like "Song of Myself," is indeed "an American lyric." *Don't Let Me Be Lonely* builds on Whitman's legacy, embracing formal innovation to explore how art illuminates our connections to each other, to lived experience, and to the "official" and personal version(s) of the story.

BIBLIOGRAPHY

Baker, Houston A., Jr. *Modernism and the Harlem Renaissance*. Chicago: University of Chicago Press, 1987.

Ellison, Ralph. "Change the Joke and Slip the Yoke." In *The Collected Essays of Ralph Ellison*, edited by John F. Callahan, 100–112. New York: Random House, 1995.

Gay, Ross. "Black Poetics and the Anti-Affirmative." Faculty lecture presented at New England College MFA residency, Henniker, N.H., June 28, 2007.

Rankine, Claudia. *Don't Let Me Be Lonely: An American Lyric*. Saint Paul, Minn.: Graywolf, 2004.

———. Interview by Jennifer Flescher and Robert N. Caspar. *Jubilat* 12 (2006). Reprinted by Poetry Daily at poems.com/special_features/prose/essay_rankine.php.

———. "Transcript: Claudia Rankine in Conversation." 2009. www.poets.org/viewmedia .php/prmMID/21017.

Whitman, Walt. "Preface to *Leaves of Grass*, 1855." In *The Portable Walt Whitman*, edited by Mark Van Doren, 5–27. New York: Penguin, 1973.

7 ～ i am not a man

CAMILLE T. DUNGY

I am not a man. In conversation with several of my male peers I was disabused even of the illusion that I was *one of the guys*. So, fine, that's clear. Here I am, writing about the black male in poetry, some kind of woman. And maybe I've been asked to write about the black male in poetry *because* I'm some kind of woman. Maybe I'm here because I'm the kind of woman people refer to as "a daddy's girl." I'm the genuine article. The kind who, at seventy-five, will still be calling my father "Daddy."

Once, after Mom complained about something my father had done, I defended him saying, "What Daddy did made perfect sense to me." And what could she say except, "*Everything* your father does makes perfect sense to you." And she was right. So far as I can see, Daddy's nearly infallible. I do dearly love that man.

So maybe I'm included here, a woman with a guest pass to this all-male club, because I can be trusted, because everyone who knows even a little about me knows there is at least one black man I believe can do no wrong. And isn't that one of the things we have to think about when we think about constructions of black American masculinity? Mustn't we think about the fact that, facing the culturally imbedded quagmires that black men in America must daily face, each one must need at least one person who believes he can do no (or at the most very little) wrong?

Mind you, it might be safer not to have too many people thinking you're the hottest thing around. Consider Etheridge Knight's "On Seeing the Black Male as #1 Sex Object in America":

> Black men in the south
> Of America / are / sooooooooo pretty—
> . . . .

> That men, and women, hide
> Under sheets and masks and ride
> And plot under the Alabama moon
> How to "cut the nut." (97)

Isn't part of the construction of black masculinity in America the myth of the perfection of his body, strength, and penis? And can't this construction work on a man in dangerous ways? So perhaps part of the responsibility for those of us who construct images of black masculinity is toward the construction of balanced portrayals. What should we call the black man's equivalent to the virgin/whore paradigm? It would be dangerous to believe that every black man must be pimp-ilicious, savage, and strong. It would be equally dangerous to assume that an individual black man might not display some or all of these attributes. It would be dangerous not to carefully examine these assumptions and others like them: what they represent and why; who they benefit and how; what they mean and when; how and where they can and cannot be applied.

One thing that a successful poem must do is push against preconstructed notions, test them, deny them, walk away from or embrace them. A sonnet; a sestina; a pantoum; a poem steeped in anaphora; one rich in whole rhyme, half rhyme, slant rhyme, or alliteration; a poem reliant on biblical allusion or the blues; a long-lined poem, a short-lined poem, a prose poem, a syllabic poem— every poem contains and is contained by a certain set of values, the boundaries it will test, dismiss, confirm. The act of writing is a process of complicating expectations. To write a sonnet is not simply to write fourteen lines of iambic pentameter in a Shakespearian or Spenserian or Miltonic rhyme scheme. To write a sonnet is to question and complicate the values set forth for the sonnet by everyone who has written a sonnet before your sonnet, and to anticipate and frustrate the expectations of any reader who picks up a sonnet after yours.

By "anticipate and frustrate" I mean the poet must predict what expectations a reader might have, adhering to them well enough so the reader will, out of pleasure or excitement, knowledge or intrigue, continue to read. To the same ends, the poem must compromise the ease with which it will be read. A thinking reader does not appreciate extreme simplicity, or the predictable and uncomplicated obvious.

A thinking reader knows every runaway slave did not sport the tattered trousers or the provision-filled, stick-slung bandana portrayed by the stereotypes that nineteenth-century typesetters used in runaway adverts. A thinking reader would thank you not to simplify the ingenuity of freedom seekers by relying on this image, these details, alone. And the uncareful reader will never turn into a careful, thinking reader if her preconceptions are not shaken, confounded, tossed out. The poet who writes about a 19th-century fugitive slave must acknowledge and subvert descriptive and stylistic boundaries established by the standard stereotype. A poet writing about any black man in any age must do the same. To not illuminate the expectations set up for each character, to not demonstrate the ways in which he falls short of, exceeds, surprises, conforms to or reconfigures these expectations, to not make a character something less than mechanically perfect and something more than simple, easy, plain, is to not show a character the respect of diligence, perception, skill, and care.

Consider, once more, my daddy. He's my dad. I see him when I see him, maybe five times a year, and I have yet to write poetry about him, so, sure he can be perfect. I mean, I don't have to actually *live* with him or, through my poems, make him live. I love him, but it's up to Mom to actually *love* him. And bless her little heart is all I have to say about that. I've loved some black men in my life.

And maybe *that's* why I've been asked to write this essay, because I've been known to love a black man or two in my time. And isn't poetry, like a relationship, a private and intimate declaration made public? And, as with any good relationship, doesn't poetry require that we notice and care for and tend to and think about those on whom we've focused our attention? And don't black men, like poems, sometimes do things that don't at first, if ever, make perfect sense to us? And isn't love, like poetry, partly about learning to incorporate that which does not make perfect sense into that which creates a sense of completion? And don't our subjects, desired even in and often because of their imperfections, live and breathe (sometimes before we've written about them and sometimes *because* we've written about them)? Maybe I'm part of this conversation because, as a poet, I've grown into and out of and over and into and out of and into the love of my subjects, which, quite often, have been black men.

I know this much: I've written two historically based collections about African American life, and neither would have been complete, in fact neither would have really gotten started, had I not found ways to balance my portrayals of black women with portrayals of black men. In America, who you are is often measured by and against who you are not. I believe that to study and understand womanhood in American culture it is crucial to study constructions of masculinity. And so maybe *that's* why I'm writing this essay, because I've taken an intellectual interest in balanced portrayals of women and men. To do this honestly, I write about complicated women and less-than-perfect men.

One of the most dangerous things about the myth of the perfection of the black male body, strength, and penis is the fact that the myth is oftentimes not true. Like the nineteenth-century typesetter's stereotype, this image of strength and virility was constructed, in part, as a means for someone else to regain and maintain control over black men. And yet, unlike the tattered-trousered fugitive, the unbreakable black man remains a model with a great deal of appeal.

Like all living beings, every black man has his flaws, and to know him well enough for true respect and love means you'll have to recognize those flaws. But too often the perceived role of those of us who live with, love, or write about black men is to keep silent about those weaknesses. To broadcast them is viewed as a betrayal. I confronted my own mother over a version of this crime. And yet, to perpetuate the stereotype by never calling it to question feeds, often unwittingly, into its original design. Men who cannot be wholly revealed because they cannot reveal their weaknesses alongside their strengths are more caricature than men.

It's *men* I want to love. *Men* I want to write about. I write toward the question I asked myself in one of the earliest poems completed for my first book: "What do I know if I don't know / what it is that would have made him a man?" Not a perfect man, not a demon man, not whatever one-sided kind of black man we grow so used to (and for some of us so weary of) seeing. Only a man. A real, live man. I want to write men who are flawed and men who are fabulous. Men who are balanced. Men who are complicated as Gwendolyn Brooks's "Satin-Legs Smith." I want to write into poems men who are able to do no, or just a little, or, if it suits the occasion, all kinds of wrong. I want to know what might make and unmake a black man, because in working toward that knowledge, in writing toward that knowledge, I move that much closer to knowing what can make and unmake me (woman, black, American, man lover, woman lover, human being). I inch that much closer to understanding what can make and unmake *us*.

BIBLIOGRAPHY

Knight, Etheridge. "On Seeing the Black Male as #1 Sex Object in America." In *The Essential Etheridge Knight*, 97. Pittsburgh: University of Pittsburgh, 1986.

II. THE UNSAYABLE & THE SUBVERSIVE

Matthew Lippman's "Shut Up and Be Black" opens with questions across race and teaching, and the ways we affect each other through poetry. An in-depth look at gender and race, Leigh Johnson's "Unsexing *I Am Joaquín* through Chicana Feminist Poetic Revisions" unpacks the feminist Chicano imagination. In "New Female Poets Writing Jewishly" Lucy Biederman explores recent dialogue and debate in Jewish American literature and champions a movement. The weighing of competing or complementary identity lenses is explored in Tim Liu's "Looking for Parnassus in America," and Liu quarrels with himself in exploring why one poet might be privileged in his work over another. Hadara Bar-Nadav in "The Radical Nature of Helene Johnson's *This Waiting for Love*" closely examines this work and asks us to consider the women poets of the Harlem Renaissance. Natasha Trethewey's poetry of historical and family violence and personal racial hybridity is the subject of Timothy Leyrson's "Writing Between Worlds," and Paula Hayes takes on the racial underlayment in A. Van Jordan's poetry in her essay "Letting Science Tell the Story." This section ends with a difficult quarrel indeed, indictment and complicity in Native American/First People's literary communities, in Travis Hedge Coke's genuinely rendered "Identity Indictment."

8 ～ shut up and be black

MATTHEW LIPPMAN

I.

How the hell am I supposed to teach black literature to high school students? I'm a white dude. Secular Jew from New York City, circa 1965. What do I know about Etheridge Knight, Patricia Smith, Ralph Ellison? Couple of poets. All poets, really.

I know this: I love their language. That's the collision. Language love slamming up against experience. I barely know what it means to be a white-dude Jew from New York City circa 1965, so how can I go into a classroom, tack up Knight's "The Idea of Ancestry" or Patricia Smith's "Skinhead," and even sound like I know what I'm talking about? I can't. That's my problem. But I gotta try, right?

2.

I brought Ralph Ellison's *Invisible Man* into the curriculum, eleventh-grade English, at a small independent school outside of Boston proper, in 2011. What I know: I am not black. What I know: *Invisible Man* has been my favorite novel since I first read it in college. Also, I know this: I am a Jew. The space between myself and the black man is huge. What do I know about him, about the black woman, to teach this novel in a way that has any sort of authenticity? Nothing. I tell the students, I can't really teach this book because I am not black. I tell them, I can only read it with you.

I have two sections of eleventh-grade English. That's thirty-eight students. Two black students. One is African. The other is from inner-city Boston. His name is Harold. When I look at him I think: How am I going to get away with teaching this book, this book I can't teach, with him in the class? He sees right through it, through me, the whole situation, the paradigm—or maybe it's just me being stupid. The student from Africa? I don't know, it just feels different.

With Harold, well, he's Harold and *Invisible Man* is his history. At least I think it's his history because he's African American. Not African. Or maybe these are all some whacked-out stereotypes that I've got running around my brain even though I used to think I had the props to talk about this stuff because I grew up in New York City in a lower-middle-class neighborhood during the 1970s, went to public school, and didn't really know what was up except that we all went into the street after school and ran around getting dirty, playing stickball, basketball, ring-a-levio, and "color" didn't seem to matter. Or maybe it did and we just weren't seeing it because everyone was kinda poor and so we were just being that, broke, and stealing candy from Gus 'n' Bernie's because we could. Truth is, I don't know anything, really, about anyone's history—cultural, political, psychological—except my own, and I've got to remember this going into the classroom every day if my teaching is going to be organic. As a teacher, well, that's all I am interested in—organic, an organic staged environment, because, come on, we're not hanging out at the playground. As a teacher I want everyone to feel as comfortable as possible in the classroom. That's primary. The material comes secondary. But, I'm outta my league here just like the white Jewish athletic director at my school who "recruited" Harold from another school to play basketball. Kid is six-foot-six and has a nice jump shot. That is the picture. It's an old picture. It's the one that the whole world of America loves to watch, to burn up, to fondle. Harold wants to go D-I, then pro. What the fuck am I supposed to do? Maybe the only history is the history that he's in my class and loves basketball, or thinks he loves basketball, and so basketball and black are at the table, again, and I'm lost. But, I don't know, see, I'm just making this up because it's been made up for me and I keep thinking: You can't teach this book. It's impossible.

3.

I got into this dumb and beautiful business of teaching because I was a poet. It's another story everyone knows. I never knew much about literature the way I knew some about poetry. I had to eat, so I figured, I like teenagers, I'll teach them. It went well for a long while, and then I decided to teach *Invisible Man*. Cool. *You love that book for so many reasons.* One day I was sitting on the sofa thinking about those reasons and I got tired. I went to YouTube and there like a shot of Red Bull into the brain was Patricia Smith reading "Skinhead" on Poetry TV. She didn't so much read it as she sang it. With my one good finger, she said, Fuck you. Uh-oh. My head blew up and I'm sitting there thinking yeah yeah, hell yeah, I gotta talk about all this black stuff, and the decision to bring Ellison's novel into my curriculum felt more explosive. Because I can't stand the fluffy stuff, and Ellison and Smith and, later, Knight all have attitude in their writing. Attitude with a capital *A*, and that is what I have been trying to get my students to understand, see, embrace—attitude. Smith's poem, her whole persona-thing in that performance of "Skinhead," is the absence of invisibility, and I thought it brilliant that an African American woman would write and read a poem from the persona of white fascist asshole. I thought, Man, that's some ballsy shit and I gotta teach Ellison because it's so damn smart and to show these kids how far we've come even though I still don't know anything about how far anyone has come.

4.

Class ends. We're all out in the hall. Harold, I say, you all right with this? pointing to the book. He looks down, says, Yeah? I say, You know, it's in the text? He says, Yeah, I know. I say, The word "nigger" is going to come up. He says, Got it. For a second I want to be Bill Withers or Miles Davis or just Carl Smithson, friend of mine from Long Island, so I can be black. I swear it, sometimes when I am up in front of the students teaching *Invisible Man*, all I want to do is shut up and be black so I can "really" teach the book. At least that way it would be authentic and rich, real, super organic. There I go again, using that word "organic" like I'm talking about peaches or just the damn butterflies so I can talk about the black experience in a way that is full of *Blackness*. Problem is, I am a white Jew in front of Harold and it freaks me out. Not him. I don't think he cares that much, or maybe he does or maybe I'm just putting all this nonsense on him because it doesn't matter. It's all some whisper of racism. Funny, when I was a younger man, a younger teacher, I had no problem teaching Toni Morrison's *Sula* or Hughes's "I, Too, Sing America" to the same population of kids—affluent Jews and gentiles, a couple of black kids, some Asians. I was stupider then, as a teacher, because I thought I knew something about something that I can never know—history. Now, though, the whole thing just feels wrong, disconnected.

5.

I read Knight's "The Idea of Ancestry" out loud. I'm reading it and look-
ing at Harold. The whole poem is about drugs and getting high and almost
kickin' the habit and the beauty of family and love. I'm looking at Harold—all
around me these white faces and half of them are asleep—and I want Harold
to get up and say, Wake the fuck up, but that's just me like I know something
about Harold. It's my problem with all this black literature. I don't know what
to say and so I want my one black student to say something because all of my
inadequacy comes straight from blindness, but, that's only half true. The other
half is that I just don't know. How could I know? How could any of us know
the person on the other side of the room who grew up speaking the funk when
I was speaking the slide and that other one near the water cooler, chatting up
his buddy in rhyme? Impossible.

When the poem is over I look up. I look toward Harold. He's kicked back
in his chair, his huge sneakers on the desk, and I say, you know what I say, I
say, Harold, can you please get your sneakers off the desk. It's because I feel
like a chump. He gives me a look that says, Don't worry, man, it's cool. You
like this, I say, about the poem. I like the line, I am all of them, they are all
of me, I am me, they are thee. Why? I ask. It flows nice, he says. Nice, I say.

6.

Every remark I make when I remark on Ellison's narrative is racist. So I de-
cide to tackle it head on. I ask the kids, How many of you are racist? I raise
my hand, answering my own question to—what? Make a point? Be honest?
Maybe both. One other girl raises her hand. She's Jewish. What she under-
stands, I think, is that she does not like other people because they are different
from her and does not mind owning that little piece of her tarnished heart.
Maybe that's the first step, no matter what tribe you belong to.

Patricia Smith came to my school. She visited. The students loved her. She
was wholly, I imagined, Patricia Smith. She was refined and raw and she em-
braced every question like it was a little baby. She came to my class. She read
some poems. We all went to a larger room for a more formal reading. Ms.
Smith wasn't into that formal thing. She asked for requests. Someone said,
"Skinhead." She recited it. The whole place fell apart. They loved her. I don't
know who they saw up at the front of the room. A woman. A black woman. A

poet. A songwriter. I was glad for them. For me. Because we all fell apart at the tension in her language. That's the point, I think. Maybe that's just the point no matter what the background of a person. But of course—and this is the thing that almost always gets me—it's exactly the background of a person that does make us fall apart. That contradiction is at the center of this conundrum.

7.

I wish Etheridge Knight could have visited my school. I would have paid top dollar for that visit. When I first read "Feelin' Fucked Up" I felt like I was put in a headlock—a sensually inviting, smack-me-down kind of headlock. Poems don't change my life. I don't believe in that mumbo-jumbo. This poem changed my life. Just like *Invisible Man* changed my life. How? They opened up a big window and said, Walk through. My own writing, of course, was what they changed. You can't mess with that. You know what's interesting, there's something about that poem that transcends black, white, Asian, Muslim. It's not that Knight uses "fuck" a thousand times. I mean that's fun and all but what what what about the poem moves past the fact that Knight is black writing about being Knight? I have asked myself the question for a long time. Harold answered it. He said, It's true. It could have been the little quiet girl, a transplant from Manhattan who goes to Shabbat services every Friday night, or the arrogant lacrosse player from Wellesley who said that, but no, it was Harold. Who's Fanon? I asked. No answer. What about Nixon? Two kids knew. Hey Lipp, Harold said, again, it don't matter. It's just true. He's right, Alex said and Mia and Veronica and Pauline and Shaquille and Kamika and Arjun. Because you can get to love easy, you just have to be open to it and then even if you don't like your brother or sister because his hair is messed up or her shirt has no collars, it's easy. Just go there. That's what Knight is saying and that was it. Feelin' fucked up feelin' so good. Class dismissed.

8.

In my school we hired a guy named Don. He was hired to be Director of Diversity—an Italian dude from the Bronx who has the heart of a nightingale, the laughter of three thousand children, the spirit of a wild dervish. He spoke a speak right out of a 1975 college seminar on "Getting to Know Your Brother." His office was filled with chocolates, books about race and commerce, race and class, race and marriage, race and race. The kids loved him, hung out on his couches, ate his candy, went to his symposiums on social justice. A well-liked man. But there was this: He ain't have any color in him except Italian color and that's not much, no disrespect. So the black science teacher moved through the crowd, nudged a bit and took over his spot, not in any mean-spirited way, just in a "made sense" way, right? History is a funny thing. People who belong to the same tribe speak the same language and that, really, is their history. It's just true if truth is anything to quantify. I think, if I know anything, language is history and, on good days, an expression of identity—personal and communal.

This is me: I am waiting by the whiteboard, waiting for the black man, the black woman, to come and nudge his/her way into my classroom, take *Invisible Man* and "Skinhead" out of my hands and tell a truth I couldn't even imagine because he or she shares the same language with Ellison. I welcome it, I think. Come into my classroom. Bring it on. I'd like to be a teacher in your class. Not for me, though, but for Harold who sits in his seat and imagines hook shots, left-handed layups, the big shorts that run past his knees. I'd just like to watch. I'd like to watch, also, the other kids in the class who, I feel, would benefit greatly from hearing the history of someone else's language. The white kids or Asian kids or the kids from Colombia and Guatemala. I imagine an English Literature classroom where a Native American teacher teaches Sherman Alexie and a Chicano teaches the poetry of Juan Felipe Herrera and a woman teaches Margaret Atwood's *The Handmaid's Tale*, et cetera. I guess, if this were the case, I'd be out of a job but, you know, things might be a lot different in the classroom. I have no answers.

9.

How's class? I ask Harold, in the foyer of the school where all the kids hang out. He smiles. Interesting, he says. Why? I ask. I don't know, he says. So tell me, I say. He says, It must be weird being you, white, talking about all this black stuff. Black stuff? I say. You know what I mean, Lipp, and I do, all too much. What am I supposed to say? You like the book? I ask him, the noise of sixty teenagers blamming off the wall. I like it, he says. It's cool, he says, then sees one of his friends and gives me a pound, says, Later, Lipp, and is off.

I had to check in. That's what I had to do. That's all I can do, really. For a long time, no lie, I wanted to be black like I wanted to be one of the Just Men in Judaism, like, when I was sixteen, I wanted to be the musician Elton John, like when I lived in Italy I wanted to be Italian and when I am with a man that is gay I want to be gay. It's an odd, messed-up thing that I have always done—trying to appropriate the language of the person sitting next to me who is not a Jew just to feel part of the tribe, to communicate (here goes that word again) in an organic way. Jew comes easy to me and there are no issues. It's not that I want to pretend to be part of another person's tribe or be included in the club, no, it's just that I have always tried to figure out a way, as a teacher, to open up the classroom and have it be the safest place that I can make it. The world, too. That's why I check in. That's, maybe, all I can do.

10.

It's impossible, I am finding as the year moves forward, to teach *Invisible Man* without feeling like a fraud. Halfway through the year I have decided to expunge it from the curriculum. It has always been important to me to teach literature by black authors, more so than Chinese authors or Muslim authors or Hispanic authors. Honestly, I have no idea why. I don't know if it matters. I just have a connection to the collective voice, the big language, that has come out of the black community. Saying anything else would be a lie. The poetry of Etheridge Knight moves me in my spine. I love his poetry so much I can't believe it. The same is true about Audre Lorde's poetry and Major Jackson and Gary Jackson and Mahalia Jackson. I don't know why. It's just the bounce-music in the language. It does something to me. Maybe I am a racist. I think I would be more of a racist, now, at this moment in my life as a teacher, if I continued to teach Ellison's brilliant and beautiful book. Oh, I understand, it is a book about transformation, about hope, about me and you and I and thou. That's true. But, really, it's a book about a black man, a man made invisible, a man who allowed himself to embrace his invisibility because of the color of his skin and I know nothing about that. I can't even get close to that.

11.

This is what Smith does in "Skinhead." She says, "I am the White Boy." From that point on, anything is possible. Maybe that's how we become invisible. We become the Other. Maybe that's how we bridge the gap. Maybe that's how I teach these books, these poems. I just pretend to be black, get all invisible out of my Jew self and become black by acknowledging the fact that I am pretending, that I am making it all up as I go along just so I can get past all the racist crap. It's an experiment I have yet to try. Probably out of fear. Hey, you know what Lippman did in English class, he pretended he was black and then talked about "The Idea of Ancestry" like he was black. I'd be fired in a second. It's a cool thought experiment, though. Smith does it in "Skinhead." It's pretty damn powerful. It's also pretty damn exciting. Think about what my teaching would be like if I could do this with every text. Pretend to be a Muslim when teaching Salman Rushdie or Japanese when teaching Murakami. Think about those conversations.

See, this is what poetry does. It allows the poet to go nuts. In the going nuts the reader gets to go nuts too. Smith's "Skinhead" disarms people—a black woman writing as a skinhead—to make a point. We are all of each other. Even though we're not, we are. Ellison does the same thing and so does Knight. It's transcendental on some level and I don't give a shit if you think it's not or that it shouldn't be. It should be. You keep your language, I'll keep me, but in doing that we can also step out and check in.

12.

Someone said, It's great that you are teaching *Invisible Man*. I tell them I took it out of the curriculum. Oh, that's too bad, he says, but does not ask me why. I am so glad he does not ask me why. I wouldn't know what to say. I have written these pages, and I still don't know if I have said anything of any merit. I'm sure I will teach it again, maybe when I am fifty-five. Maybe I will read it with my students and we will just listen to the music, to the language, without saying a damn word about the text. Just last night I ran into an old student who told me the most memorable and resonant thing that happened for him in high school was in one of my classes. It was a class called Music and Literature. I had forgotten this but for one whole class period we listened to Van Morrison's *Astral Weeks*. Not a word was said about it before or after. I think if I teach *Invisible Man* again it will be in a class called Music and Literature. Each class will be dedicated, simply, to reading books out loud, no matter what the author's race, religion, cultural background, sexual orientation. When the recitations are complete, there will be no discussion, just the quiet of the silence in the air as the words take some kind of root and shape and form and then disappear for the moment into more pressing matters like weekend plans, dates, parties, text messages to the crush who is in science class and half asleep.

13.

At the beginning of this schoolyear, the first day of classes, I saw Harold in the front circle, smiling, happy, laughing. He caught my eye. I caught his. We walked up to one another and did that man hug thing. He bent his 6' 8" frame (he grew) down to my 5' 1" frame (I shrunk) and exchanged pleasantries. A few minutes passed and it was time to split. He grabbed my hand, looked down at me, and said, I love you, Lipp, then took off. I love you too, Harold, I said, and he turned back and smiled. Because that's what this essay is, a smile. It's a damn love story. I know. It has to be, right? Who cares if I know your language, you know mine? Truth is, we are never going to get it right anyway so why the hell should we begin to even try? We've just got to check in. That's the whole damn point anyway and then, really, all the rest of it just flies off the desks and computers and notebooks and the world is an all-right place and we can come together and be all right with one another and then go our big and beautiful and blistering and separate ways and then wake up the next morning and do it all over again.

9 ∼ unsexing *i am joaquín* through chicana feminist poetic revisions

LEIGH JOHNSON

Rodolfo "Corky" Gonzales's *I Am Joaquín* (written with small distribution in 1967, published by Bantam Books in 1972) is one of the most widely recognized cornerstones of the Chicano literary canon. Undeniably the poem is manifesto, epic, and heralded literary production all in one. However, because *I Am Joaquín* purports to speak for the Chicano Movement, yet largely leaves out women's contributions, the poem has elicited many responses—poetic, scholarly, and artistic—almost since its initial publication. While the issues of sexism and Chicano Movement discourse are not new, the discussion of Chicana poetic responses to *I Am Joaquín* adds consideration of new poems and addresses how these poems use archetypes and naming in ways that other discussions of responses to *I Am Joaquín* have not considered as thoroughly.

Chicana poets have resisted archetypal representations of women, and contemporary poets have also responded to the residual antifeminism of the Chicano Movement. In a representative revisioning of *I Am Joaquín*, several poets—Carmen Tafolla, Sylvia Alicia Gonzales, Lorna Dee Cervantes, and Sandra Cisneros—have explicitly addressed the misogyny they see in *I Am Joaquín*. The poets use the cultural locator *I Am Joaquín* to position women's voices and experiences in the Chicano/a collective identity.

In his thorough explication of *I Am Joaquín*, Juan Bruce-Novoa argues: "The Chicano Everyman, Joaquín, retreats first into his people, and then into history to seek essential knowledge" (49). That essential knowledge, though, leaves women out, or relegates them to weeping widows, raped wives, or passive mothers. The Chicana feminist responses to *I Am Joaquín* engage these clichés to insert specific historical, social, and political importance of women from pre-Conquest to post-Movement. Meant to be recited at Movement rallies, meetings, and marches, *I Am Joaquín* is best experienced aurally. Daniel Belgrad argues that the poem is an original example of performing Chicanismo and situates power relations to "elicit a cultural response in which assimilation is seen as treason, and accessibility as capitulation" (251). Because the poem takes up rape of land, culture, and women, it alludes to La Malinche and all women as cultural traitors, an image that Chicanas have contested through poetry, essays, and fiction.

I Am Joaquín engages cultural archetypes of Chicanos that have existed for five hundred years—or two thousand, depending on one's critical interpretation of whether the poem begins at the Spanish Conquest of Mexico or earlier, with the Aztecs. The poem expresses hybridity through paradoxes, making the speaker both "the sword and flame of Cortez / the despot" and "the Eagle and Serpent of / the Aztec civilization" (17). The textual history of *I Am Joaquín* explains some of these images. The original version came as part of the Colorado Crusade for Justice, and the 1967 printing contained several heavy charcoal drawings. Silvio Torres-Saillant shores up the paradoxes of the symbols in the poem: "The volume's cover shows the full-length face of an adult male wearing a penetrating look, with the small whole body figure of a peasant boy placed on the lower left hand corner of the large face. One assumes the face to represent the titular character of the poem" (453). Even though *I Am Joaquín* was used as an epic poem to inspire crowds, it was also a piece of visual culture. Those readers outside the scope of the Chicano Movement because of gender, location, or age might have experienced it visually. In 1969 Luis Valdez recorded a film version of the poem, reading the text while pictures of the Chicano Movement, murals from Mexico, and other images appear on the screen, further blending the aural and visual experience of the text.

Chicana poets draw on comparable images as they attach new meanings to the significant metaphors of *I Am Joaquín*, including poverty, resistance, and history. In revising the images, Chicana poets also insert women into the narrative of the Chicano Movement, rectifying the omission of women from the Movement canon. As Vicki L. Ruíz's foundational study *From Out of the Shadows: Mexican Women in Twentieth-Century America* explains the problem, women's participation "has been reduced to a cursory discussion of sexism within the movimiento," yet "a growing body of scholarly studies and literary works offer eloquent testimonios of Chicana feminist thought" (100). The poems discussed here reveal women's literary participation and un-silencing in the Movement.

One of the first and most explicit revisions of *I Am Joaquín* is Carmen Tafolla's 1978 poem "La Malinche." As other scholars have pointed out, the opening line of the poem, "Yo soy Malinche" echoes the opening of *I Am Joaquín*. Mary Louise Pratt argues that Gonzales's poem "had the effect of anchoring Chicano identity in a series of cultural coordinates that included land, agriculture, spirituality, and links to the indigenous . . . in a normative male subject" and that Tafolla's poem is an "analogous foundational project" (868–69). As "La Malinche" seeks to subvert the normative male subject speaking for women into a woman asserting her identity and speaking for herself, the text of the poem also offers a different interpretation of Malinche. *I Am Joaquín* does not specifically address the Malinche figure, but her image haunts Chicano/a literary production.

Literary depictions of La Malinche (sometimes called La Chingada) depend on retelling the circumstances of her relationship with Hernán Cortés, the fate of her children, and her place as the mother of a mestiza race. Almost all writers are, on some level, responding to Octavio Paz's 1950 essay *The Labyrinth of Solitude* which claimed: "And as a small boy will not forgive his mother if she abandons him to search for his father, the Mexican people have not forgiven La Malinche for her betrayal" (86). Chicana poets have had to contend with this image of Malinche in order to subvert the argument that women are responsible for the selling out of indigenous peoples to the Europeans and the Chicano Movement to the Anglo feminists. Emma Pérez shows that by sympathizing with the colonizer father, Paz makes Malinche the "dreaded phallic mother who will devour him, castrate him, usurp him" (107). Most of the widely read, taught, and studied poems about Malinche have been written since the Chicano Movement, when Chicana feminists sought to gain awareness of issues impacting women that had been marginalized by the same activists.

By making Malinche speak for the Chicana experience as Joaquín speaks for the male, Tafolla reclaims Malinche's voice—a mode of exchange—as a tool for Chicana agency. Tey Diana Rebolledo and Eliana S. Rivero argue that Chicana writers see La Malinche as a survivor—a woman who "cast her lot with the Spaniards in order to ensure survival of her race and a woman who lives on in every Chicana today" (193). Perhaps this is the most important element the revisions of Malinche reveal—the fact that she can say, as Tafolla's speaker does, "I was not a traitor to myself" (199), productively challenging cultural memories that are racist, misogynist, or homophobic.

Revising Malinche in the context of the Chicano Movement, especially in light of the way Chicana feminists were viewed as cultural traitors by the Movement, is a daring and subversive act. It is also a necessary act. *I Am Joaquín* relies on images of the pre-Conquest Aztec society to establish the royal native society, a trope Tafolla rejects with the reality of Malinche's speech, "I was sold into slavery by MY ROYAL FAMILY—so / that my brother could get my inheritance" (198). In rendering this perception of Native unity problematic, "La Malinche" asserts women's voices and, says Vicki Ruíz, "casts her as a woman who dared to dream" of a better world (107).

The most epic undertaking of the Chicana revisions of *I Am Joaquín* is Sylvia Alicia Gonzales's "Chicana Evolution," first published in 1978. The poem begins with the lines "I am Chicana / Something inside revolts" (418) and is split into three parts which are biblical in scope and representative of past, present, and future. By beginning with and repeating the refrain "I am Chicana," Gonzales self-consciously echoes *I Am Joaquín* with a crucial difference. While *I Am Joaquín* is supposed to speak for the Chicano Movement bringing people together as brothers in struggle, "Chicana Evolution" genders the declaration and immediately suggests revolt against a patriarchal structure. Mirroring Corky Gonzales's declaration that Joaquín is both "the sword and flame of Cortez" and "the Eagle and Serpent of the Aztec" (17), "Chicana Evolution" proclaims,

> I am Chicana
> A blistering Indian sun
> waiting to be sacrificed.
> A pale Catholic virgin,
> waiting to be baptized. (421)

While this statement seems passively constructed, it sets up the revelation at the end of the second section: the speaker sees Malinche as a Christlike figure who will come (and already has come once) to sacrifice herself "in redemption of all her forsaken daughters" (422). The recognition that Malinche is both savior and betrayer is crucial to the future that the poem imagines. Norma Alarcón reads the return of Malinche as "gloomy" in that Sylvia Alicia Gonzales's act of "writing itself is empowering, yet she postpones the daughters' actual enablement, as if the appropriation of language were still to take place" (76). For one thing, the future is in Spanish, but it comes with a full recognition of the Malinche in all Chicanas and the poet's assertion that she makes them strong in their position as "MUJER" (424). "Mujer" is the feminist articulation of Chicana identity, and it is the last word of her poem; mirrored against the last word of *I Am Joaquín*—"ENDURE!" (29)—it takes on an urgency and force that would be lost without the knowledge that her poem is a response to Corky Gonzales's. When these poems are read together, the critic sees that "Chicana Evolution" posits both a positive role for Malinche and a revision to the masculinist view of *I Am Joaquín*.

Lorna Dee Cervantes's poem "Para un Revolucionario," initially published in 1975, critically examines the themes and images in *I Am Joaquín*. The opening stanzas describe the romantic persuasion of the sentiments in *I Am Joaquín*, especially the love of land, art, and the Chicano soul and body, yet the speaker quickly deflects the overly nostalgic romanticism of this nationalist vision by pointing out, in a mix of Spanish and English, the realities of women in the Movement. Sheila Marie Contreras characterizes the poem as "a pointed poetic critique of the gender politics within movement communities that confined women to domestic work, without recognizing the centrality of that labor to the success of the movement" (133). The speaker says that the revolucionario's voice is lost in the wail of children, clatter of dishes, and noise of a house. More significantly, he has rejected her as his equal, not accepting her claim "I too am Raza" (382). He views her as a sex object, and she declares, "I can only touch you / with my body" (382). Cervantes's repetition of images from *I Am Joaquín* such as blood, Raza, freedom, dream, brown, sun, spirit, and art all serve to underscore how "Para un Revolucionario" is a revision of the Chicano nationalist poem. She subverts these images by suggesting that unless the male revolutionary recognizes her as Raza too, the dream of the revolution will elude both of them. Cervantes's poem does not attempt to recuperate an image of a woman, as Tafolla's "La Malinche" does; rather it points out the ways that Chicanas are already part of the struggle for racial and sexual equality through their building of communities and families with their own hands.

Most of the previous poems were written in the fifteen years following the publication of *I Am Joaquín* and seemed to carry a direct sense of urgency in revising the narrative to include women in the story of Chicano/a resistance. More recently, Chicana poets have been interested in revising archetypes of women in Mexican American literature and culture, experimenting with form and voice, and writing a different experience than countering *I Am Joaquín* suggests. However, subtle revisions to it exist in poems like "Loose Woman" by Sandra Cisneros. The speaker describes those who would try to silence or discount her before coming into her own space, when she declares, "I am the woman of myth and bullshit. / (True. I authored some of it.) / I built my house of ill repute" (113). These lines draw on the maligning of women in the Movement, the distrust of La Malinche, and the speaker in Lorna Dee Cervantes's "Beneath the Shadow of the Freeway" who only trusts what she builds for herself. In "Loose Woman" the speaker claims ownership over the good and bad that she has created and participated in, yet she also disrupts the silencing of women in *I Am Joaquín* by ending with opposition to the line "I WILL ENDURE" (29). Cisneros's speaker proclaims, "I break things" (115). The things she breaks are those things that hurt her or hold her back—stereotypes about women, legal inequality, religious doctrines, and more. In this radical alteration of *I Am Joaquín*, Cisneros destabilizes the narrative voice that assumes endurance and prowess. The female speaker of "Loose Woman" is sexually dangerous to men, but she is also well aware of her reputation, which she exploits as a potential for glorious revolution against patriarchy and racism.

These Chicana revisions of Corky Gonzales's epic *I Am Joaquín* create new ways of inserting women into the Chicano Movement, but more than that, the poems address the lost identity of the Chicana. They suggest that not only is she not lost, she has the potential for inciting a revolution of her own to overthrow patriarchy and sexism. Rafael Pérez-Torres observes that *I Am Joaquín* reveals "an anxiety about the Chicano/a cultural condition that emerges from a lack" and creates "a socio-cultural condition . . . whereby the Chicano imaginary moves among sites of naming and loss" (206). The poems by Carmen Tafolla, Sylvia Alicia Gonzales, Lorna Dee Cervantes, and Sandra Cisneros rectify the lack of naming a powerful Chicana presence in the original epic poem. There is room for these revisions in the Chicano literary canon without diminishing the impact of Corky Gonzales's poem; rather, there is value added in a naming that is expansive—*Soy mujer*, to build oneself, to break out, to be Raza in one's own way—and not lacking.

BIBLIOGRAPHY

Alarcón, Norma. "Traddutora, Traditora: A Paradigmatic Figure of Chicana Feminism." *Cultural Critique* 13 (Autumn 1989): 57–87.

Belgrad, Daniel. "Performing *Lo Chicano*." *MELUS* 29, no. 2 (2004): 249–64.

Bruce-Novoa, Juan. *Chicano Poetry: A Response to Chaos*. Austin: University of Texas Press, 1982.

Cervantes, Lorna Dee. "Para un Revolucionario." In Fisher, *The Third Woman*, 381–83.

Cisneros, Sandra. "Loose Woman." In *Loose Woman: Poems*, 112–15. New York: Alfred A. Knopf, 1994.

Contreras, Sheila Marie. *Blood Lines: Myth, Indigenism, and Chicana/o Literature*. Austin: University of Texas Press, 2008.

Fisher, Dexter, ed. *The Third Woman: Minority Women Writers of the United States*. Boston: Houghton Mifflin, 1980.

Gonzales, Rodolfo "Corky." *I Am Joaquín*. In *Message to Aztlán: Selected Writings*, 16–29. Houston: Arte Público Press, 2001.

Gonzales, Sylvia Alicia. "Chicana Evolution." In Fisher, *The Third Woman*, 418–26.

Paz, Octavio. *The Labyrinth of Solitude: Life and Thought in Mexico*. Translated by Lysander Kemp. New York: Grove Press, 1961.

Pérez, Emma. *The Decolonial Imaginary: Writing Chicanas into History*. Bloomington: Indiana University Press, 1999.

Pérez-Torres, Rafael. *Mestizaje: Critical Uses of Race in Chicano Culture*. Minneapolis: University of Minnesota Press, 2006.

Pratt, Mary Louise. "'Yo Soy La Malinche': Chicana Writers and the Poetics of Ethnonationalism." *Callaloo* 16, no. 4 (1993): 859–73.

Rebolledo, Tey Diana, and Eliana S. Rivero, eds. *Infinite Divisions: An Anthology of Chicana Literature*. Tucson: University of Arizona Press, 1993.

Ruíz, Vicki L. *From Out of the Shadows: Mexican Women in Twentieth-Century America*. New York: Oxford University Press, 1998.

Tafolla, Carmen. "La Malinche." In Rebolledo and Rivero, *Infinite Divisions*, 198–99.

Torres-Saillant, Silvio. "Páginas Recuperadas: Political Roots of Chicano Discourse." *Latino Studies* 4, no. 4 (2006): 452–64.

10 ～ new female poets writing jewishly

LUCY BIEDERMAN

In 1994 in "How Jews Became White," Karen Brodkin Sacks traced the so-ciological, historical, and institutional forces through which American Jews attained whiteness in the mid-twentieth century, countering the enduring narrative that Jewish immigrants to America possessed special qualities that allowed them to move up the social ladder. Sacks argued that "the Jews who were upwardly mobile were special among Jews (and were also well placed to write the story)" (85). David Biale and others have since complicated Sacks's assertion of Jewish whiteness, arguing that American Jews have continued to take stances that assume or take advantage of the notion of Jews as nonwhite. "But this strategy is full of ironic contradictions," Biale writes, arguing that American Jews "seek to be marked at once as part of the majority culture, by linking their history to the institutions of America, and as different, by insist-ing on the particularity of this history as a persecuted minority" (28). Cheryl Greenberg summarizes this condition as "the tension between Jewish self-perception of vulnerability and external perception of Jewish security" (61).

Perhaps in that tension—between the social, or external, views of Jewish-ness and internal, or personal, definitions and questions regarding Jewish iden-tity—American Jewishness can be located. Recent criticism regarding Jewish American literature takes place in the context, or in the shadow, of these ten-sions and conditions and conversations, especially when it comes to depictions of and references to the Holocaust. Where some critics see Jewish Americans as having been silenced, others see them as having been given special treatment. Either way, it can be difficult to establish an agreed-on set of Jewish American literary traditions or methods in literature when fundamental questions remain in play, including what constitutes a Jew and how one performs Jewishness in literature.

Fittingly, recent criticism about new Jewish literature often begins with questions, as if conceding that the ground on which such criticism stands is shaky, or constantly shifting. The essays in *Radical Poetics and Secular Jewish Culture*, a collection concerning the effect of cultural Judaism on contemporary American poetics, seem invested in the work of unsettling or disrupting fundamental issues. Charles Bernstein asks: "Am I Jewish? Is this Jewish?" (13). Rachel Blau DuPlessis asks, "What is secular Judaism?" (2010, 209). Hank Lazer in an essay titled "Who or What Is a Jewish American Poet?" notes that multiple poet-critics invoke Kafka's quip "What have I in common with Jews? I have hardly anything in common with myself" (19). (Kafka's, "of course, is an extraordinarily Jewish statement," Jerome Rothenberg writes (34).)

But when criticism of Jewish American poetry is impelled toward questions, definitions, and the work of establishing legitimacy or explanation for why Jewish American poetry can or should be studied, perhaps this stands in the way of *reading* Jewish American poetry as such. Alicia Ostriker has noted that the term "Jewish Literature" tends to exclude Jewish poetry (148). However, reading new female poets like Arielle Greenberg and Sabrina Orah Mark in a Jewish American context can potentially allow for deeper, broader, or clearer readings.

In an article for her series about contemporary poetry in *American Poetry Review*, Greenberg focuses on spirituality, making a distinction between spirituality and "words like *religion, belief, faith*, or *divinity*" (39). As opposed to those other terms, spirituality, she argues, can be seen as less doctrinal, more open to a variety of connections. Spirituality is offered not only by Greenberg but by poet-critics like DuPlessis and Lazer as a potentially more permissive site of ontological exploration. DuPlessis, a self-defined cultural Jew, describes being told she is not a real Jew by a culturally conservative academic and "fully affiliated Jew." Such poses of offense and defense are an example of how Judaism is performed or proven in an academic context. Greenberg points out that "MFA programs, writing retreats and artists' colonies are generally thought of as safe spaces for various 'alternative' viewpoints and lifestyles, but are not necessarily great places in which to be a devout person of faith" (39).

Considering the fraught atmosphere in which these conversations take place, then, Greenberg's decision to discuss spirituality rather than religion in her criticism is understandable. At the beginning of the article, Greenberg writes that spirituality "is about *connection*, and connection is what is interesting me most these days" (39). By identifying or associating herself with the spiritual as opposed to the religious from the start, Greenberg distances herself from the types of "attacks" and counterattacks that DuPlessis describes. But perhaps Greenberg's identification with spirituality also could be read as cousin to the tendency toward self-erasure that Bernstein considers distinctly Jewish. "While Jewish secular culture has sometimes—well maybe often, well sometimes or often, I really can't be sure—wanted to erase—or shall we say put under erasure?—its explicit Jewishness, especially insofar as such identity-politic might remove or ghettoize us from the larger culture of which we are an integral part—nonetheless there is no particular reason, in other words, no necessity, to take such bracketing of Jewishness as anything other than Jewish" (14). Bernstein's comically hedging tone in "well maybe often, well sometimes or often, I really can't be sure" and even in his dash-heavy punctuation enacts the kind of "bracketing of Jewishness" that he diagnoses as a clear, if ironic, quality of being Jewish. Jewishness being bracketed can have multiple and opposing meanings: to bracket can mean, as Bernstein suggests, to "remove or ghettoize," or to put in a special, prized position; to choose; to hide—all of which have specific and freighted connotations in Jewish religious and historical contexts. Through this lens, Greenberg's elision or avoidance of explicitly religious discussion could be read as a "bracketing" of her Jewishness.

In an interview on the online journal *Melusine*, Greenberg says that she decided to write about Jewish identity and themes in her second book, *My Kafka Century*, when she realized she had not addressed her Jewish upbringing in her debut, *Given*. Burt Kimmelman suggests how secularism can "highlight, paradoxically" Jewishness, in that it enacts the sense of exile that is central to Judaism, "an exile, ultimately, from the word, even from the Word of God— which has been epitomized in the historical fact of the Diaspora" (32). It may be that Greenberg's Jewishness can be located not in the explicit Jewish themes in *My Kafka Century* but in Greenberg's dynamically shifting degree of engagement with Jewish themes between the two books.

Another surprising and unexpected site of American Jewishness in Greenberg's poetics is the presence of what could be called "counterlives." This term is borrowed here from Andrew Furman, who borrows it from Philip Roth's novel *The Counterlife* to describe Roth's use of a variety of Jewish perspectives, which Furman reads as Roth's way of depicting a single multifaceted self and thus addressing "the slipperiness of Jewish American identity" (30). For Furman the sense of Jewish identity bleeding into the identities of others is fundamental to American Jewishness. "To be a Jewish American in the twentieth century is to ask a series of 'what if' questions. What if I had been born in 1933 in Germany or Czechoslovakia or Poland? What if my parents or grandparents fled to Israel rather than to the United States?" (30). Even the title of Greenberg's *My Kafka Century* suggests a speaker with an impulse to ask those questions, and an identity "slippery" enough to try on different centuries. It signals a sense of history, time, and self that encompasses more than one lifetime. After all, how many centuries can one claim as "mine"? To define or seek to understand oneself as *not* oneself—as containing opposing desires, or as being present at various and impossible or improbable times and places— could be a way of articulating a distinctly Jewish self. Mark Heller in defining his own Jewish poetics writes, "If, like Adonis, I search for the self, I also seek that exodus from it" (172). In Greenberg's poetics, counterlives become a bold expression of the ambivalence and abstracted darkness that come with asking those questions as a Jewish American female in the twenty-first century.

Another example of counterlives in Greenberg's *My Kafka Century* is her poem "Me and Peter Lorre Down by the Schoolyard," which begins with the line "Me and my sidekick, we're both pederasts. Like you" (10). There are at least four different selves in the brief space of this line—me, my sidekick, you, and we (composed of "me and my sidekick")—all of whom are directly associated with the poem's "me." Thus the poem announces its task of self-definition, and immediately intertwines that task with a sense of the self as many. The phrase "Like you" appears two more times in the poem's nineteen lines, and "Like I" reappears once. These "likenings" underscore the poem's task of defining the self in or as others. Lazer in a 2009 article speaks to the poem's work of defining through repetition and retrial when he writes, "In my own delineation of a Jewish poetics, part of why I am so determined to fail at this task of definition is that if there is such a thing it is antithetical to any encompassing and fixed singularity" (78). Here Lazer suggests that to seek to define, and to not only "fail at this task of definition" but to be determined to do so, is Jewish. In Greenberg's poem, the speaker's grammatically incorrect "Like I" is a likening to oneself that fails, a defunct self-definition, a broken connection between oneself and another—and yet here it is, existing anyway in this poem, defying the reader's recoil at its wrongness. It also, especially coming after the phrase "The little girls, they cry," evokes the cadences of a nonnative speaker. Hannah Wirth-Nesher shows how Grace Paley uses such syntactic inversions to suggest "the Yiddish source language" of the speaker (220). By using the ostentatiously incorrect "Like I," Greenberg underscores a sense of discomfort with the English language. Thus exile from the surface of the poem itself is established.

This poem's task of definition does not end at self-definition. Consider the line "*Kindermurder*—it sounds sweet as a game and we want food," which invites comparison with the poem's first line. Aside from both lines being definitions (the first line defining "me and my sidekick," this later line defining *Kindermurder*) the two lines speak to each other formally and thematically. Both are fully end-stopped, both are organized around the narrative and linguistic power provided by their longest, most loaded word (pederast, *Kindermurder*). The "rhyme" between these two lines indicates that defining is one of the poem's central drives, and associates that drive with a sense of depravity. In addition to "*Kindermurder*" and "pederasty," there are words and phrases in these lines and throughout the poem that, when taken together, seem to definitively place the speaker(s) in the Holocaust, like "non-Jews," "hang," "Hungarians," "terrible noses," "no papers," "rat-hole," "difference," "ink," "policeman," "six-sided star," "ledger," "hoof," "we want food," "knives," "gash," "tubercular rag," and "*nein*." However, that context is not immediately clear because of the tonal distance between the body of the poem and its title, which alludes to the Paul Simon song title "Me and Julio Down by the Schoolyard" and to the early Hollywood horror actor Peter Lorre. That distinction between the selves of the title and the body of the poem is an example of Greenberg's use of counterlives throughout the poem, and of her location of Jewish identity in variety.

Sabrina Orah Mark's poetics employ counterlives as well, and to similar effect. In a 2010 interview on the blog *Faith in the Unseen*, Mark says, "The idea behind *The Babies* was that its poems were supposed to be a collection of the imagined voices of those who never lived because of disaster—with *The Babies*, specifically, the Holocaust." Mark introduces the more general word "disaster" before honing in on the specific disaster of the Holocaust. Perhaps that beat of hesitation or reluctance is evidence of the tension that Cheryl Greenberg describes, between external and internal perceptions of Jewishness. Even though, as Mark says, *The Babies* concerns the Holocaust, most of her responses in the interview lead away from Shoah-related themes and topics. Perhaps Mark's reluctance to discuss those themes in conversation as directly as she discusses them in her poetry is a response to the controversy in literary studies regarding Holocaust content.

Interestingly, while Mark's two full-length books, especially *Tsim Tsum* (2009), have been reviewed relatively widely for small-press poetry, few of the reviews mention the Holocaust. Of the six reviews found that mention the character Walter B, who appears in several poems throughout both *Tsim Tsum* and *The Babies*, only one suggests that, at the very least in name, the character is an allusion to Walter Benjamin, the philosopher and essayist who committed suicide fleeing the Nazis. Of course, Mark's engagement with the Holocaust and figures from that era in *The Babies* and *Tsim Tsum* is not what makes her a Jewish poet; rather, the literary methods and forebears Mark calls on to evoke Holocaust themes can be considered distinctly Jewish American. For example, *The Babies* begins with an epigraph from Paul Celan, who, as Marjorie Perloff puts it, has been placed "in a kind of solitary confinement," in that he and all his poems have come to represent the Holocaust—and that alone—for contemporary readers (287). And the Jewishness of *Tsim Tsum* is evoked even earlier, in its title, a Kabbalistic term that critics like Norman Finkelstein have engaged in their readings of Jewish poetry. Of five reviews found for *Tsim Tsum*, two mentioned the meaning of the book's title, but none related that meaning to a Jewish reading of the book.

Instead of positing Mark's writing in a Jewish American context, reviewers have taken the more received route of assuming that what is not immediately lucid or familiar in Mark's poetry is intentionally and permanently obscure. But to place this obscurity in the context of Jewish American methods and techniques would have entirely different implications than to state that the writing is "bizarre" (as does one review) and leave it at that. The only review that considered Mark in a Jewish American context is Stephen A. Allen's online review in *Rattle*, which begins, "When an American Jewish author quotes Paul Celan, references Walter Benjamin, and drops German words into her poems, certain historical events inevitably come to mind." Allen is correct, to the point where it seems conspicuous that so few other reviewers have brought up the Shoah in their discussions of Mark's poetry. Perhaps to mention the book's obvious Jewish themes invites new readings, or challenges expected readings of Mark's work in ways for which reviewers are not prepared. Whatever the reason, the reception of Mark's work suggests that stronger vocabularies or frameworks for discussing new Jewish American writing are needed.

In addition to engaging the Shoah via oblique references to some of its major literary voices like Celan and Benjamin, throughout her work Mark draws from the techniques that critics identify as distinctly Jewish American. Kimmelman writes of George Oppen's skepticism "about the possibility of knowing and conveying anything other than a partial intention or meaning—

which writing, in its finitude of signification, exemplifies. This skepticism is, I would say, typically Jewish" (34).

That same skepticism is present throughout Mark's work. "Black Market" portrays a world in which various types of exchange, including economic exchanges and linguistic exchanges like metaphor, are broken. Nearly every sentence of the poem can be read as a depiction of a broken connection or bad trade. "Cheat the rubble collector out of old rage and oranges," Mark writes. Here two unlike entities, "rage" and "oranges," are likened, because they are both things out of which to "cheat the rubble collector." Usually such simile functions to expose an otherwise hidden truth, but here Mark gestures at metaphorical language only to further obfuscate or disrupt the relationship between objects and their real-world meaning or value—if, she seems to suggest, they have any real-world meaning or value at all. Another trade later in the poem reads: "I watch you trade our mattress for a miniature boxcar." This poem is a "market" where a toy, or "miniature" of an object from the outdoor world of work, is tradable for a large, indoor, domestic object. Metaphor, perhaps our primary tool for depicting human experience through language, is useless here; some switch has been left off, it seems, a screw left unturned.

The final moments of the poem relate this sense of a broken system of exchange to the slipperiness of identity that pervades this poem and contemporary Jewish American poetics in general: "I want to . . . barter away everything you've ever called me: burnt string, broken ladder, violent one, until I am unrecognizable. Even to myself." Perhaps becoming "unrecognizable" to oneself—cutting away the violent, broken, burnt strings to which is tied—is the ultimate goal of writing counterlives. However, considering the contradictions and contraindications present in Jewish American literature, it seems possible to read counterlives as both a means of severing a connection to oneself and a means of connecting with alternate versions of oneself.

Recent controversies and conversations about Jewish American literature can lead to new readings of and perspectives on young writers who engage with American Jewishness. What is misunderstood or disregarded in the reception of Greenberg's and Mark's writing feels related to the anxieties and complexities with which American Jewishness and recent Jewish history, including the Holocaust, are received. Bernstein writes, "The whole secular Jewish culture in Europe was completely wiped out between 1937 and 1945, along with the rest of European Jewish culture. What would have become of all these intellectuals and artists?" (16). Perhaps to write Jewishly as a female poet in contemporary America is to write into the negative capability that Bernstein identifies.

BIBLIOGRAPHY

Allen, Stephen A. Review of *The Babies*, by Sabrina Orah Mark. *Rattle*, n.d. rattle.com/ereviews/markso.htm.

Bernstein, Charles. "Radical Jewish Culture / Secular Jewish Practice." In Miller and Morris, *Radical Poetics and Secular Jewish Culture*, 12–17.

Biale, David. "The Melting Pot and Beyond: Jews and the Politics of American Identity." In Biale, Galchinsky, and Heschel, *Insider/Outsider*, 17–33.

Biale, David, Michael Galchinsky, and Susannah Heschel, eds. *Insider/Outsider: American Jews and Multiculturalism*. Berkeley: University of California Press, 1998.

DuPlessis, Rachel Blau. "Midrashic Sensibilities: Secular Judaism and Radical Poetics (A Personal Essay in Several Chapters)." In Miller and Morris, *Radical Poetics and Secular Jewish Culture*, 199–224.

Finkelstein, Norman. "Secular Jewish Culture and Its Radical Poetical Discontents." In Miller and Morris, *Radical Poetics and Secular Jewish Culture*, 225–44

Franklin, Ruth. "Identity Theft: True Memory, False Memory, and the Holocaust." *New Republic*, May 31, 2004, 31–37.

Furman, Andrew. "What Drives Philip Roth?" In *Contemporary Jewish American Writers and the Multicultural Dilemma*, 22–39. Syracuse, N.Y.: Syracuse University Press, 2000.

Greenberg, Arielle. *Given*. Amherst, Mass.: Verse Press, 2002.

——. Interview. *Melusine* 1, no. 2 (Summer 2009). melusine21cent.com/mag/node/91.

——. *My Kafka Century*. Tuscaloosa, Ala.: Action Books, 2005.

——. "Revelatory and Complex: 'Plain, Free-Flowing' Spirituality." *American Poetry Review*, May/June 2012, 39–42.

Greenberg, Cheryl. "Pluralism and Its Discontents: The Case of Blacks and Jews." In Biale, Galchinsky, and Heschel, *Insider/Outsider*, 55–87.

Gubar, Susan. *Poetry After Auschwitz: Remembering What One Never Knew*. Bloomington: Indiana University Press, 2003.

Heller, Michael. "Remains of the Diaspora: A Personal Meditation." In Miller and Morris, *Radical Poetics and Secular Jewish Culture*, 170–83.

Kimmelman, Burt. "Tracking the Word: Judaism's Exile and the Writerly Poetics of George Oppen, Armand Schwerner, Michael Heller, and Norman Finkelstein." *Shofar* 27, no. 3 (2009): 30–51.

Lazer, Hank. "Is There a Distinctive Jewish Poetics? Several? Many? Is There Any Question?" *Shofar* 27, no. 3 (2009): 72–90.

——. "Who or What Is a Jewish American Poet, with Specific Reference to David Antin, Charles Bernstein, Rachel Blau DuPlessis, and Jerome Rothenberg." In Miller and Morris, *Radical Poetics and Secular Jewish Culture*, 18–31.

Mark, Sabrina Orah. 2004. *The Babies*. Philadelphia: Saturnalia.

————. Interview by Juan Carlos Reyes. November 21, 2010. faithintheunseen.wordpress.com/
2010/11.

————. 2009. *Tsim Tsum*. Philadelphia: Saturnalia.

Miller, Stephen Paul, and Daniel Morris, eds. *Radical Poetics and Secular Jewish Culture*. Tusca-
loosa: University of Alabama Press, 2010.

Ostriker, Alicia. "American Jewish Poetry, Familiar and Strange: A Review." *Shofar* 27, no. 3
(2009): 148–50.

Perloff, Marjorie. "'Sound Scraps, Vision Scraps': Paul Celan's Poetic Practice." In Miller and
Morris, *Radical Poetics and Secular Jewish Culture*, 287–309.

Rothenberg, Jerome. "The House of Jews: Experimental Modernism and Traditional Jewish
Practice." In Miller and Morris, *Radical Poetics and Secular Jewish Culture*, 32–39.

Sacks, Karen Brodkin. "How Jews Became White." In *Race*, edited by Steven Gregory and
Roger Sanjek, 78–102. New Brunswick, N.J.: Rutgers University Press, 1994.

Wirth-Nesher, Hannah. "Language as Homeland in Jewish-American Literature." In Biale,
Galchinsky, and Heschel, *Insider/Outsider*, 212–30.

11 ∼ looking for parnassus in america

TIM LIU

On a recent trip to Morocco where I wanted nothing more than to "disappear" on my long walks through an unfamiliar landscape, I found myself dismayed inside the walls of the medina in Marrakech (where I was staying) because I couldn't walk more than ten or twenty yards without someone accosting me with *Hey Japan!* or *Jackie Chan!* (I concede that I do look like the film star) or *Ko-nee-chee-wah!* In all of my travels, including tourist-trodden cities such as Istanbul or Venice, I've never encountered such an unrelenting onslaught from the locals (men of all ages), the reminder that I was an *eternal outsider*. Only on the day when I hired a native guide did this verbal barrage suddenly cease and desist; even when I walked a good ten or twenty paces behind my guide, everyone knew that I was already "taken," accompanied and chaperoned. It was then I realized that in this country I was essentially a *woman*, a target for harassment unless properly attached. Things got better out on the coast in Essaouira (a.k.a. Mogador), but by then I was feeling pretty battered.

In America, as an Asian American, I am among other things a *model minority*, an *eternal outsider*. The absence of any ESL or fresh-off-the-boat accent (which both of my parents had) might tip someone off that I was born here, but then again, I've gotten used to being asked the question *Where are you from?* and when I say the Bay Area or California or South San Jose or the Almaden Valley, depending on my many moods, I wait for the other shoe to drop: *But where are you really from?* So I repeat myself while adding: *And you, where are you* really *from?* Nine times out of ten, I get the *Oh! I didn't mean anything by that*, to which I respond, *No worries, neither did I.*

In Hong Kong, when I lived there as a Mormon missionary, my Cantonese was so atrocious that the natives thought that I was either (1) retarded; (2) Japanese (and very ambitious in trying to learn how to speak Cantonese!); (3) Korean (on account of my moonlike face); or (4) Hawaiian (because I butchered Cantonese like an American).

In America, when I was a kid, other kids would often ask: *What are you? Chinese? Japanese? How can you tell the difference?* And of course the big joke was that we all pretty much *looked the same.*

In Shanghai, on my first trip there when I was thirteen years old, my Chinese cousins looked through my eighth-grade yearbook and exclaimed that my white-devil classmates also all *looked the same.*

At the Bread Loaf Writers' Conference back in 1990 when I served as a waiter, my mentor was Donald Justice. In our one-on-one conference, he told me that not only was I serious about poetry but I had a *subject*, that being gay and Asian and Mormon was *wide-open turf* in American poetry. He then asked if I had read any Marilyn Chin, a former student who was also *making it*. It turned out that I hadn't, though I had read the first books by Li-Young Lee (*Rose*), Garrett Hongo (*Yellow Light*), and Cathy Song (*Picture Bride*).

Back then, the chancellors of the Academy of American Poets included Richard Wilbur, Stanley Kunitz, Daniel Hoffman, Anthony Hecht, Howard Nemerov, David Wagoner, James Merrill, May Swenson, John Hollander, Mona Van Duyn, John Ashbery, W. S. Merwin, Amy Clampitt, and (from 1991) Richard Howard (my mentor at the University of Houston where I attended grad school). Back then, I was still trying to imagine if I had a place at the table in the hallowed halls of an American Parnassus. It wasn't until 1999 that Lucille Clifton and Yusef Komunyakaa accepted the invitation to cross the color barrier for Academy chancellors that had been in place since 1946. And if I'm not mistaken, it would take another thirteen years to see our first Asian American chancellor, Arthur Sze, when he was elected in 2012.

When I was growing up in California, I was one of a handful of Asian American students at a high school where more than two thousand attended. I remember asking my best friend Dave, who was white and Mormon, if he saw me as Asian, to which he responded, "Of course not! I see you as Tim."

As it turns out, Donald Justice was partially right in what he imagined I would be writing about. For whatever reason, that fraught intersection of being gay *and* Mormon was something that, borrowing from Charles Wright's "Laguna Blues," seemed to "bother me all the time" and trouble me into speech, whereas being a Chinese American, while troublesome at times, did not ultimately pierce my lyric sensibilities.

I've always believed that we read and write out of and through our obsessions.

Each of us has a personal psychology that is colored by race but also by myriads of other cultural mirrors and markers, and which of these impinge on our poetics and our daily practice of poetry is up for grabs.

Over the past two decades, in addition to the work of Arthur Sze, Cathy Song, Garrett Hongo, and Li-Young Lee, I have also spent a good amount of time with poems written by Tan Lin, Myung Mi Kim, Theresa Cha, Mei-mei Berssenbrugge, John Yau, David Mura, Linh Dinh, Pamela Lu, Monica Youn, Mông-Lan, Cathy Park Hong, Srikanth Reddy, Paisley Rekdal, and Brenda Shaughnessy, to name just a few. Their poetic craft, their personal obsessions and warped visions, are what feed me as an artist rather than their racial identities per se.

During this same period, my loyalties (and enthusiasms!) remain for poems written by Linda Gregg, Jack Gilbert, Louise Glück, Jean Valentine, Michael Palmer, Susan Howe, Gustaf Sobin, Charles Wright, Adrienne Rich, and Allen Ginsberg, to name just a few contemporary others, not to mention the roll call of the great dead that include Milton, Blake, Keats, Hopkins, Whitman, Dickinson, Stevens, Crane, Moore, Pound, Bishop, Plath. That all these English-language poets are *white* is not entirely lost on me even if, in the end, this fact finally matters only a little, if at all.

When searching for a yoga class, I am looking to deepen my yogic practice. If my instructor happens to be Asian and/or Mormon and/or gay and/or male, I suppose I might take some comfort in seeing some part of myself (or selves) mirrored back, but these markers per se would not serve as essentials to keep me going back. Same thing could be said for deepening my own poetic practice.

12 ∼ the radical nature of helene johnson's *this waiting for love*

HADARA BAR-NADAV

Helene Johnson (1906–1995) was an award-winning poet of the Harlem Renaissance. Her posthumously published book of poetry *This Waiting for Love* reveals her subtly stated philosophies of poetry, a subversive response to the American literary tradition that attempted to exclude and silence her along with other women poets of the period. In one of the few reviews of *This Waiting for Love*, Lesley Wheeler refers to Johnson's literary career as "notoriously abbreviated" (340). Considering the lack of critical attention to Johnson's work, "notorious" surely is an overstatement. Facing the challenges of a literary establishment largely controlled by white men, Harlem Renaissance women poets had few models and less support for their craft than men did. In his essay "Women Poets of the Harlem Renaissance," T. J. Bryan sardonically states: "the major difference between Harlem Renaissance women poets and their male counterparts is that literary history has, for the most part, excluded the women" (113). A striking number of well-regarded women authors of the period who also wrote poetry, including Gwendolyn B. Bennett, Alice Dunbar-Nelson, Jessie Redmon Fauset, Angelina Weld Grimké, and Anne Spencer, did not publish poetry collections in their lifetimes. Black women writers were largely outnumbered by men in anthologies of the day, such as Alain Locke's *The New Negro*, Countee Cullen's *Caroling Dusk*, and James Weldon Johnson's *Book of American Negro Poetry*, and omitted from other (white) mainstream publishing venues. Poetry by women of the Harlem Renaissance also commonly appeared in marginalized or poorly distributed journals (see Lucky 91; Honey, *Shadowed* xxvii). Johnson only had twenty-six poems published in her lifetime, many of which were not reprinted until Verner D. Mitchell edited her collection *This Waiting for Love*, to which he added thirteen previously unpublished poems. Recognizing the bold complexity of Johnson's work, Mitchell notes that she "challenged accepted boundaries" and that her favorite subjects included "protest, female sexual awakening, the importance of the African past, the sensuousness of nature, and black cultural pride—matters considered inappropriate by the genteel readers of the early twentieth century" (12). Bryan similarly acknowledges Johnson's fierce creative spirit and admits her to a group of rebellious poets from the Harlem Renaissance who advanced toward "poetic freedom and away from the restrictive Ideal of True Negro Womanhood" ("Women" 107). Johnson's daring subject matter also manifested itself formally. Though she wrote in some traditional forms, she favored the free verse stylings that dominated modernist poetry. As such, Johnson's limited publishing record and critical neglect may be less an indication of quality and more a reflection of the precarious aesthetic and social conditions with which women writers of the Harlem Renaissance struggled.

Though some Harlem Renaissance women poets achieved limited success, critics often dismissed their seemingly conventional lyrical and pastoral verse as imitating European traditions and contributing little to black literature (Honey, *Shadowed* xxxiii). Other critics dismissed their poetry by comparing it to the more experimental, race-conscious poetry written by black men (Bryan, "Black" 3). Lacking sufficient critical support and recognition, and facing racism outside the Harlem Renaissance and sexism within, some women poets of the period responded by metaphorically going underground—and to nature itself. Margo Natalie Crawford posits that these women poets sometimes insisted on "the sheer freedom" of writing "about the beauty of nature as opposed to being burdened by heavy racial or gendered themes" (127). Though Crawford may be correct to a degree, I would argue that a closer look at these pastoral poems reveals subversive, radical ideologies and alternative models of creativity. According to Maureen Honey, black women writers of the Harlem Renaissance identified with a "natural landscape that men dominated and violated," an identification that "afforded them metaphors for describing their oppression in ways subversive of white male power yet indirect enough not to offend that very group" (*Shadowed* xli). In critical discussions of the work of Harlem Renaissance women poets, it is therefore necessary to consider "the coherent rebellious messages" in their verse even though their subjects and strategies may appear on the surface to be conventional (Honey, "Survival"

310). Critics tend to focus on Johnson's more obvious breaks with convention in which she uses urban vernacular language; however, it is in her pastoral poems that she is most radical, articulating a bold aesthetic vision while paying poetic lip service to the master. In Johnson's pastoral poetry, she constructs a revisionist model of poetics that envisions creative support among women; alternatives to the power dynamics of the traditional artist-muse relationship; alliances between women and nature, and women and poetry; and nature as a key subject through which subversive messages can be coded and accessed by others.

Among Johnson's contributions to literature of the Harlem Renaissance is her use of nature as a means to revise conventional models of creativity. The poem "Magula" begins: "Oh Magula, come! Take my hand and I'll read you poetry, / Chromatic words, / Seraphic symphonies" (34). This invitation from the speaker to Magula suggests that the creative interaction between these two women will result in a heavenly, musical language. Johnson not only exalts collaboration among women but speaks to the joy inherent in poetry that will fill Magula with a sensual and aesthetically nourishing song. The speaker offers language to Magula, thereby acting as a sort of muse. Johnson revises the traditional muse figure, the woman who inspires the male artist but does not herself create art, and presents an alternative model in which women find inspiration in each other. Moreover, the speaker does not silence her friend, but rather acknowledges Magula's own voice. Magula is described as "Eager-lipped" but threatened into silence by "a man with a white collar / And a small black book with a cross on it" (34). At this crucial moment of silence on the verge of song, the speaker helps Magula recognize the potential of language and warns her about the man armed with symbols of power and authority. According to the speaker, the man will rob Magula of her own sense of beauty and joy, thereby threatening the world in which she lives and creates. Mitchell rightly refers to the poem's speaker as a "poetic guide" who enables Magula to reject "societally imposed definitions and constraints for black female sexuality and personhood" (16), to which I would add constraints on creativity. The male figure might represent the spiritual, social, and political forces that oppress women writers. His small book acts as a constrained, rigid, boxlike text that threatens to silence Magula and sharply contrasts with her colorful world—her expansive text of poetry, song, dance, and nature. Poetry as offered by the speaker serves as an alternative, spiritually informed, creative praxis that allows for artistic collaboration among women who are "Eager-lipped," in which Magula can speak her own words, aver with her body and its movement through dance, and experience beauty and joy on her own terms.

Johnson complicates assumptions about women's creativity in her poem "Invocation." In her revisionist invocation, Johnson claims nature as muse to women writers and embraces the natural world in all its variations and cycles. The speaker asks to be buried in the rain under the "warm wet breast of Earth." She wishes to commune with nature, which is personified as sensual and female. She calls to the weeds, flowers, and trees to grow "[r]iotous, rampant, wild and free" above her grave (Johnson 2000, 46). Even though an invocation is commonly depicted as life-affirming and creative, Johnson strategically associates it with death—but then challenges the notion of death as a finite ending and claims it as part of a regenerative cycle. As the poet-speaker dies and is buried, her body will fertilize the earth and thus give birth to lush, wild foliage (or language). Johnson portrays a highly symbiotic relationship between nature and the woman poet who requires no man for inspiration. However, Johnson also suggests that a journey through death is somehow essential to women's creativity. As an invocation, this poem likely calls for the metaphoric death of those societal or cultural systems that are not life-affirming and that thwart women's creativity.

Johnson continues to ally poetry and nature in her poem "Let Me Sing My Song" in which the speaker calls on the rain, mud, and moon to help her sing. This poem opens as a plea in which the speaker wishes for the freedom to speak, implying that this freedom is being threatened. Johnson models a useful and functional reliance on nature as seen through the poem's speaker, who momentarily experiences a creative catharsis as she considers a gleaming stream: "Groping, untaught, / Flexing the cramped mind / In thought" (62). Johnson ultimately claims poetry as the space in which the speaker can express herself, unadulterated by what she has been taught, perhaps by the literary establishment or by anyone who would challenge her creativity.

Johnson also marks "Let Me Sing My Song" with urgency by repeating its title twice in the body of the poem and by invoking death. The speaker turns to nature for help in part because she fears "the barren drought of death" (62). Johnson metaphorically uses death to signify the potential destruction of the woman poet, who fears for her creative life and struggles to fulfill it. As the speaker finds her own voice, she models for her readers ways in which they can similarly find support through nature and through poetry itself.

"Let Me Sing My Song," which appeared in the notable literary journal *Challenge* in 1935, was the last poem Helene Johnson published in her lifetime

(Wall, foreword xiii). The final line, "I fear the barren drought of death," rings as an ironic closing to Johnson's publishing career, though she did continue to write in the decades that followed (Mitchell 3). Johnson had been poised for a promising literary career, and her early work was well received. She published in the Harlem Renaissance journals *Opportunity* and *Crisis*; her poem "Bottled" appeared in *Vanity Fair*. She was also the cousin of fiction writer Dorothy West and was close friends with Zora Neale Hurston (Mitchell 6–8). She was considered by some to be a rising star. James Weldon Johnson called her "a genuine poet" who "possesses true lyric talent" (279). Considering her promising start and abrupt exit from the literary world, Patricia Liggins Hill wonders "what the literary fate of this talented poet would have been if she had received the patronage and critical attention enjoyed by several of the male poets of the time" (918). The publication of *This Waiting for Love* offers insight into the variety, complexity, and rebellious spirit of Johnson's poetic vision and demands that the literary fate of this poet be revisited. Helene Johnson and other women poets of the Harlem Renaissance undeniably created revolutions through their poetry, simultaneously appealing to those who might dismiss poetry that takes on themes deemed inappropriate for women and to those readers who understood the ingeniously crafted messages imbedded in their texts.

BIBLIOGRAPHY

Bryan, T. J. "Black American Women Poets from 1915 to 1930: Products of a Cultural Milieu." *Obsidian II* 3, no. 2 (1988): 1–10.

———. "Women Poets of the Harlem Renaissance." In *Gender, Culture, and the Arts: Women, the Arts, and Society*, edited by Ronald Dotterer and Susan Bowers, 99–114. Selingsgrove, Pa.: Susquehanna University Press, 1993.

Crawford, Margo Natalie. "'Perhaps Buddha Was a Woman': Women's Poetry in the Harlem Renaissance." In *The Cambridge Companion to the Harlem Renaissance*, edited by George Hutchinson, 126–40. Cambridge: Cambridge University Press, 2007.

Hill, Patricia Liggins, ed. *Call & Response: The Riverside Anthology of the African American Literary Tradition*. Boston: Houghton Mifflin, 1998.

Honey, Maureen, ed. *Shadowed Dreams: Women's Poetry of the Harlem Renaissance*. 2nd ed. New Brunswick, N.J.: Rutgers University Press, 2006.

———. "Survival and Song: Women Poets of the Harlem Renaissance." *Women's Studies* 16 (1989): 293–315.

Johnson, Helene. *This Waiting for Love*. Edited by Verner D. Mitchell. Amherst: University of Massachusetts Press, 2000.

Johnson, James Weldon, ed. *The Book of American Negro Poetry*. Rev. ed. 1931. San Diego: Harcourt Brace Jovanovich, 1983.

Lucky, Crystal J. "Black Women Writers of the Harlem Renaissance." In *Challenging Boundaries: Gender and Periodization*, edited by Joyce W. Warren and Margaret Dickie, 91–106. Athens: University of Georgia Press, 2000.

Mitchell, Verner D. Introduction to H. Johnson, *This Waiting for Love*, 3–19.

Wall, Cheryl A. "'Chromatic Words': The Poetry of Helene Johnson." Foreword to H. Johnson, *This Waiting for Love*, ix–xiii.

———. "Poets and Versifiers, Singers and Signifiers: Women of the Harlem Renaissance." In *Women, the Arts, and the 1920s in Paris and New York*, edited by Kenneth W. Wheeler and Virginia Lee Lussier, 74–98. New Brunswick, N.J.: Transaction, 1982.

Wheeler, Lesley. Review of *This Waiting for Love*, by Helene Johnson. *African American Review* 36, no. 2 (2002): 340–42.

13 ~ writing between worlds

TIMOTHY LEYRSON

In 2006 in an early critique of Natasha Trethewey's third collection of poems, *Native Guard*, which would go on to win the Pulitzer Prize, William Logan opened with the statement "Natasha Trethewey's well-mannered, well-meaning poems are as confused about race as the rest of us." Trethewey's poetry represented the strange position of being biracial during a time when laws and societal attitudes were shifting at a rapid pace. All of humanity was just as confused then about race, and what race meant beyond a method of identifying ourselves and others by skin color or national origin, as we are currently.

There is a long tradition of American writers of African heritage who have used writing to present their view of the world based on personal experiences, dating back at least to *Narrative of the Life of Frederick Douglass, an American Slave*. Later, during the Harlem Renaissance, with the rise of intellectual leaders like W. E. B. Du Bois and poets such as Langston Hughes, writers often addressed the issues of being black, biracial, or multiracial during their era, but they were still living in a period when they were considered in the eyes of the law "black" due to the "one drop rule" which allowed for a wide range of social discrimination and even violence. Yet, as African Americans gained more and more social and political freedom, their writing remained a method of expressing their personal life challenges in order to relate to other communities.

Additionally, civil rights progresses, allowing greater freedom to individuals of all races to take part in the discourse of theories of literary interpretation, social awareness, and defining one's own identity. This shift in view has allowed individuals to embrace the multiple aspects of their own ancestry, and many writers have taken up the tradition of expressing their own lived experience of racial identity within their writing. However, a limited number of critics have addressed Trethewey's work, and none has taken an in-depth look at her work from the standpoint of how her biracial background has impacted her poetry's subject matter, imagery, and tone. This issue should be addressed for a variety of reasons. First, her biracial background, and her parents' breaking of miscegenation laws in the state of Mississippi at the time of their marriage, has a rich historical context within the United States. Trethewey's life story also grants her a unique perspective on race relations during the civil rights movement because her formative years occurred in the late 1960s and 1970s. Trethewey uses her position as a person of African and Caucasian heritage to express a hybrid racial identity that carries through much of her work. While her catalog of work is expanding at a rapid pace, this essay will focus on her books *Domestic Work* and *Native Guard*, chosen for the sheer overlap between historical racial issues and Trethewey's perspectives on being of mixed heritage.

To understand Trethewey's work regarding her views of her own racial background in the fullest detail, one needs to first understand the context of previous writers, gaining a yardstick against which to examine how her poetry and her views of the black experience—or, more accurately, her views of the mixed-race experience—expand upon those ideas that came before. In his book *The Souls of Black Folk*, W. E. B. Du Bois set forth a concept that a majority of whites had, more than likely, never considered. Du Bois wrote that blacks (and one could easily argue that Du Bois's concepts can be applied to all other minority races as well) view themselves through a "double-consciousness," a "sense of always looking at one's self through the eyes of others" (3). It is a striking observation, this idea that blacks not only view themselves as black but also are constantly aware that whites view them as black as well. From Du Bois's perspective "the Negro is . . . born with a veil. . . . One ever feels his twoness,—an American, a Negro; two souls, two thoughts, two unreconciled strivings; two warring ideals in one dark body" (3).

This is one of the concepts that Trethewey uses in her poetry, especially in the poems written from a historical perspective, such as those representing working-class black culture. "Speculation, 1939" from *Domestic Work* describes the thoughts of a black female elevator operator as she contemplates how her life will change with the New Deal. Trethewey insinuates that the woman is currently in a tense situation due to race relations by using lines such as "she's tired of the elevator switch, // those closed-in spaces, white men's / sideways stares" (14). The idea of the elevator being a "closed-in space" also acts as a contrast in opportunity juxtaposed with the "open" possibilities that the character warily hopes may come from "this New Deal." Trethewey beautifully crafts the sense of limbo that may be felt by the woman with the final two lines, "not this all day standing around, / not that elevator lurching up, then down" (14). This further establishes a sense of in-between as she contrasts the monotony of being stuck in one place and the simultaneous "lurching" between places, much like the double consciousness described by Du Bois.

Trethewey's work does not just show her characters, or the speakers of the poems, reflecting on how race relations change. Her poetry is also able to demonstrate the views held within the various periods when her poems occur. Her ability to do this is important because Trethewey was born in 1966, one year before the *Loving v. Virginia* Supreme Court case which legalized interracial marriage in the seventeen states where it still was banned. Being born at this time grants Trethewey a unique perspective on the evolution of civil rights throughout her life.

In her 2009 interview by Terry Gross on NPR's *Fresh Air*, Trethewey reflected on how views of race are changing. Barack Obama's inauguration as the nation's first nonwhite president was discussed, with Trethewey noting that he was

> only five years older than I am. That we are of the same generation is significant, I think, because we are of a generation that came out of that moment when there were still over twenty states that had antimiscegenation laws, and that we grew up in a time when those laws were gradually changing and being done away with. And it seems to me that I have come of age at the same time that the nation has come of age in a certain way.

The importance of her views about her parents' relationship stands out especially in *Native Guard*. Poems such as "Miscegenation" recount the details of her parents' marrying outside the state and then returning, despite the fact that Mississippi did not recognize interracial marriages as legal. The potentially confusing opening couplet from the poem, "In 1965 my parents broke two laws of Mississippi, / they went to Ohio to marry, returned to Mississippi" (36) was explained in greater detail by Trethewey in her *Fresh Air* interview: "when my parents got married, it was not only illegal in the state of Mississippi for interracial couples to marry, it was also illegal for them to leave the state of Mississippi, get married somewhere else that allowed it—in their case, Ohio—and then return to the state married."

Trethewey continues her own themes of the in-between within her descriptions of her life as a series of paradoxical ideas. The form of the poem that establishes her parents' marriage is the ghazal, which traditionally is identified by the poem's theme of unattainable love. In addition to the context of her parents' marriage, Trethewey contrasts the time of her birth, "near Easter," and the idea that "Natasha . . . means *Christmas child*" (36). While the holidays are undeniably important within Christianity, the time of year in which they occur is equally noteworthy, with Christmas falling near the winter solstice, the longest night of the year, and Easter near the spring equinox, when daylight and night are of equal length. This juxtaposition may be viewed as another paradox.

In *Native Guard* Trethewey continues to examine her parents' relationship, herself, and how the rest of the world viewed them as a family, with poems such as "Southern Gothic" and "Incident." To establish the link between the violence and the psychological fear associated with the burning of a cross on her family's lawn in "Incident," Trethewey uses the pantoum form, which creates a refrain to start and end the poem: "We tell the story every year." The literal physical danger, however, comes into relief against the repeated telling of the story through the use of the refrain "Nothing really happened."

This concept is explained by Trethewey herself in her 2008 interview with Wendy Anderson. Trethewey said of the choice of form for the poem, "I tried writing 'Incident' for a long time with a straight narrative lyric, but it kept getting bogged down by the incident, reduced to a little incident about the cross burning. It wasn't until I turned to that other envelope of form and repetition that I even understood what the poem was about"—that it was not centered on the incident but on "how we remember the incident."

What is most important about the concept of remembering incidents from one's life is that the memory itself is a place of in-between. Memories exist neither in the realm of what actually happened, as most memories are flawed, nor in what could have happened, but solely in the realm of expressing how events from the past shape one's view of the world.

Possibly the most skillful aspect of "Incident" is that while using the pantoum form Trethewey quickly alternates between events occurring inside the home and the details of the outdoors. While these shifts do not occur in a perfect sequence, they do happen in approximate couplets, causing each stanza to describe two lines of "inside" events and two lines of "outside" events. Obviously the act of burning a cross was purely racially motivated, but Trethewey truly makes it *her* incident of in-between through imagery such as "the cross trussed like a Christmas tree" (41), as well as tying the events outside and inside together through focusing on her family lighting hurricane lamps in contrast to the cross's burning. She writes of both that "by morning the flames had all dimmed" (41).

The light imagery from "Incident" extends to the poem "Southern Gothic" from *Native Guard*. Light from the fire of the cross may represent the illumination of fear, while the light of the oil lamps illuminates feelings of safety. "Southern Gothic" places Trethewey between the races of her parents who "sleep, their bodies curved—parentheses / framing the separate lives they'll wake to," while Trethewey herself lies between them. This may be yet another view of Trethewey placing herself in the in-between of her parents' racial differences. Trethewey goes on to recall insults hurled at her, "*peckerwood* and *nigger / lover*, *half-breed* and *zebra*" (40). While the bed is an island of safety for young Trethewey and her parents, she is able to decipher that how they *appear* as a family is more important to outsiders than what they *actually* are: "Oil lamps flicker / around us—our shadows, dark glyphs on the wall, / bigger and stranger than we are" (40).

Trethewey's poems about her childhood, like "Southern Gothic," often show her being able to recognize in her youth that she was a child of the in-between. This view of her personal experiences is seen primarily in the poems "History Lesson," "White Lies," and "Flounder" from *Domestic Work* and "Blond" from *Native Guard*. These poems are set during her childhood, and reflect on race in a very specific manner. Trethewey addresses her own racial background through the lens of each of her parents, never really seeming to side with one or the other, but rather making certain that both sides are represented to some degree. While there is emphasis placed on how she was perceived by others, much like Du Bois's idea of double consciousness, the focus of the poems surrounding her childhood tends to be on how Trethewey viewed herself. Addressing these poems in approximate chronological order, the reader is able to better understand Trethewey's view of her own mixed race and to witness how the perspective is first acknowledged, then mulled over, and finally accepted.

In "History Lesson" Trethewey recounts her grandmother taking her photograph in 1970, when Trethewey was four years old: "they opened / the rest of this beach to us, . . . on a narrow plot / of sand marked *colored*" (45). Here Trethewey is acknowledging her "black" or, at a minimum, "not white" background. She is aware that she would not have been allowed to venture across the beach's entirety, perhaps even not allowed to have the photo taken where she stood.

This view is expanded upon in "Flounder," which details her fishing with her aunt and describes the polarity of her own background. The poem may also be viewed as a meditation on how others perceive someone of mixed racial background. Trethewey sets the scene of her aunt "reeling and tugging hard at the fish / that wriggled and tried to fight back. / *A flounder*, she said, *and you can tell / 'cause one of its sides is black. // The other side is white*, she said" (35–36). Trethewey's depiction of the fish *trying* to fight back is an important, and easily overlooked, detail in that the fish is fighting against being taken out of the milieu it is accustomed to, striving to stay within a realm of comfort, where its dual colors serve as a natural camouflage. Another important note is that the flounder itself is literally incapable of seeing both of its own colors, and therefore the duality of color does not matter to the flounder. The only reason the color is brought into question is because this is a method of recognition for those viewing the flounder from the outside, those who find a need to name, or be able to identify, a fish using colors as a reference. This poem, it seems to me, is the beginning of Trethewey's interpretation of an idea I refer to as "triple consciousness," in that Trethewey is aware that she is viewed by whites as being black, while also being viewed by blacks as still being Other.

In "White Lies" Trethewey extends the idea that how others view someone is important, and also begins to examine racial identity through the filter of what can and cannot be changed. The poem examines the ideas of "passing," an idea that in itself has a rich history within the black community, for good and ill. For people of mixed heritage, passing as white was a marker of having an easier life, of being able to slide into "being white" as long as they never let their actual genealogy be known. Trethewey even begins the poem with colloquialisms indicating that the lies themselves were merely passing for white lies. While white lies have no real consequence in theory, Trethewey goes on to describe the lies she would tell, most of them indications of her own stature and upbringing. These lies are more of a false indication of who she was—some may argue this even indicates a lack of pride in herself and her "blackness"—yet it should be noted that Trethewey was coming of age in a time and place when passing was not a forgotten memory but rather something that grandparents, and perhaps even parents, would have done. The poem concludes with a veiled reference to the practices of forebears who passed, such as the taking of low doses of arsenic to cause the skin to pale, when Trethewey writes her mother's response to catching her in lies: "She . . . washed out my mouth / with Ivory soap . . . I swallowed suds / thinking they'd work / from the inside out" (37).

The idea of passing also appears in *Native Guard* in the poem "Blond," and is in fact stated outright in the opening stanza: "Certainly it was possible— somewhere / in my parents' genes the recessive traits / that might have given me a different look . . . like a good tan—an even mix of my parents'— / I could have passed for white" (39).

As Trethewey's poems move toward the present, one can begin to gauge quite easily how she not only views race relations as a whole but, perhaps more important, uses markers within her own life to explore the effects of being of mixed race on an individual, from just after the height of the civil rights movement forward.

Again addressing the poems in a quasi-chronological format, "Signs, Oakvale, Mississippi, 1941" in *Domestic Work* sets the scene of a woman leaving home. While it is not clearly established whether she is recently married, elop- ing, or simply leaving to be with the unnamed man referenced in the poem, it is openly stated that he has offered her a level of financial security. Interest- ingly, race is never contemplated in this poem; what is provided to the reader is symbols of southern, if not specifically black, culture with lines such as "she knows to watch the signs for luck" (16). This poem signifies the in-between in that the viewpoint character in the poem is literally traveling between places, and her focus is torn between the present at the beginning and end of the poem and her hopes for the future seen in the midsection of the piece.

Once more using the sonnet form to show her skill and craft, Trethewey is able to push past the typical conveying of a sweeping generalized emotion. While the idea of hope is applicable to many readers, Trethewey's specific images play tug-of-war with the reader's expectations as well as the character's emotions. Reference to "signs" is common within the black culture, primarily in the South with its traditions of voodoo, and these concepts are used quite purposefully. "The cards said *go*," the character believes; however, Trethewey contrasts this idea of certainty with the poem's final sentence, appropriately using the turn to maximum effect: "Outside her window, / nothing but cotton and road signs—*stop* or *slow*" (16). This contention between the signs of hope, relying on the cards, and the markings of "staying in one's place" provided by the signs/symbols of the South allows the reader to feel some of the ambiguity and uncertainty that plague the character within the poem.

Turning to *Native Guard*, in "Photograph: Ice Storm, 1971" Trethewey also offers opposing perceptions of the world as she moves the reader in and out of the home repeatedly, extending a sense of duality, or perhaps of purgatory. The poem's second stanza acknowledges the storm and shows the speaker trapped inside the home, where things are unstable. The description then shifts to the setting outside. The imagery is of a landscape that is in-between, hidden by winter's fury and yet vibrant enough that it "glistens beneath a glaze of ice" while the leaves showcase themselves through their "glassy case." The contrasting of the serenity outside with uncomfortable imagery inside the home is explained in the final sentence of the poem, which reveals that the photograph itself holds some details and leaves others out: "the date, the event: nothing / of what's inside—mother, stepfather's fist?" (10).

Her mother plays many important roles within Trethewey's work, but perhaps one of the more important pieces treating the contrast of her mother's blackness and Trethewey's mixed background is "My Mother Dreams Another Country." This poem goes beyond the surface by portraying Trethewey's mother as a woman who examines what race may, or may not, mean for her daughter's life: "from *colored* to *negro*, *black* still years ahead . . . and there are more names for what grows inside her . . . while flipping through a book of baby names" (37).

This specific imagery was addressed by Trethewey in her *Fresh Air* interview. Terry Gross has Trethewey read "My Mother Dreams Another Country" and then says: "In the poem that you just read, you imagine your mother thinking about the word 'mongrel' and how that will be used against you, and this is as she's thinking of names to name you. I remember at a press conference, Obama used the word 'mutt'; he was talking about the dogs he was going to get for his girls. And in describing one of them, he said, he's a mutt like me. What did you think about when you heard that?" Trethewey responds with an explanation of the importance and history of the word choice: "Well, I thought it was very funny. I appreciated that sense of humor that actually points to a word like 'mongrel' and ideas about mongrelization that were very much on the minds of certain Mississippians at the time. To be able to use it tongue-in-cheek at this point suggests that we've come a long way."

While her statement regarding how far America has come is true, the idea itself is represented within the context of the poem through Trethewey's use of specific color imagery. The theme of color is contrasted between the beginning and the end of the poem. Using the colors "black" and "white" creates a starkness, while the terms used for the colors in between are those that were/ are typically slurs on those of mixed heritage. However, at the end of the poem Trethewey uses the image of the television station "broadcasting its nightly salutation: / the waving Stars and Stripes, our national anthem" (37). While the colors of the flag are not directly stated, the words automatically evoke red, white, and blue woven together to create one united image in the reader's mind.

Unification of identity in her being biracial occurs for Trethewey in the poem "Pastoral." The speaker acknowledges in the opening line that the events of the poem are a dream, but then shifts gears by introducing the Fugitive Poets, who were not only real but in favor of segregation. If we read this through a historical lens, we can see why Trethewey would feel conflicted. In one sense she *should* be with the Fugitive Poets, as she is also southern and shares their craft. She even attempts to reason with them in line 13: "*My father's white*, I tell them, *and rural*" (35). She, conversely, is not white, a condition further examined when she writes, "*Say 'race,'* the photographer croons. I'm in / blackface again when the flash freezes us." This last sentence is made especially haunting by the word "again," as if blackface is something that the speaker constantly takes off, or puts on, or has thrust upon her by those around her. This returns us to one of the most powerful expressions of Trethewey's triple consciousness: while the Fugitive Poets view her as black, inside she is keenly aware that she doesn't feel entirely, or only, black, and therefore blackface is required for her to identify as such.

Trethewey's views of her biracial identity, and of race relations overall, are beneficial for a number of reasons. By embracing these concepts she is able to create deeper meaning in her own expression; for her readers who are biracial she develops a common bond; and readers of a singular racial background are forced to examine the world beyond their own perception. But perhaps the highest level of understanding is that her views may be acting as a method of transformation. The idea of being united in one's own mind, as well as to others, is explained by Trethewey herself in a lecture she delivered in Emory University's Distinguished Faculty Lecture series on February 3, 2010. Trethewey stated:

> I believe, after all, that poetry is the best repository for our most humane, ethical, and just expressions of feeling. This is because poetry ennobles the human soul, that it opens—not closes—our hearts. Poetry matters not only because of its aesthetic beauty, but also because of the possibility of humane intelligence—its ability to teach us what we have not known, to show us what we have been blind to, to ask of us the most difficult questions regarding our own humanity and that of others. Across time and space, it shows us how we are alike, not that we are different. It asks

of us that we approach the world with more openness than we might employ in our daily lives. It asks that we be more observant, more compassionate, empathetic. I write because I cannot stand by and say nothing, because I strive to make sense of the world I've been given, because the soul sings for justice and the song is poetry.

BIBLIOGRAPHY

Anderson, Wendy. "An Interview with Natasha Trethewey." *BookSlut*, February 2008. bookslut.com/features/2008_02_012353.php.

DuBois, William Edward Burghardt. *The Souls of Black Folk*. Chicago: A. C. McClurg, 1903.

Logan, William. "God's Chatter." *New Criterion*, December 2006. newcriterion.com/articles.cfm/gods-chatter-2545.

Trethewey, Natasha. *Domestic Work*. Saint Paul, Minn.: Graywolf, 2000.

———. Interview by Terry Gross. *Fresh Air*, NPR, January 29, 2009. npr.org/templates/story/story.php?storyId=99474984.

———. *Native Guard*. Boston: Houghton Mifflin, 2006.

———. "'Why I Write': Poetry, History, and Social Justice." Lecture given at Emory University, Atlanta, Ga., February 3, 2010. www.waccamawjournal.com/pages.php?x=323.

14 ～ letting science tell the story

PAULA HAYES

Contemporary African American poet A. Van Jordan, in his third collection of poems, *Quantum Lyrics* (2007), pursues matters of race by turning to the cultural history of science. As readers, we are swept into a labyrinth of physics and mathematics, and in the very next breath we are met with science fiction, film, and music. Unlikely and surprising characters like Albert Einstein, Erwin Schrödinger, and Richard Feynman walk beside *DC Comics* superheroes Flash, the Atom, and the Green Lantern as historical truth, subjective truth, and popular culture traverse the boundaries of time and space. Holding together such a diverse range of ideas is Van Jordan's use of the montage.

Jordan positions his "Quantum Lyrics Montage," a subset within the larger work *Quantum Lyrics*, in a rich history of African American modernism; we may think here of Langston Hughes's *Montage of a Dream Deferred*, Derek Walcott's *Omeros*, and the writings of Melvin Tolson and Amiri Baraka. In part because of the expansiveness of the form, the montage becomes a poetic tool for deconstructing American narratives on race and identity, whether self-identity or communal identity. Very similar to a collage, the montage allows for a poet to bring together contradictory and conflicting images in startling, novel contexts by linking the images, with the effect of demonstrating continuity where there might otherwise be only disparity and difference. The montage allows a poet to bend time, transgress limitations of form, and enter into multiple social worlds all at once.

In "Quantum Lyrics Montage" Jordan creates associations in the poetic text between the racial ideologies of American society in the 1920s–1950s and German society in the 1920s–1940s. By discussing race within multiple contexts, Jordan reminds us of poetry's enormous capacity for being a public art form and of the civic function of poetry. Can poetry, in some sense, lead the way to more provocative dialogues about race? Through reconstructing historical dialogues in poetic form, does it make it any easier for us to imagine a world where new dialogues on race can emerge?

When we read Jordan's montage, it is as though we are entering into other artistic mediums; a poem melds into another form, it becomes like a snapshot, a still frame, or a scene from a silent film. As part of his montage technique, Jordan consistently reminds his readers of how poetry may pull from music, photography, and cinema, as he alludes to Louis Armstrong, Miles Davis, *City Lights*, *The Battleship Potemkin*, and *Triumph of the Will*. Poems contained in the "Quantum Lyrics Montage" frequently open with language such as "Fade in," "Flashback," "Interior," "Cut to," and "Interior Shot." By using this kind of cinematic language, Jordan is able to direct his readers to move in and out of different scenes, glide between time periods, and absorb multiple places, cultures, and geographies. Jordan's references to music, photography, and cinema additionally function as reminders of African American contributions within these fields. Or, as Jordan describes American culture in the first half of the twentieth century, it was "a jazz improvisation / of languages: strident, cool, chaotic / order" (62).

In "Quantum Lyrics Montage" Jordan adopts the dual role of historian and storyteller. At the heart of the story stands Albert Einstein, depicted as a compassionate scientist who possesses unrelenting faith in humanity. It is tempting to ask why Jordan decides to use Einstein as *the* central figure in the montage. What is the significance of Einstein in a poetic context that engages race? In what is a very telling interview with Anna Clark, Jordan explains why he discusses Einstein at such length: "If physics had a Race Theory, my hypothesis would be that we have more to fight for together than we have reasons for which to fight each other" and that "Einstein embodies this theory." In this interview Jordan poses the question, "Who would think that a Jewish immigrant from Germany and Switzerland would be a champion of civil rights in America before World War II?" It is the concept of solidarity between races, of communities working with one another, that Jordan observes in the life of Einstein.

The poems in "Quantum Lyrics Montage" carry a moral weight, as Einstein's friendships with Marian Anderson and Paul Robeson are told as part of the story of Einstein's participation in civil rights activities. We see the risks that such friendships carried for Einstein. Alluding to the files the FBI kept on Einstein as a result of his civil rights involvement and his personal friendships with prominent African Americans, Jordan writes, "How revolutionary an act— / for saying, simply, what's complicated / about love and war" (68). Einstein's staunchness as a civil rights advocate is contrasted in the montage with his personal weaknesses as a man. The montage traces Einstein's first marriage to Mileva Marić, his second marriage to his cousin Elsa, and his betrayals. Einstein's passions are shown to be only human, for "love is born not out of deceit but from the quest for light" (65). Einstein's trust in the inherent possibilities of humanity to overcome its own limitations is set against the uglier side of history—its prejudices, biases, and racism. If the self-destructive proclivities in human nature are not dealt with and transcended, what can be the results? Observing Einstein's contributions to quantum theory, the montage calls attention to how quantum theory is within itself a double-edged sword that can lead either to peace or to annihilation. A world overcome by prejudices, racism, and hatred for others can become in an instant, in the twinkling of an eye, a nonexistent world; that is why "We need to slay the quantum dragon / of atomic war" (59). But the dragon is not only the threat of nuclear weaponry. The dragon represents all of the negative emotions that lead to a path of devastation. The dragon is racism as much as it is any other form of animosity.

"Quantum Lyrics Montage" points to the fact that twentieth-century attitudes toward race exceed national boundaries, and to better understand racism in twentieth-century America it helps to place it within a larger context of transnationalism. In Germany in the early 1920s, Einstein's theories fell under the scrutiny of several anti-Jewish German scientists and physicists, some of whom would later become Nazi scientists under Hitler. The turning point for Einstein came in 1921 when he was publicly denounced at the Berlin Philharmonic by the anti-Jewish physicist Philipp Lenard. Lenard's primary contribution to physics lay in his research on cathode rays and empty spaces in atomic particles. Lenard's public rebuke of Einstein was one of the first steps toward the establishment of the infamous Anti-Einstein and Anti-Relativity League. As historian Fred Jerome explains in *Einstein on Israel and Zionism*, after World War I the cultural climate of Germany and its anti-Jewish propaganda had penetrated into science: "Einstein himself had been the target of that postwar German anti-Semitism. In 1920, when the whole world was hailing his name and inviting him to visit, a small group of Germans organized a series of public meetings in Berlin to denounce the theory of relativity as a 'Jewish perversion'" (10).

Jordan's "Einstein: Berlin's Philharmonic Hall" captures the racial tension between Einstein and Lenard; there Jordan writes, "To stretch the light of their strained spirits, / Frozen in time, in this temple of intolerance" (51). The image of the light being pulled apart, constrained, halted and stalled in time, points to what becomes of the mind once bigotry seeps in and takes hold. But the poem, contained in the montage, also retells the historical circumstances Einstein faced in Germany in the 1920s. In a letter Einstein penned in 1921—incidentally the year he received the Nobel Prize for physics—he expresses his growing concern over the place of Jews in Germany. He writes, "Until a generation ago, Jews in Germany did not regard themselves as part of the Jewish people" (Jerome, *Israel* 43). During the 1920s Einstein began to support the idea of establishing a Jewish state in Palestine. Einstein did not practice Judaism and had not really identified himself with Zionist concepts until 1921, following the intellectual and cultural exclusion he experienced in Germany. The basis of Einstein's Zionism was a desire to see the Jewish people create a nation of their own so that they might experience cultural autonomy and political sovereignty. For Einstein, a nation of Israel would mean a place where a renaissance of Jewish intellectualism could occur. Yet, as Jordan reminds us in "Einstein on World Government," another of the poems in the montage sequence, Einstein was not an isolationist, and his views on Zionism evolved in the 1930s to a much broader scope as he embraced the political hope that the world might one day see the establishment of global cooperation for world peace.

Although one might think that America's entry into World War II would have led to an increase in racial tolerance in America, this was not the case. Jordan in his montage, by placing Europe and America side by side for comparison, reveals the hypocrisy of America on its home front. As Jerome observes, "In the first fifteen months after Hitler's defeat, a wave of lynching and other anti-black violence—mostly, but not only, in the Southern states—killed more than fifty African-Americans, with recently returned veterans the targets of some of the most bestial lynch mobs" (*File* 72).

Einstein immigrated to America in 1933, the year that Hitler came to power under Germany's Enabling Act. After his move to America, Einstein did not forget the terrible incidents he had witnessed in Germany; in fact, what he witnessed became an impetus for his work in civil rights in America. "Quantum Lyrics Montage" calls attention to Einstein's role in working with civil rights leaders Paul Robeson and W. E. B. Du Bois as they campaigned for the establishment of an antilynching law in America. Jordan's short poem titled simply "Anti-Lynching" recalls Einstein's participation in the ACEL (American Campaign to End Lynching) as well as Einstein's 1946 letter urging Truman to put forward an antilynching law (Jerome and Taylor 143). The law was never passed. Jordan's plea "Let's cut branches of men from trees" (66) presents us with a brutal image revealing the fissures, the cuts, and the depth of the psychological wounds lynching produced in the minds of African Americans, particularly men. Equally telling from "Quantum Lyrics Montage" is "Mr. W.E. Burghardt du Bois"; the short, thirteen-line poem alludes to an editorial piece written by Einstein and published in Du Bois's *Crisis* magazine in 1931. In the editorial Einstein expressed his concerns over the Scottsboro Trial, in which nine teenage African American boys in Alabama were falsely accused and convicted of raping a white woman. The Scottsboro Trial called into question whether slavery had truly ended or whether another form of slavery had not been instituted, an *invisible slavery* within the legal system. Jordan's poem imagines Du Bois and Einstein discussing "the problem of the color line" in America; evoking Du Bois's *The Souls of Black Folk* (1903) as an implied subtext of the poem, the intersubjective, interracial dialogue between the two leaders concludes that, sadly, "There exists no erasure for race" in America (54).

While "Quantum Lyrics Montage" consists of historical material, other sections of *Quantum Lyrics* rely on the poet's autobiographical memories. Race is not merely a historical problem to be analytically solved. Race also is profoundly experiential, a part of self-identity. "Remembrance," autobiographical and personal for Jordan, allows the poet to recall the painful memory of watching a childhood classmate being mercilessly beaten by three boys. The poem delivers a strong sense of moral ineffectualness, while at the same time describing a need to return to an innocence that is irretrievably lost. "Remembrance" does not come right out and specify that the boy was beaten because of race; in fact, the most direct reading of the poem would indicate that the bullies and the victim were of the same race. However, at a subtextual level, the poem's *energy*, emotive vibes, and tone all reveal the dread and hesitation, the suppression of action, and the repression of fear that is associated with the psychological effects of racial segregation. "Remembrance" digs deep into the trenches of the psyche to try and come to terms with why the poet did nothing to rescue the boy, Milton McKnight, from being *symbolically lynched and rendered voiceless*:

> A kid we said was a little slow;
> He was tied to a tree.
> Three guys, for fun, were beating him
>
> Like a pedal on a bass drum,
> But no music was coming out. (30)

The silence and the boy's muteness contrast with the "bass drum" that *cannot* speak for the boy, as language becomes subtly transfigured into an abnormality and disquiet. Jordan finds that in recalling the event he is rendered spiritually impotent (the poem hints at physical impotence, too, in the moments when the memory of the tragic event resurfaces in the poet's mind).

There is an underlying question that runs throughout the poem "Remembrance," and this question, in many ways, runs throughout a good portion of the entire text of *Quantum Lyrics*. It is the question, or matter, of moral obligation. Does a person, either unaffected or affected by another's pain, suffering, or oppression, turn a blind eye? Is it not preferable, better for the human race as a whole, when individuals and communities get involved in contesting oppression? Jordan approaches the question of moral action from the perspective of science fiction and popular culture in the poem "The Green Lantern Unlocks the Secrets of the Black Body." The poem is a meditation upon the black body and black aesthetics. Alluding to a 1959 issue of *DC Comics*, the poet dreams of the superhero the Green Lantern swooping down to earth and discovering moral chaos, America on the brink of a war, and then having to decide: "Should I get involved? / I have to answer: / whether I'm born here or just / passing through" (33). As both "Remembrance" and "The Green Lantern Unlocks the Secrets of the Black Body" indicate, there are always moral questions that have to be answered. The issue becomes, how will individuals choose to respond?

There are additional ways we should consider *Quantum Lyrics*. Besides Jordan's use of science and the autobiographical, his poetry portrays the *orality* of African American culture and the relationship of the African griot or spiritual leader to the prophetic function of spoken language. In the poem "Sculpting the Head of Miles Davis," Jordan compares the strength of the musicality of poetry to the great trumpeter's ability to incite and arouse the senses with one "mute drop from his horn" (100). The poem looks at race from a positive perspective instead of retracing racial traumas. In praise of the physical form of Miles Davis's African features, the poem implicitly compares Western definitions of art and beauty to those of African aesthetics. Dreaming of what a sculpted figure of Miles Davis's head would look like, the speaker of the poem imagines how he would mold the clay to bring out the alignment between physical form and musical notes; metaphorically, the poem extends this concept to consider how the lyricism of poetry is also an alignment of form and sound. Or, as Jordan writes, "pull back and follow the rhythm / of the jawline" (99).

In A. Van Jordan's poetry, music is cultural, and as such it is an expression of the contributions of African Americans to the cultural landscape of America. But cultural signifiers can also become interpolated as personal signifiers of the consciousness and memory. In "R&B," where Jordan reminisces about his father's dying, music crosses the generational gap between father and son. The poem posits a comparison, or contrast, between the poet's generation and its love for hip-hop and the father's love of jazz. Incorporating both African American musical art forms in the poem, Jordan slips back in time to feel the movement of what drove his father's life. Making an association between the beat of jazz and the life rhythms of his father, Jordan describes how, overwhelmed after his father's funeral, he finds himself driving through the streets of Akron, Ohio, channel surfing on the radio. Unable to find a radio station that plays anything but hip-hop or rap, the poet lets his mind go back in time, easing into the soft memories of jazz—"I am falling deeper under the spell of singers / who can still play piano" (104). Connecting with the world of jazz in "R&B" means a ceaseless connection to the soul of the father, as art moves from the impersonal, static realm of form into the subjective, fluid realm of the poet's emotions.

There is, lastly, the question of how lyricism, whether in jazz or blues or poetics, becomes an expression of beauty. In poems like "Richard P. Feynman Lecture: Intro to Symmetry," the idea of form is taken to the sublime level of the universe's structure, but eventually brought back down to the human level of the "symmetry" of "bodies" and relationships; or, as Jordan writes, what we call life is nothing more than a sum of "mysteries inside mysteries in our own bodies" (15). Riffing off the concept of Richard Feynman's famous 1960s Cal Tech lectures on the nature of the universe and physics, Jordan pulls the idea of physics apart, searching theories of physics for clues about human behavior. What the poet finds is that if we dig deeply enough into these mysteries that the universe offers, there is *no physics of race*. And if there is no physics of race, there must be a way to transcend the social boundaries of race.

WORKS CITED

Baraka, Amiri. *Transbluesency: Selected Poems.* New York: Marsilio, 1995.

Bell, Derrick. *Faces at the Bottom of the Well: The Permanence of Racism.* New York: BasicBooks, 1992.

Clark, Anna. "Where Physics, Poetry, and Politics Collide." Interview with A. Van Jordan. *American Prospect*, November 2, 2007. prospect.org/article/where-physics-poetry-and -politics-collide.

Clearfield, Andrew M. *These Fragments I Have Shored: Collage and Montage in Early Modernist Poetry*. Ann Arbor: UMI Research Press, 1984.

Jerome, Fred. *The Einstein File: J. Edgar Hoover's Secret War against the World's Most Famous Scientist*. New York: St. Martin's Press, 2002.

———. *Einstein on Israel and Zionism*. New York: St. Martin's Press, 2009.

Jerome, Fred, and Rodger Taylor. *Einstein on Race and Racism*. New Brunswick, N.J.: Rutgers University Press, 2005.

Jordan, A. Van. *M-A-C-N-O-L-I-A*. New York : W. W. Norton, 2004.

———. *Quantum Lyrics: Poems*. New York: W. W. Norton, 2007.

Rowell, Charles H., and A. Van Jordan. "The Poem Is Smarter Than the Poet." *Callaloo* 27, no. 4 (2004): 908–19.

15 ～ identity indictment

TRAVIS HEDGE COKE

Pop quiz: Do you identify a Native American by skin color, lineage, religion, blood quanta, community involvement, cultural participation, tribal membership, or how much fry bread a person eats? How do you disqualify? Is a Native American an Indian, Amerind, First Nations, Native, NDN, Indigenous American? Is Native Poetry a genre, or just a shelf designation in a marketing system? Is poetry a genre or a technique? Is a writer who writes in many modes including poetry a poet? Is a mixed-lineage poet of Native descent a Native poet or just a poet who is Native? Who is the judge of cultural participation? Which culture, the one from a hundred and thirty years ago, eighty years ago, or right now, today?

Any editor who okays a bio claiming Native identity or lineage is faced with that quiz, because it can turn into a fight pretty easily. It can turn to more than a fight, more than a casual indictment, it can become a legal issue. I know for a fact some editors avoid work by authors who self-identify, but then, I know some editors who avoid anyone who implies or outright states an ethnicity in their bio or work. It's chancy.

As Native poets, if we are not prepared to take that fight if it comes, we have to worry it out of the whole package of our identity as writers, to keep it from coming up. Some do. Some say "Native descent" to be safe or point out they are from this region, this rez, or that town. Give a tribal affiliation. Give a percentage. Give an ancestral name. I like self-identifying as NDN because it sounds like a word but it isn't a proper word, and it annoys the grammarians. I don't have any fair answers, but I can point to my family, my ancestors, places I've lived, people I have worked with, or I can just say "Fuck you" and leave it at that. Yeah, maybe *fuck you* lacks the veracity of a family tree full of percentage breakdowns between different tribes and non-Native lines coming together, two or three Venn diagrams. One of the sisters at St. Catherine's Indian School in Santa Fe told me, in seventh grade, that saying "eff you" was a sign you'd lost the argument, but another sister, who'd come over from Ireland, said it just showed you cared.

"They only need one Indian" is common knowledge in Native circles. *They*, whoever They are, only need one token to feel comforted and blank the rest. So you need to be more Indian, or differently Native, because being Native and something else is not going to cut it. You have to lose the Native aspect for that. (Which some writers, some entertainers, do. Why do you think Benjamin Bratt, Danny Trejo, and Tommy Lee Jones self-identify personally, but marketing is a different issue? Passing is alive and well in the marketing machine.) What do we do when we hear singers or poets are self-IDing but we've never seen it in their promo materials, we never see loud shout-outs to an ethnic dish or political movement in their work? We laugh it off. They're *trying* to pass as Indian.

Somebody got us to police ourselves. I read at a very good venue once, audience was over a hundred strong, and there's maybe four, five Native people there, so sure enough, when I return to my seat, some guy comes over to where I'm sitting with another Cherokee and a Lakota, both poets, and proceeds to explain to us how my poetry isn't genuinely Indian, and how the two women need to both shut up and let him talk. He wasn't trying to be an asshole, he was trying to do his job as he saw it and happened to be an asshole at the same time. He thought his job was policing other Indians, making sure we don't get out of bounds with our word choices or write about things that took place in the last twenty years. He needed us to know that all tribes were one tribe and that true Indianicity looks like someone posed for a photo in 1884.

When I and several writers who'd done an issue of the *Florida Review* together read for the Smithsonian Museum of the American Indian—this was recorded live, and is sometimes streaming at their website—there was a question-and-answer session after the reading. Most of the questions were solid. But one woman could not allow herself to hear the answers she was getting. She wanted to claim that prior to meeting white people, Native Americans—again, this is half the planet she's talking about here, two continents, one whole hemisphere of people—had no writing at all, and no poetry. We're on a stage, looking out, knowing this is recorded. I'm perched beside the others because there weren't enough seats when we got a late arrival, but regardless, the others are sitting, staring out at the audience, having all just read poetry, prose, some prose poetry, and this woman would like us to just admit we owe it to white people.

I'm cool with owing things to white people and owning up to that. White people have done a lot of good things for the world. But they didn't invent rhythm, they weren't the first to recognize that imagery in spoken or written storytelling is powerful, they didn't create the idea of pattern or progression, or that the strongest word choice and arrangement is more important than all the grammar in existence.

Other poets tried to explain this to her. To his credit, Orlando White tried to calmly, seriously address and then address again this question, as well as one can speak for the literary and artistic history of two continents of nations and cultures. And she interrupted him while he was talking to tell him, no, she's right. She wasn't asking. She may have used an asking tone, occasionally, but she was not asking. She was telling with the inflection of a question. She was begging the question. She was baiting her argument.

So, I stood up, which is easier to do fast from crouching than sitting, and without a mic I try to save her from embarrassing herself any further, from insulting this other writer any more than she has. I don't tell her she's full of it, I don't tell her to sit down and shut up, I just tell her she's wrong. All writing, all speaking that is preplanned comes back to poetry. Poetry is efficacy in words. The best prose is poetry, the best speeches, the best songs that use words are poetry. They are rooted in poetry and grown in its soil. And that poetry, that inclination, has been arrived at independently by uncountable human beings. All the tired structures and "that's not a real word" indictments we hear are to train us away from poetry, not to teach it. Poetry isn't a white thing, an Asian thing, an American Indian thing, a modern thing, an ancient thing. When children learn words and try to communicate ideas beyond their immediate grasp by selecting the best words they have, that is poetry. It is reinvented independently when nearly everyone learns to speak or to write.

I was talking on the fly, just to put some distance between her presumptions and the very earnest answers she had just received from other writers. Maybe I got through to her. Maybe she reflected later on what Orlando had said. Unfortunately, none of us may have had an effect on her. I don't believe she really cared who invented poetry. She just didn't want Indians to have it. Maybe it wasn't romantic-savage enough for her.

And, unfortunately, we can buy into that, too. We start to cull each other, in house, as Native poets, to cancel one another out. I've got a rejection e-mail from an editor that says, literally, "It's more a gay poem, than an Indian one." I have had work rejected because the editor couldn't really "see Indians sitting around watching *Predator*," as if we don't own TVs or something. They honestly suggested I change it to a cowboy movie or *Pow-Wow Highway*.

How many response poems do we have, with one Native poet calling out the common tropes of another as false or a sell? And how frequently do such poets, in their own lives, actually reflect the things they're calling out as a sell? It is not that the commercialized aspects are inaccurate, or perhaps even inaccurate in their emphasis or frequency, but we already lost our hemisphere to conquest, we lost our ability to define ourselves to governments, to BIAS and equivalents, and we lost our face to the movie version. Isn't it somewhat petty, and downright reactionary, to write response poems decrying reasonable representations simply because they are dangerously becoming the dominant representation?

The real pretenders don't have to care that much. If it's just a sell, it's not going to matter if the smarter outsiders catch your lie, and those in (the broader Native) community know; you can still sell books to the gullible. Inside community, the weight of representing the whole is too heavy for that noise unless you really, really want it. You can't fake it, you can't stretch, without your cousins finding out, people back home will know, and you understand, somewhere inside and cemented firm by a thousand reminders, that when non-Native people see you, they think every other Native person they meet is you (and conversely, any Native person they met before you, even if it was a white guy in makeup on TV, is how they see you). Those of you in the conversation know, but for those outside, for the sake of this essay, let me clarify: When someone sells out big, we know. Word gets around. People talk. If you're selling out to fit a niche, marketing your neighbors, fictionalizing a myth a non-Native audience wants to the detriment of your family? We know.

Most broad, multinational cultures, or cultural meshes, have this awareness. It's not a purely Native thing, certainly, but we cannot downplay it for that. "Indian time" is a phrase and thing in India, too, after all, to differentiate from Anglo time, and so, too, there's Tulsa time, so important they wrote a song about it. I'm in Weihai, China, writing this, and they have fry bread here! In recent Native lit, that's been the big sell, the big icon, our love of fry bread. We luuuuuurv our fry bread. But it isn't isolated to Native culture. We got drums. Everybody's got drums. Heck, we got guitars, too, and today everyone has guitars. There's only one continent on earth you cannot buy a guitar on, and it is the same one you can't buy corn or chili on.

While it feels, perhaps, that arresting Native culture to a pre-contact or pre-assimilation time is a separate issue, it isn't. It feels that way because it is an immense restriction, one not typically placed in America on any other in-America culture. It is immense and it is pervasive. That Native culture happened one hundred years ago or further back is an understood. When you see a specifically Native portrayal on television, in a movie, today, it is almost required that it hark back to *an older, purer time*, even if it's directed by a Native person. I deliberately did not hand over my poem "God and Pony Show" to a good magazine, because the guest editor asking for it told me it was my "most authentic poem." It's not. It's a goddamned parody, and it's a goddamned western.

With that specter hanging on us like a giant vampire bat, though, we grow to avoid any authentic representation that nears the commercial sell. You see smart, good-hearted Native writers who laugh off "poverty porn" and who won't go near the conversation, while their siblings die huffing gasoline, their childhood friends are resigned to taking what comes and not trying because it ain't worth trying, and some of us are so glad we got to keep the land that was our prison camps as we continually lost wars to the United States of America, to Canada, to Texas, to all these nations, that we will go tooth and nail to keep anyone from pointing out that they were, after all, prison camps and never intended to be places of good living. Which is not to say reservations suck, and not to imply that all Native people are suffering intensely at all times, but we are discouraged from commenting on it, turned away from representing it, encouraged not to deal with it by the sheer inanity of non-Native coverage.

We sold bats to German tourists, once, when I was young. The youth of Kyle, South Dakota, sold a busload of German tourists with feathers in their hair and plastic faux-bone chokers on, some dead bats that had, previous to dying, nested up at the school by a store that sold, genuinely, five-cent candies. Bread cost four times as much at that store as it did in Rapid, but the candy was one nickel per piece, and that summer you could get twenty-five for a dollar. So we collected dead bats on a wooden board and sold them to the tourists for probably twenty bucks, selling these poor dead things for the "medicine" they possessed. And, of course, they do have power, they do have worth—do, not did—and I'll work to remember those bats the rest of my life. But what we sold them was not the bats, it was some comfort.

And, maybe some misanthropes will tell you that's what Native lit looks like today. Maybe some of it does. We have been abused, scared, shamed, and pigeonholed unless we mimic the fakery, and the thing that was faking is us, to begin with. Authenticity's a sham. When Andy Rooney said Native cultures had never contributed anything significant, we should have blasted Jimi Hendrix at him until his ears bled with joy and love. Authenticity is only a word. A shelf designation to help with marketing. Some people will tell you early Rolling Stones was more authentic than early Beatles, but what makes some art school dropouts doing lifted blues riffs more authentic than working-class Scousers singing about wanting to hold their sweetheart's hand? Which Beatles song is Indianest? (They weren't Indians. The end.) Which Jimi Hendrix songs are Native songs? (All of them.) What poems of Joy Harjo's are more Native? (All of them.) If we weighed Laura Mann's Indianicity against Ai's Nativeness, which side would have more weight and which would fly?

Indianicity ain't a word. Nativeness is almost semantically null. Authenticity is a come-on, a tease. I like self-identifying as NDN because it sounds like a word but it isn't a proper word, and it isn't the one it sounds like, either. You will be found out by your cousins, your sisters, mothers, your sons and neighbors. Maybe you will find yourself therein, as well. That's you, as in all of you, not only the Native poets, for no matter how neurotically we divvy up the world and desperately claim separations, there's more mixing than there is divides. The ground and the air are intermixed things, and on this earth, one always pulls you closer to it and the other is constantly surrounding you, forever touching your skin, your mouth, and your blood.

III. IMPERIALISM & EXPERIMENTS

Comedy, Confession, Collage, Conscience

Philip Metres begins this section by delving into a community and poetic arena still heavily silenced in America in his eye-opening essay "Carrying Continents in Our Eyes: Arab American Poetry after 9/11." In 2007 Major Jackson's essay on race in poetry, "A Mystifying Silence: Big and Black," cracked open the silence on this topic and made many discussions, many poems, and indeed this collection of essays ultimately possible. In "Writing White," Martha Collins, known for her own poems exploring whiteness and race, seeks to respond to Jackson's essay. Jaswinder Bolina takes on the normative white male figure and explores the margins around it in his deeply considered essay "Writing like a White Guy." Working to make "Whiteness Visible," Tess Taylor, herself a descendant of Thomas Jefferson, examines poetry that addresses racialization from a white perspective. In counterpoint—contrapuntally, if you will—Ailish Hopper's "The Gentle Art of Making Enemies" considers the destabilizing, reassembling, and re-visioning of race through poetry, and the gestures, strategies, and maneuvers of many poets currently working in this vein. The provocative poet Tony Hoagland considers poly-historical poetic issues, such as race and the National Book Critics Circle Award, and also the cathartic role that humor plays in poetry in "No Laughing Matter: Race, Poetry, and Humor." This section closes with Patrick S. Lawrence looking deeply into one African American poetic landscape of contigency, alienation, and American reanimation in "The Unfinished Politics of Nathaniel Mackey's *Splay Anthem.*"

16 ~ carrying continents in our eyes

Arab American Poetry after 9/11

PHILIP METRES

Denial, my psychologist father likes to quip, *is not just a river in Egypt.* I keep wanting to assert that anti-Arab racism in the United States is not as bad as it used to be; that "sand nigger" is not an epithet "increasingly used," that internment camps for Arabs are not just around the corner. I keep wanting to assert that while racism and xenophobia exist in the United States, racism against Arabs is no longer the last *acceptable* prejudice, as Edward Said posited back in 1978. After all, just days after the attacks of September 11, 2001, President George W. Bush—in what may have been his most courageous statement in office—admonished those who would equate Islam with terrorism. To be sure, that didn't stop scores of hate-crime attacks against Arabs and Muslims, as Hayan Charara's "Going Places" recounts, in the weeks after the 9/11 attacks— the ugly consequences of fear-mongering, Orientalism, and white supremacy.

Of course, racism still exists. Switching on Fox News, listening to Christian talk radio, or cruising the Internet, we don't need long to notice how anti-Arab and anti-Muslim paranoia seethes in the discourse of the far right. In a 2012 video, "The Real Gabriela Mercer," the Republican Tea Party candidate says, "If you know Middle Easterners, a lot of them look Mexican . . . dark skin, dark hair, brown eyes—and they *mix,* they mix in. And those people, their only goal in life is to cause harm to the United States. So why do we want them here—either legally or illegally?" In another portion of the video, in front of a border wall that reminds one of the wall in Palestine, she says, "and these are radical Muslims who . . . want to kill us." Displacing the fear of the Latin American immigrant onto the Middle Eastern immigrant, Mercer notes conspiratorially that prayer rugs were found in the desert borderlands between

Mexico and the United States used by smugglers. As if prayer were an ominous precursor to murder.

Neither a Muslim nor a member of al-Qaeda, a third-generation Arab American, I nevertheless found myself, in the weeks following the attacks of 2001, on a university panel called "Making Sense of September 11th," articulating the laundry list of grievances that the Muslim world had against U.S. foreign policy. I was not asked to do so, but I felt I had to. As if I were engaging in a kind of representative performance—apropos of Deleuze and Guattari's notion of "minor literature"—my every utterance felt immediately political, and connected intimately to how fellow Arabs and Arab Americans might be treated. I knew then, and know now, that I can speak. Though I will not joke about bombs on phone calls or anywhere else, I know that I have certain rights as a citizen—and a reputation for nonviolence—that precede and follow any utterance I make. Many first-generation Arab Americans—and noncitizens— do not share that confidence, and in fact live in terror of losing the hold they have on life here.

For many Arab American writers, 9/11 became a moment in which we "outed" ourselves—that is, claimed solidarity with fellow Arab Americans and with those struggling against oppression and injustice throughout the Arab world. But it would be false to overstate the importance of 9/11 to Arab American literature. Since at least the 1980s Arab American poets have negotiated a complex double consciousness that translates and troubles both the American and the Arab, from literary traditions to political ideologies. In this essay, I'll explore how Arab American poets such as Lawrence Joseph, Naomi Shihab Nye, Suheir Hammad, Mohja Kahf, Fady Joudah, Khaled Mattawa, and Deema Shehabi (with Marilyn Hacker) attempt to rewrite the Orientalist narrative of Arab life, engage in modes of political and aesthetic resistance, and worry their connection to and complicity with the nation. For these poets, a cosmopolitan vision of human connection and global citizenship is haunted by the knowledge of U.S. privilege and the national liberation struggles in the postcolonial Middle East.

Though Arab Americans—who legally had been considered "white" but who often faced discrimination based on immigrant status and religious/cultural difference—often chose the path of quiet assimilation, Arab American writers did not long remain politically quiescent. Emboldened by the ethnic liberation movements and by the courageous work of Edward Said, whose landmark *Orientalism* (1978) was followed by groundbreaking critiques of empire, Zionism, and representations of Islam, Arab American poets such as Melhem, Lawrence Joseph, Naomi Shihab Nye, Samuel Hazo, and Elmaz Abinader began to write about Arab American life in a way that began to get serious attention in the 1990s.

Steven Salaita has observed that the recent post-9/11 profusion of Arab American literature has come with a remarkably robust multiplicity of styles and themes. In his words, "there is no such thing as diversity in Arab America: there are diversities. We do not adhere to a singular body politic: we engage in all sorts of politics. We do not occupy an Arab American culture: we belong to numerous cultures" (2). Yet certain themes recur throughout the body of work, as he notes: not only immigration and assimilation but also U.S. racism, xenophobia, and marginalization. And more particularly, Arab American literature returns to the paroxysm of the Israeli-Palestinian conflict, the Lebanese civil war, Islam, and patriarchy/homophobia—all themes exacerbated and irritated by empire and the reactions to empire.

Read alongside *Orientalism*, Deleuze and Guattari's articulation of "minor literature" is a particularly useful lens through which to examine Arab American poetry. First, minor literature is marked by the deterritorialization of language by a minority writer. Second, in minor literature the "cramped space" of the writer's world "forces each individual intrigue to connect immediately to politics. The individual concern thus becomes all the more necessary, indispensable, magnified, because a whole other story is vibrating within it" (17). This hyper-politicization is further pressured by the ways in which the "minor" writer constantly writes not merely for herself but for a collective whose agency is compromised by its minority status. Finally, in minor literature an "individuated enunciation" cannot "be separated from a collective enunciation" (17).

Arab American poetry compels a slight reordering, which emphasizes the problematics of reception and the politics of representation that complicate and often threaten to silence or domesticate Arab American subjectivity. First and foremost, there is the politicization of all things Arab. This politicization is inextricably connected to U.S. foreign policy in the Middle East, driven by the geopolitical thirst for oil and desire to support Israel and the Gulf States at almost any cost. Nearly every articulation or representation of the Israeli-Palestinian conflict must face the condemnatory force of Israel apologists and the smear of anti-Semitism, silencing dialogue. Arab American experience and the experience of other ethnic Americans are analogous, but the particularity of U.S. foreign policy toward the Middle East—which far predates the 9/11 attacks—is the backdrop against which Arab American literature finds itself.

Second, Orientalism, or the repertory of ready-made stereotypes about those in the Middle East, continues to haunt the U.S. imagination of Arabs. U.S. cultural, racial, and religious xenophobia rhyme with this Orientalism. This system of stereotyping, of course, provides the bulwark and justification for an aggressive U.S. foreign policy that favors two primary material and geopolitical interests: oil and Israel. Recently, when I posted on Facebook a link to a performance by a young British Palestinian poet, Rafeef Ziadah, a colleague who teaches at a local private high school noted that his "students are doing an oral poetry recitation as part of their final next week. How I'd love to share this and how I know I'd get run out of the building if I did. Too bad, for sure."

Given the politicization of all things Arab, Arab American writers cannot escape the pressure of the political, and the desire to represent, as these anec-dotes illustrate. They merely confirm what Jack Shaheen demonstrated in his landmark study *Reel Bad Arabs* (2001), which analyzed 10,000 American films and found that fewer than a dozen had positive, nuanced representations of Arabs. In light of limited or limiting representations, Deleuze and Guattari's notion of minor literature privileges literature without "subject"—that which is "non-representative, deterritorializing" (21). Yet Arab American literature extends from mainstream modes all the way to that experimental horizon. In other words, some Arab American writers employ the radically deconstruc-tive modes of language-deterritorializing in an effort toward a globalist vision of literature. But Arab American poets have responded to these conditions through a broad range of poetic strategies, not just through Deleuze and Guat-tari's postmodern privileging of nonrepresentational subjectless assemblages and language defamiliarization.

Given the predominance of stereotypical representations in the mass media and popular culture, Arab American writers have had a lot of work to do, and therefore their use of mainstream poetic tactics of autobiographical lyric and anecdotal narrative seem as useful as experimental methods of minor litera-ture. Some poets, such as Naomi Shihab Nye and Mohja Kahf, actively court the dangers of self-commodification and strategically employ dominant or mainstream poetic modes. Others, such as Suheir Hammad, identify with and employ African American strategies of engaged political poetry. Some, among them Hammad, Fady Joudah, and Deema Shehabi, hybridize American poetry with Arab language and poetic traditions. Still others attempt experimental assemblages of collage, such as the recent work of Khaled Mattawa. In short, Arab American poets have used *any means necessary*. But let's begin with Lawrence Joseph, whose poetry has evolved as his vision of poetry's possibilities has dilated—from personal narrative to prophetic critique of empire and global capital.

A lawyer from Detroit, Lawrence Joseph emerged in the 1980s as an important poet whose work was inflected by the working-class storytelling of Philip Levine and his own ethnic roots. "Sand Nigger" dramatizes Levine's influence, articulated to the cultural experience of Arab American immigrants:

> the name fits: I am
> the light-skinned nigger
> with black eyes and the look
> difficult to figure—a look
> of indifference, a look to kill—
> . . . an enthusiastically
> bad-tempered sand nigger
> who waves his hands, nice enough
> to pass, Lebanese enough
> to be against his brother,
> with his brother against his cousin,
> with cousin and brother
> against the stranger. (2005a, 92)

Joseph's fifth book of poems, *Into It* (2005), propelled him into the position of visionary poet, not limited to autobiography. These poems employ a gyring consciousness that sees the war embedded in a geography of global capitalism, military specularity, and Old Testament imagery. Here Joseph explicitly implicates himself, as if he were prophet and drone pilot:

> Zoom in close enough—the shadows
> of statues, the swimming pools of palaces . . .
> closer—a garden of palm trees,
> oranges and lemons, chickens, sheep . . .
>
> Yes, that's it. I've become
> too clear-sighted—the mechanics of power
> are too transparent. (41)

Joseph's ability to situate himself in the place of complicity marks his poetic project as particularly *American*, intriguingly assuming the position of citizen of empire at a time when Arabness was suspect.

From the same generation, by contrast, Naomi Shihab Nye, one of the best-known Arab American poets, has worked to demonstrate the human-ity of Arabs, both in the lyrical representation of her nonviolent vision and in her narrative depictions of Arab and Arab American life. Shortly after the 2001 terrorist attacks, Nye published an open letter "To Any Would-Be Terrorists," demonstrating the particular pain that these attacks caused Arab Americans, who had worked for years to be part of the fabric of a suspicious society. Relatedly, she published a selection of her Arab-themed poems called *19 Varieties of Gazelle: Poems of the Middle East* (2002). Even the title of the book is a testament to the beauty, diversity, and multiplicity of Arab culture and being. To her credit, her work does not spare critique of American im-perial meddling, outright censorship, and cultural ignorance, as a poem like "All Things *Not* Considered" aptly announces: "you cannot stitch the breath / back into this boy" (133). But the way she grounds her poetic depiction of Palestine so often through her beloved father, Aziz Shihab, in her elegiac *Transfer* (2011) makes it nearly impossible not to think of Aziz when one hears any story of Palestinian refugees. In "Scared, Scarred, Sacred," Nye writes of her father:

> All your life you were flying back to your lost life
> dropping down like the Oz house.
> You kept the key, as Palestinians do.
> You kept the doorknocker.
> And now you are homeless for real.
> Fire ate your body, you became as big as the sky. (23)

It is a commonplace among Palestinian refugees to have the keys to the houses from which they were exiled, along with title deeds and other papers, which bring them no closer to their desired return. Nye's familiarly American image of Dorothy's whirling house in *The Wizard of Oz* offers Americans a way of feeling about Palestinian exile that evokes its utter strangeness. The final image, describing a cremation, at once feels like a liberatory release and an uneasy evocation of the Holocaust.

From a younger generation, Palestinian American poet Suheir Hammad began her poetry by employing the Black Arts poetics of June Jordan and hip-hop, registering her identification between Arab American and African

American oppression and political-cultural struggle: "carry continents in our eyes / survivors of the middle passage" (81). In *Born Palestinian, Born Black* (1996), Hammad's "Dedication" is a poetry of militant outrage, that

> sees Palestine over the sea
> feels her uncle's heart join hers
> thinks of exchanging her books and pencil
> for a knife a small pistol (13)

The early poetic, like Black Arts poetry, occasionally overrelies upon strict binaries: white/black, evil/good, Israeli/Palestinian. If, in the words of Deleuze and Guattari, "the political domain has contaminated every statement" (17), Hammad's early work suffers, at times, from this stain. However, by the time she began to appear on *Def Poetry Jam* just after 9/11, her work had changed, measuring its distance between audiences more carefully; through her compelling performances on HBO, Arab American poetry and culture reached new audiences. Her role in popular culture marked a sea change from the narratives of self-Orientalism and assimilation and proposed that Arab American identity is by no means uncomplex. In fact, her recent collection *Breaking Poems* (2008) moves close to minor literature in its syncretic combinations of Arabic and English, in its globalist broken embodiments: "moon / same in ramallah wa new orleans wa jerusalem wa johannesburg wa beirut same moon" (34). The "wa" simply means "and" in Arabic, but its repetitions begin to sound like a suturing cry.

Published in the same year as the hoax-text *Honor Lost*, Mohja Kahf's *E-mails from Scheherazad* (2003) supplements Hammad's radical ferocity with poignantly comical portrayals of Arab American feminist subjectivity. In "My Grandmother Washes Her Feet in the Sink of the Bathroom at Sears," Kahf re-creates the comic-awkward panic of trying to explain her grandmother's ablutions to scandalized midwestern women, who

> shake their heads and frown
> as they notice what my grandmother is doing,
> an affront to American porcelain,
> a contamination of American Standards
> by something foreign and unhygienic
> requiring civic action and possible use of disinfectant spray
> They fluster about and flutter their hands and I can see
> a clash of civilizations brewing in the Sears bathroom. (26)

The global reach of the grandmother's practice extends back, in Kahf's poem, to Aleppo, Damascus, and Istanbul, and relies upon the porcelain of China—widening our cultural sense of what cleanliness might mean, and how cultural practices are rarely narrowly nationalistic.

Fady Joudah's *The Earth in the Attic* (2008), the first Arab American winner of the Yale Younger Poets prize, centrally concerns itself with life in exile, life as exile. The son of Palestinian refugees, Joudah blends hard-edged poetic witness with the dreamlike evanescence of Mahmoud Darwish (whose poems he translates brilliantly). Joudah composes a narrative poetry that defies the linearity of dull narration; instead he braids multiple lines of narrative, enacting multiple departures and longed-for returns of the exiled.

In "Along Came a Spider," Joudah references those early-morning moments when the earth is secured for the spider to create its web, its home space:

> On mornings of this refugee settlement,
> After the rain falls in stalks
> Of mushroom clouds,
> The spiders bloom anywhere there's a web-hold
> And the earth is like an attic. (57)

Like Walt Whitman in "A Noiseless Patient Spider," Joudah sees the spider as a slightly ludicrous figure of indomitable faith, of home-seeking in an inhospitable world. In this poem the "refugee settlement" resonates doubly, as both an African and a Palestinian experience seen simultaneously.

This double resonance happens hauntingly in "Scarecrow," as if the poet's work in Zambia and the Sudan somehow were a repetition of familial history. The refugees have "no time to look for anyone" and are nearly run over by army trucks, yet

> Later, they will accuse you of giving up your land.
>
> Later, you will stand in distribution lines and won't receive enough
>   to eat.
> Your mother will weave you new underwear from flour sacks.
>
> And they'll give you plastic tents, cooking pots,
> Vaccine cards, white pills, and wool blankets.
>
> And you will keep your cool.
> Standing with eyes shut tight like you've got soap in them.
>
> Arms stretched wide like you're catching rain. (45)

While the opening of the book is presented principally, in the harrowing sequence "Pulse," from the point of view of a doctor treating refugees in Africa, the poems of the second section deliver the hauntingly palimpsestic trauma where the two conflicts in Darfur and Palestine come to resemble each other, though one is widely termed a genocide and the other something else. Joudah's ethical delicacy is to avoid "The Name of the Place," as one poem is called, but also to refuse to exoticize or reify what Darfur has come to represent in American liberal consciousness. In this refusal of names, he refuses the gradations of suffering—that some events are tragedies, others atrocities, that some policies are civil wars, others genocides.

We can see the sudden solidarities between exiled people, whether displaced Arab Americans or Africans, in Joudah's very first poem, where a taxi driver notes that if you see the hoopoe as a good omen, you are one of us. Identity is fluid, and what we believe and who we stand with can be as important as who we are or how others think of us.

Khaled Mattawa, in his essay "Freeways and Rest Houses" from the anthology *Post Gibran*, has called for a similarly complex Arab American literature, one that moves beyond post-assimilation nostalgia and post-Gibran self-Orientalism. In his words, "the staples of grandmotherly aphorism, thickly accented patriarchal traditionalism, culinary nostalgia, religious dogma, belly dancing and adoration of Kahlil Gibran are meager nourishments for cultural identity, let alone a cultural revival and a subsequent engagement with the larger American culture" (61). Avoiding the safe ethnic-identity tropes of food and family, Mattawa has begun to create in his own poetry the answer to his critical call.

Tocqueville (2010), Mattawa's fourth book of poems, enters the philosophical territory of Lawrence Joseph's *Into It*, meditating on what it means to be a poet at the center of American power. But *Tocqueville*, in contrast to Mattawa's lyrically driven previous work, pronounces that it no longer suffices to sing, even to sing of dark times, as Bertolt Brecht proposed. Rather, through the experimentally daring poetry of Mattawa—born in Libya and long an American citizen—we become witnesses to our own implicatedness, our own vulnerable privilege.

While the first poem is titled "Lyric" and begins "Will answers be found / like seeds / planted among rows of song?" the lyric "I" of the poet pulses through the entire collection, through its wider networks of imperial history, global economic flows, and Machiavellian politics, emerging in the diverse voices of a Somali singer, a Sierra Leonean victim/perpetrator of atrocity, a gallery viewer of photographs of Palestinian exile, a factory worker in Georgia, Ecclesiastes as insurance salesman, a terrorist, a State Department insider.

The keynote poem of the book is "On the Difficulty of Documentation," a dialogic meditation on the role of art in a world of violence. The poem takes as its mediating occasion a photographic exhibit of Palestinian refugees. Here Mattawa quotes liberally from two poets, as if in dialogue: Sir Thomas Wyatt, of the Renaissance courtly love tradition, and Bertolt Brecht, of the school of alienation and political action. As the poem reflects on the refugee pictures, Mattawa zigs and zags between poetry's desire to herald the beautiful and its desire to be truthful—between art and history, between transcendence and wound. It ends with Wyatt rather than Brecht, but such a tilt does not suggest that beauty wins. The deft collage of photographs and poetry quotes builds, until Wyatt's own words—"they flee from me"—become more than a courtly love elegy:

> And what of that look, and the all too human?
>
> To be enthralled
>
>   and fain know what she hath deserved (Wyatt)
>
>   the squalor that makes the brow grow stern
>   the just anger that turns a voice harsh. (Brecht)
>
> What else could she do, as she parts, but softly say,
>
>   Oh dear heart, how like you this? (Wyatt) (5)

In the end Wyatt's lament becomes a lament of the political poet, who sees the refugees themselves disappear from his language, from the wider narrative of human rights, displaced by a state that was meant to instantiate the rights of another genocided people.

Tocqueville's central poem, "Tocqueville," is a tour-de-force globalist polyphonic collage that extends through the middle twenty-six pages of the book. Here we feel the poet linger on the dark abyss of globalization—how its purported connectedness has come with profound alienation. Mattawa re-creates the poet's role as global Tocqueville, but this prophetic Tocqueville has none of the adoring tone of the original Frenchman; he has seen too much. Instead, among other things, we are made witness to the words of a man who is compelled by soldiers to beat his baby son to death: "They found me in the house with my baby child. They'd already killed my wife in the field. They told me to place the child in the mortar we used to mash cassava. Then they handed me the club and told me to bludgeon my child, or they would kill me. And I did as they said. Afterwards, they cut off both my arms and let me go" (29). In this poem, Brechtian alienation trumps the poet's longing for the beautiful. *Tocqueville* is a lyric that repudiates lyricism, an unrepeatable experiment, a witness to blindness, a shooting script without camera or bullet. Mattawa takes no cynical distance from the operations of empire; he situates himself, and all of us, in the middle of it, and asks us not to look away, but to lean in and bear its weighty implications.

It would be impossible to avoid the Israeli-Palestinian issue in a discussion of Arab American poetry. One of the more poignant aspects of the Israeli-Palestinian conflict is how the existence of the Jewish state attenuates the rich history of exilic and cosmopolitan thinking of Jewish culture even as it has produced yet another experience of exile—for Palestinians. The unpublished sequence "Diaspo/Renga," a collaborative sequence written by Marilyn Hacker and Deema Shehabi, offers a paradigmatic cosmopoetic example of how Jewish and Palestinian experience of exile provides a window into imaginative empathy for and identification with oppressed and displaced peoples throughout the world—often with the aid of U.S. imperial muscle. Hacker, the celebrated poet and expatriate American Jew who's the leading translator of Arab Francophone poetry, began an e-mail correspondence with Palestinian American poet Deema Shehabi, in the Japanese form called renga. From the very first alternating exchanges, the poets lift and shift our gaze from site to site, and from sight to sight, beginning in Gaza, the archetypal geography of immobility and imprisonment:

> Five, six—and righteous,
> the child in green in Gaza
> stands in her wrecked home,
>
> grubby, indignant. Her hands
> point; she explains what was done
>
> bombed, burned. It all smells
> like gas! We had to throw our clothes
> away! The earrings my
>
> father gave me . . . No martyr,
> resistant. The burnt cradle . . .

breaks over the cold mountains
of North Carolina where a Cherokee
poet huddles in a cottage

by an indigo fire. She sees
the child and says:

This is the new Trail of Tears.
Calls out: Oh outspread Indian nation
let's braid our hair

with the pulverized
gravel of Palestine.

Witness, she says, the unpinned
knuckles of this child. Feel
the burlap curtains whip across . . .

the third floor window
in Belleville, dyed blue-purple
like the hyacinth

on the windowsill. Nedjma
does math homework. Strike today;

but school tomorrow.
Coming back from the demo
they sang in the street—

Rêve Générale!—the slogan
makes her smile. Wan winter sun

Hacker initiates our journey in Gaza, where a child becomes spokesperson for the depradations of Israeli bombing, and Shehabi—whose grandfather was once the mayor of Gaza—sends us to North Carolina, where a Cherokee poet sees this child (presumably on television or in a news story) and sutures her own experience of dispossession (the "Trail of Tears") to the Palestinian *nakba*. The connection between colonialisms has been a regular motif in Palestinian literature, famously in Mahmoud Darwish's "Address of the Red Indian." Then, almost as quickly, Hacker brings us back to her Paris, richly populated by Arabs such as Nedjma, and the city's vital tradition of general strikes.

Hacker and Shehabi cocreate a meeting place in poetic language of their multiple word-worlds, inflected by exile but not silenced by it. When Shehabi writes of the experience of reading Arabic to Hacker, who is a student of Arabic, they meet in the raw sensuality of the lips and teeth and tongue and ear.

For Arab American poetry, cosmopolitan belonging is always complicated by the very real vulnerabilities and griefs of the refugee, of the exile who, in the words of Hacker and Shehabi, "grabs a fistful of ground." Though any place can come to be called home, Arab American poetry contains a thirst for connection to belonging and place that urban cosmopolitanism cannot slake.

The cosmopolitanism that Ameen Rihani aimed for in the first salvo of Arab American literature remains the direction toward which some of the best of Arab American poetry is now tending. But we must continue to distinguish such globality or cosmopoetics from mere cheerleading for globalization, neoliberalism, and empire. On the contrary, critically engaged globalism does not reject the idea of the nation-state, nor does it accept the so-called Clash of Civilizations. Given the ongoing colonialism in Israel-Palestine, the tenuous postrevolutionary conditions in Egypt and Libya, and the civil war in Syria, the poetic cosmopolitanism of Arab American poetry necessarily holds a space for the work of national liberation.

Since the terrorist attacks of 2001, Arab American poets have spoken against the paranoia and fear-mongering of the Right in complex and clarifying ways. As the title of a Lawrence Joseph poem became the title of a crucial anthology of Arab American poetry edited by poet Hayan Charara, these writers were "inclined to speak." Maxine Hong Kingston, echoing François Fénelon, wrote after 9/11, "All our wars are civil wars" (222), since the United States contains people from every nation in the world. The ongoing wars in the Middle East compel us to remind Americans that humanity does not end at the national border, and to interrogate all "comfort zones" in light of "conflict zones."

Arab American poets will continue to play a key role in confronting the imperial temperament, reminding us that the machinations of power are neither distant nor without consequence. Poetry may not stop tanks or drone attacks, but Arab American poetry can leap the gulf between the dominant narrative of the United States and the realities experienced on the ground. Denial is not a river in Egypt, and it's not just residual anger from the shadows of the Twin Towers. It's also the ideological blindness of imperial privilege, supplemented by Orientalism. What Arab American poets show us is a way to see again through our unclarity of vision—through empathic identification, provocative confrontation, the tonic of comedy, the honesty of confession, the collage of subaltern voices. What we do with this new sight is another question entirely.

BIBLIOGRAPHY

Akash, Munir, and Khaled Mattawa, eds. *Post Gibran: Anthology of New Arab American Writing*. West Bethesda, Md.: Kitab, 2000.

Charara, Hayan. "Going Places." *Witness* 24, no. 3 (Fall 2011). witness.blackmountaininstitute .org/issues/volume-24-number-3-fall-2011/going-places/.

———, ed. *Inclined to Speak: An Anthology of Contemporary Arab American Poetry*. Fayetteville: University of Arkansas Press, 2008.

Deleuze, Gilles, and Félix Guattari. *Kafka: Toward a Minor Literature*. Translated by Dana Polan. Minneapolis: University of Minnesota Press, 1986.

Gibran, Kahlil. *The Prophet*. 1923. New York: Alfred A. Knopf, 1989.

Hammad, Suheir. *Born Palestinian, Born Black*. New York: Harlem River Press, 1996.

———. *Breaking Poems*. New York: Cypher Books, 2008.

Heyen, William, ed. *September 11, 2001: American Writers Respond*. Silver Springs, Md.: Etruscan, 2002.

Joseph, Lawrence. *Into It*. New York: Farrar, Straus & Giroux, 2005.

———. "Sand Nigger." In *Codes, Precepts, Biases and Taboos: Poems, 1973–1993*, 90–92. New York: Farrar, Straus & Giroux, 2005.

Joudah, Fady. *The Earth in the Attic*. New Haven, Conn.: Yale University Press, 2008.

Kahf, Mohja. *E-mails from Scheherazad*. Gainesville: University Press of Florida, 2003.

Kingston, Maxine Hong. "Memorial." In Heyen, *September 11, 2001*, 222.

Hacker, Marilyn, and Deema Shehabi. *Diaspo/Renga*. Unpublished mauscript, 2012.

Mattawa, Khaled. "Freeways and Rest Houses." In Akash and Mattawa, *Post Gibran*, 49–61.

———. *Tocqueville*. Kalamazoo, Mich.: New Issues, 2010.

Nye, Naomi Shihab. *19 Varieties of Gazelle: Poems of the Middle East*. New York: Greenwillow Books, 2002.

———. "To Any Would-Be Terrorists." In Heyen, *September 11, 2001*, 287–91.

———. *Transfer*. Rochester, N.Y.: BOA Editions, 2011.

"The Real Gabriela Mercer." Video clip. youtube.com/watch?v=0pUyLoRWe5I&feature =youtu.be.

Rihani, Ameen. *The Book of Khalid*. 1911. New York: Melville House, 2012.

Said, Edward W. *Orientalism*. New York: Pantheon, 1978.

Salaita, Steven. *Arab American Literary Fictions, Cultures, and Politics*. New York: Palgrave Macmillan, 2007.

Shaheen, Jack G. *Reel Bad Arabs: How Hollywood Vilifies a People*. New York: Olive Branch Press, 2001.

17 ~ a mystifying silence: big and black

MAJOR JACKSON

> Nigger, your breed ain't metaphysical.
>   *Robert Penn Warren, "Pondy Woods"*

Beginning in earnest his long and preeminent literary career in the 1930s, it is safe to say poet and novelist Robert Penn Warren never envisioned a black readership, then or today. Yet the above excerpted line of verse from his poem "Pondy Woods," inspired by the 1926 lynching of Primus Kirby in Todd County, Kentucky (Grimshaw 114), has prompted over the years varied responses from black readers, literary artists, and scholars, if not oft cited as an example of the workings of racist ideology in twentieth-century American literature. Writing for the *African American Review*, critic Mark Sanders remarks that Warren "compressed into five deceptively economic feet nearly a half-millennium of white hegemonic philosophy, both its rhetorical strategies and underlying presuppositions" (393). In an interview for the *Washington Star* nearly half a century after Warren penned his infamous rebuke, poet and Howard University professor Sterling Brown famously retorted, "Cracker, your breed ain't exegetical."

Warren could not have imagined or predicted such posthumous and contemptuous comebacks from such distinguished and alien quarters as a black literary critical establishment. The question of the poem's audience, interesting enough, belies its irony; although the admonition, farcically spoken by a buzzard, is addressed to a fugitive black man on the run from a posse after apparently assaulting a white woman, more likely than not Warren had in mind as his ideal audience for his poem-fable that notorious gang of poets and scholars known as the Fugitives who launched New Criticism from their perch at Vanderbilt University in Nashville, Tennessee: Donald Davidson, Randall

Jarrell, Merrill Moore, John Crowe Ransom, and Allen Tate—in short, white, literate southern men like himself. The provocative poem is a performative argument that attempts to deify and consecrate the dominance and superiority of white, intelligent men over perceived instinct-driven black men.

However, were Robert Penn Warren writing in today's highly policed culture and exchange of ideas, and thus to a more ethnically diverse and politically sensitive audience of readers and critics, rest assured he would be hard pressed and most likely excoriated for such retrograde beliefs about black folk and explicit representations of white racist thought. A reading public today, despite the author's intention, would likely receive the speaker in the poem as an embodiment and mouthpiece of the author's own narrow-minded ideas about nonwhite peoples. I confess; I am among that censorious group, yet wonder if such a hypercritical vigilance actually endangers writers' freedom to fully characterize with great candor the complexity of their full humanity. Does it not benefit us to have even the most disdainful beliefs and opinions represented in our art? I wonder how much self-censorship or ambivalence is at work among white poets with respect to writing about race.

Last year in June, my inaugural teaching semester at Bennington Writing Seminars found me very ill and bedridden for a few days due to food poisoning. Laid up in the Alumni House, while the activities of creative writing workshops, lectures, and readings swirled about me, I groaned in my upstairs bedroom. I had to reschedule my poetry reading to a later date in the residency. Originally I was slated to present with the famed southern writer Barry Hannah. Being the younger and emergent writer, likely I would have had to read first.

My illness turned out to be a mild blessing. Barry began his reading without any contextualization or prefatory remarks with an opening paragraph that contained this sentence from his classic short story collection *Airships*: "This nigger was eating a banana, hanging his leg out the front seat on the curb" (169), which evoked a hesitant then hearty spurt of nervous laughter from those in attendance in the humid barn on the pastoral Bennington campus where readings are held in the summer, and as one could have predicted, roundly alienated the few black people in the audience. Too often and still, all across corporate boardrooms, military barracks, and college dorm rooms in America, women, poor folk, gays and lesbians, and people of color are expected to exhibit "a sense of humor" and to quietly laugh and joke along when the very core of their humanity is being assaulted.

The rational, appreciative writer and collegial humanist in me would have recognized that the Alabama-born and Mississippi-bred Pulitzer Prize nominee, novelist, and short story writer with the languorous southern lilt in his voice was simply accomplishing what any fiction writer worth his ink would execute in constructing his story, the building of character through diction and setting, but this would not have prevented me, especially in my younger years, from wanting to open up a can of kick-ass and whip some Barry Hannah butt.

Regretfully (and, at times, proudly), I have a history of reacting violently to being called the N-word; once, in Columbus, Ohio, the hip-hop dancer and choreographer Rennie Harris and I found ourselves crossing six lanes of highway traffic one late morning, fleeing after I punched a beefy white guy in the nose for hurling that all too familiar and uninventive epithet across a counter at me; the other occasion occurred when I was eighteen years old in a fraternity house on a college campus in Philadelphia as rap music was being played.

Fortunately, I was spared the self-conscious awareness and dilemma of wondering if somehow Barry and the roomful of largely white aspiring writers at Bennington who revered him as a model man of letters were in cahoots and making me and other black people in the barn the recipients of some cruel, inside literary joke. Having matured somewhat from my more explosive younger self, truth is, had I been present for Barry's reading, I likely would have been, in the end, grateful for his representation of a white southern racist (which I hear he renders well), even if it struck me initially as offensive, provided the story were artfully written and elegantly sought to earn my empathy. However, I would not have laughed.

Contemporary fiction writers, it seems to me, are more willing than poets to take risks and explore reigning racial attitudes of today and yesterday; of late, among them one thinks of Susan Straight, Richard Ford, Colson Whitehead, Richard Powers, and Edward P. Jones. In my opinion, fiction writers anticipate less severe criticism and aim for an enviable verisimilitude that allows readers to survey and delve into the interior motivations and psychic terrain of their characters. Poets, in contrast, are content to create "speakers" in their poems who merely serve as stand-ins for their interior selves. Evident in the most experimentally driven poems, even there one detects the construction of an alter being. Only a few poets consistently and consciously avoid this strategy, but they strike me as mere monologists.

Whereas Robert Penn Warren under-envisioned his reading audience, contemporary poets lag precisely behind fiction writers because we over-envision a readership. I do not mean by this that we give great consideration to whole groups of people different from us or as our audience, but that we are less willing to be repulsive and repugnant in our poems, so caught up in our quest for linguistic and emotional beauty and earnestness—so earnest are we in the vision of poetry as the province of communal good that we fail to create "speakers" in our poems who are contemptible and dishonorable. Add to this our knee-jerk desire to hide our faults or the less admirable parts of our own lives in our poetry. There's a little racist, sexist, classist, ageist, homophobe in all of us. So we expose ourselves in more acceptable and overly mined areas of embarrassment and shame, even then seeking the redemptive glow of self-reflection and the post-epiphanic splendor of personal triumph and enlightenment. If we do not suffer from any of the above isms, we definitely do not write poems that reflect our personal growth. But more important, the readership we envision prevents us from wanting to offend, not a group, but the overwhelmingly progressive times in which we live and write.

Some might inaccurately allege that such a self-guarded and disapproving milieu is the result of writing for a recovery/therapy-driven culture against the backdrop of "political correctness." I disagree and contend that poets and writers, when away from their pencils and writing pads or laptops, like everyone else, have the option of behaving as decent human beings, of being thoughtful and considerate, which is not a question of "politics" or "correctness," or even the invisible forces that make one self-aware about one's moral groundings or lack thereof. It is quite the cliché to assert some of America's most superb writers leave much to be desired in their social interaction with their families and others; at least, the shadow of their lives is not eclipsed by the false appearance of normality. Yet for artists, endowed with gifts and the responsibility of giving full expression to the range of human beliefs, thoughts, experiences, and possibilities, the yellow, lined legal pages or the blank screens are fair game. The imagination should know no moral bounds—only seek its greatest aesthetic heights. The formal demands of writing poetry will naturally resolve the moral questions.

In his winning book *Democracy, Culture, and the Voice of Poetry*, poet Robert Pinsky asserts, "Poetry is not the voice of virtue and right thinking—not the rhyme department of any progressive movement" (79). Maybe some of that unacknowledged legislating Shelley speaks of as poets' work involves acknowledging and giving form to the dark impressions of which we are constituted, including the quiet moments in which we enact our bigoted beliefs and fears.

The success of the Lions Gate film *Crash* directed by Paul Haggis, which grossed $54.5 million in box office receipts in 2005, owed its success, supposedly, to tapping into those uniquely American prejudices.

All this to say, in a country whose professed strength is best observed in its plurality of cultures, what seems odd to me (and this I find most appalling about contemporary American poetry) is the dearth of poems written by white poets that address racial issues, that chronicle our struggle as a democracy to find tranquility and harmony as a nation containing many nations. Why is this? How is it that poetry does not reflect and serve as a record of the evolution of our racial attitudes and progress much like American fiction from Harriet Beecher Stowe's *Uncle Tom's Cabin* to Philip Roth's *The Human Stain*? Well, it does to some extent, but the canon is severely lopsided and asymmetrical. And without that complete, wide-ranging and far-reaching racial dialogue as a literary and cultural legacy reflected in our poetry, discussions of race and ethnicity will forever be a spectator sport.

We are a country shaped and defined by ethnic stories of strife and victory. Yesterday, the enslavement of African peoples, the Civil War, Emancipation, a violent post-Reconstruction, European immigration, the Jewish Holocaust, Japanese internment, and two world wars determined the political and moral grounds by which our art, literature, and culture achieved their greatest moments. Today, the aftermath of wars in Vietnam and Korea, global conflicts in South America, Africa, and the Middle East, the Iraq war, corporate greed, world poverty, immigration, and militarism now serve as the terrain upon which we journey today in imagining humanity writ large and individually in our works of art. It seems incongruous, then, to have such a lack of poems written by white poets that address our cultural plurality, for the road to diversity has had an impact on us all, whether we care to acknowledge it or not.

We can delude ourselves if we like, but we undeniably harbor racialized views and suppressed thoughts about various ethnic groups. Race is still the most controversial social phenomenon that defines America as a country. A foreign policy such as a "War on Terror" and the resultant influx of immigrants from the Middle East spotlights ethnic difference and race as well as our attitudes toward diversity and inclusion in unique but all too familiar ways; racial profiling took on a whole new meaning shortly after the tragedy of September 11 and still guides Americans' feelings about Arab American men in turbans. Earlier this year, CNN reported that 60 percent of white people and 84 percent of black people consider racism a problem in America. As I write, the nation's highest court is justifying the decision to rule against measures that once guaranteed equal opportunity in education to all races, by saying such assurances violate the principle of a "color-blind" legal system. As Nobel laureate Toni Morrison makes clear in her popular meditation on the subject, *Playing in the Dark: Whiteness and the Literary Imagination*, "Statements to the contrary, insisting on the meaninglessness of race to the American identity, are themselves full of meaning" (46).

To some extent I understand the assertion "race is a social construct," and the less theoretical reasons as to why race has gone the way of religion and politics, conversation stoppers and unpleasant matter for any intimate gathering, especially the hallowed lines of American verse. We pretend a world of racelessness out of interest in the greater good, the democratic spirit in action, or we follow the invisible, liberal mission of seeing the virtue and worth of all people despite their ethnic and racial origins. But, for real, the differences remain, and often they are materially evident, never more so than when we discuss illegal immigration and revisit the topic of reforming the nation's Immigration Bill, which, truth be told, is an affront to the Hispanic community.

So deeply embedded are our racial views, it takes some public figure's blunder to ignite a firestorm of criticism that triggers us to vaguely confront our own intolerance and prejudiced beliefs or, worse, our cosmic indifference. In this setting, the persistence of race in public dialogue seems reserved solely for nightly news and talk radio and occurs only after controversial remarks are made, merely for the purpose of ensuring viewer/listener ratings. Moreover, we discover the unpopular view is not so unpopular and, in fact, is widely held.

When, earlier in the year, the radio announcer referred to a group of young, black, and academically gifted student-athletes as "nappy-headed ho's," what we experienced was not only the continued denigration and hostility toward women but another predictable media reaction to an exhausted topic in desperate need of new and honest perspectives. Similarly, the washed-up comedian who spewed a volcanic tirade of racial epithets at a group of black and Latino audience members at a comedy club in reaction to being heckled also triggered another empty series of news-hour specials, as we attempted to come to grips with yet another distasteful display of suppressed racial loathing. The comedian's comfort at shouting such hate-filled words only evidenced, once again, the reduction of etiquette regarding language in our culture and an unmasked anger at having to conform to an age of civility and regard toward others of different ethnic origins. The very words he used that evening reveal his nostalgia for a past of less decency and consideration: "Fifty years ago we'd have you upside down with a f-- fork up your a--." We feel a false sense of purging only after such renegade figures are publicly fired or themselves extend public apologies. The charade repeats ad nauseam.

So why should I expect our experiences and innate feelings about others different from us to find their way into our poetry? Our inchoate identities and words oversimplify our actual selves. As a result, when we attempt to give expression to our thoughts about race, we collapse into frustration and cannot quite articulate what exactly we feel based on our experiences. Donald Hall wrote that "when we wish to embody in language a complex of feelings or sensations or ideas, we fall into inarticulateness; attempting to speak, in the heat or love of argument, we say nothing or we say what we do not intend," and, more profoundly, that poems "exist to say the unsayable" (6). Poetry gives a far richer sensate experience and representation of nuanced opinions and lives that are far too easily summarized with the racial joke or prejudiced view.

More, I believe in poetry's power to enact empathy. If lyric poetry allows us, as Helen Vendler has pointed out, to inhabit the consciousness of others, then it follows that poetry becomes a means by which we leave ourselves, for a moment, and become someone else. That escape and entering widens our humanity. I am William Butler Yeats when I read out loud "Easter, 1916," and memorialize, too, those who sacrificed their lives for a cause they believed in. The poem becomes a window for me to understand martyrdom in our own time. With each poem ingested, our interiority grows and expands toward inclusivity, how we come to bridge differences between us.

On the other hand, quite possibly, there is a limit to our empathy. Do we really possess an appetite for nuanced representations of racial attitudes and experiences in our poetry for the purpose of cultivating compassion in our nation? There is a disturbing and relative silence in American poetry that refuses to be filled by the majority of white American poets. Needless to say, pages of poetry written by black, Latino, Native, and Asian American poets do great service. Well, it's not like people of color have a choice, now do they?—especially if they are being true to themselves and writing their lives. All else is manufactured. Over the centuries, many American poets of various ethnicities, from Rita Dove to Jessica Hagedorn and Agha Shahid Ali to Sherman Alexie, have deemed it aesthetically fertile, socially and politically relevant even, to portray fraught and enlightening encounters of ethnic difference, to explore joyful nuances of the color line, while white poets have been more reluctant to address the subject with veracity and candor. Why?

I posed this question to many white American poets over the past year. In their own voices, some responses included: not wanting to cause discomfort in the reader, highlighting poetry's entertainment value in the Age of Billy Collins; others point to a lack of encounter and experience with nonwhite peoples, feeling they would not authoritatively contribute much in the discussion of race relations; in the Era of Confession, some believe writing about race is opportunistic and disingenuous, for it is not a white issue, but an issue for black people and other people of color; while others fear embarrassment and the negative reaction of friends and strangers, once again envisioning a liberal-minded and retributive readership that would conduct a virtual public lynching or a poeticized Truth and Reconciliation trial.

As stated earlier, the presence of a perceived hypercritical audience actually imperils well-meaning people from fervently expressing with candor their true feelings and opinions. A friend who is an executive director of a nonprofit organization noticed the willingness of her board members to discuss openly questions of race, but once a Latino man joined the board, the chatty trustees suddenly felt stifled and unable to freely argue and debate for fear of being erroneously accused of possessing racist views.

I will add another reason: perhaps the complexities of race in the twenty-first century far outreach our imaginative capability. Another friend, who is a Foreign Service Officer in the State Department, called me up with an experience she felt I should write about. Having entered a hired car after work in Washington, D.C., where she was learning to speak Urdu in preparation for her next tour of duty, she happily put her new language acquisition to work by asking the driver, who had been speaking on his cell phone, from what region of southeast Asia did he immigrate? Exuberantly the man named his native country and was quite pleased that this young black woman from Louisiana could converse in his native tongue. Language brought them together. He praised her for her clarity and diction, told her that his elderly mother was quite lonely in this country, and wondered, if she had time, would she consider visiting her for an hour in the evenings, while he drove his taxi; that way she could further her proficiency in speaking Urdu prior to her departure overseas, and his mother would be a little less lonely. He would pay her.

Then, at a stoplight in the far right lane of a busy intersection, in which the light was green, her new friend was unable to turn due to heavy traffic. A taxi driver honked and honked behind them. Suddenly the irritated taxi driver, who looked to be from West Africa, pulled alongside them and yelled, "Nigger. Go back where you came from?" Her new friend shouted back as he was turning the car, "Nigger! You go back where you came from?" They sat and spoke not another word in English or Urdu the remainder of the taxi ride.

Whatever the reason, the mystifying silence around race highlights white American poets' unsettling and conspicuous unresponsiveness and ambivalence toward a very important aspect of social life in America, one given heft by our founding documents, by our history of immigration and war, and by our being a beacon for so many disenfranchised peoples across the globe who arrive here with the hope of interweaving into the fabric of our democracy. At least Robert Penn Warren and the other Fugitives took a stand and compellingly wrote poems and novels, albeit at times reprehensibly, from the position of being white male Americans. We knew where they stood regarding the "race question," which could allow us to substantively engage the tradition of white southern identity in American letters, and thus each other, quite candidly.

Luckily, a few contemporary white poets writing today, even at the risk of criticism from contrarian black poet-critics such as myself, actually do exhibit great hubris and are willing to take the risk of censure and disapproval. They eschew a vigilant readership and welcome the challenge of finding new figures, innovative language, and expressive forms to explore their own attitudes about race while thoughtfully redressing some of the racial imbalance in American life. These writers include Sharon Olds, Ed Pavlic, Sean Thomas Daugherty, Henry Taylor, Philip Levine, Jake Adam York, C. K. Williams, Tony Hoagland, T. R. Hummer, and a few others for whom race is a consistently vital and crucial subject. Poet Jim Daniels has also done a great service in putting together a multiracial anthology of poems about race, *Letters to America: Contemporary American Poetry on Race*.

Thus far, white poets have been content to: populate their poems with people of color (see Elizabeth Bishop's "In the Waiting Room"); exoticize and extol the virtues of ethnic life and so-called primitive cultures (see Vachel Lindsay's "The Congo" or any number of jazz poems written by white poets); make passing presumptive and ostracizing remarks about nonwhites (see Tony Hoagland's "Poem in Which I Make the Mistake of Comparing Billie Holiday to a Cosmic Washerwoman"); or cunningly profit from the loaded meanings and connotative power that black and other dark-skinned peoples have come to signify in white readers' imagination (see John Berryman's *Dream Songs* and many works of literary art by American writers). Contemporary poets replicate some of the same strategies but also are beginning to frame contemporary situations and map new emotional and psychic terrain as well as aesthetic approaches to discuss difference in this country and for us as a public readership to take delight in, to debate and argue. In my very nonacademic survey of some of these poems, I discovered a few surprising and interesting patterns.

Many white contemporary poets do not have black friends. If they do enjoy the bonds and frustrations of friendship with people of other races, those poems are not being written. Rather, many poems about race capture "encounters" with people of color. These poems normally take place in public, on a street corner, or a job site, but frequently on public transportation, and never in a white poet's home. Both parties are literally and figuratively in motion, being shuttled to their separate neighborhoods and segregated destinations. One such poem, "I Am Not a Racist," which appears in Kathryn Maris's debut collection *The Book of Jobs*, takes place on the "Brooklyn-bound express." In the opening section of the four-part poem, whose unrelenting couplets echo the gap but also the interconnectedness between her and the black people on the train, the speaker looks around at the "Blank, humorless faces / on fast-fed bodies" and thinks to herself "what happened to you / ain't my fault" (42), a popular sentiment uttered by white people who scoff at the idea of reparations or federal apologies to black people. Many white people wonder why they should be held accountable for their ancestors' crimes. The speaker, pondering this, then hears the click of a Walkman button being depressed and mistakes it for a gun being cocked. In a subsequent section, the speaker walks through fresh snow down a New York street "in love with this city—jubilant, freezing, sane" when suddenly she is jolted out of her ambulatory revelry.

> But ahead, a lupine
> pack of youths takes plucking steps on my street.
> I'm almost home. I won't ostentatiously retreat,
>
> be suspicious unfairly, fear this brotherhood
> of saunterers, or judge them by a neighborhood. (43)

The scene is too familiar to comment on at length. But I'll assert Maris achieves an astonishing tension by giving resonance to the imagined void between the speaker and the young men congregating on the street. The speaker fears and expresses trepidation but the rhyming couplets reinforce the fact that they are involuntarily locked in an awkward dance of public racial guesswork and, dare I say, desire.

In many poems authored by white poets, as in the larger society, fear of black people and innate feelings of guilt are dominant emotions. That fear has a long history in America, going all the way back to the fear of slave uprisings on southern plantations. Reports of Toussaint Louverture's Haitian rebellion in American newspapers in the 1790s, which contained vivid descriptions of massacres of white plantation owners and their families, had the effect of spurring many plantation owners in the southern United States to counter with greater forms of brutality as a means of controlling enslaved Africans and containing insurrections.

Sharon Olds's extraordinarily written poem "On the Subway," a classic poem when discussing race and poetry, situates a terrified speaker across from a young black male, whose "feet are huge" and whose countenance is described as the "casual cold look of a mugger." The fear of physical violence between this woman and the black man sitting across from her as they are "rapidly moving through darkness" is palpable and, as the speaker suggests, justifiable, for "he is black / and I am white, and without meaning or / trying to I must profit from his darkness. / . . . There is / no way to know how easy this / white skin makes my life" (5). His white shoelaces laced through black sneakers are described as a "set of international scars."

Ever since first encountering Elizabeth Bishop's "In the Waiting Room," I have been interested in how black bodies are represented and/or how "blackness" is signified in American poetry. I collect these poems as others collect poems about dogs or jazz. I attempt to identify what is gained as a result of differentiating race, and almost always imagine the poems without racial signifiers.

The most popular strategy of representing blackness is to write about black music or some popular musician, entertainer, or sports figure. This is sensible; however, rarely do poems written by white poets feature black lawyers, political leaders, or eminent scientists, which is why Robert Lowell's "For the Union Dead" ranks as one of his most important poems. Other poems that signify blackness will simply announce that the person is black, as if no other shades exist to describe people of color, which has me wonder if white poets can truly see black people:

> because the young man was
> black speaking black
>> *C. K. Williams, "The Singing," 4*

> Well, we found two black boys up there
> in the wild cliff garden.
>> *James Wright, "On a Phrase from Southern Ohio," 300*

> And the cause of death no mystery: two bullet holes
> in the breast of a well-dressed black woman
> in perhaps her mid-thirties.
>> *Henry Taylor, "Landscape with Tractor," 3*

The insistent lack of imaginative language to describe the full spectrum of people of color reveals how overreliant we are on the structures of language and received thinking. Rest assured that when a white person describes a black person, you'll almost always read the words "big" and "black" somewhere in close proximity to each other; I guess a dwarfish black person does not invite fear in the imagination—either that or the images of the black nanny and Mandingo still loom large in the collective psyche of America:

> and because the black girl was so big
> and so black,
>> so unintimidated,
>> *Tony Hoagland, "The Change," 12*

> The nurse was big and black
> and really pissed at me,
> the only kid on the burn ward.
>
> .   .   .   .
>
> since I was zonked on morphine
> most of that time, Mother believed
> I dreamed up the big black nurse.
> Still, she was a messenger, my angel.
>> *Patricia Dobler, "Some Heretics"*

Many black bodies get figured as horrific in the process of naming:

> black, naked women with necks
> wound round and round with wire
> like the necks of light bulbs.
>> *Elizabeth Bishop, "In the Waiting Room," 4*

Or nonhuman, animal-like, as in Maris's above "lupine / pack of youths," which is reminiscent of the group of young boys who brutally raped a Central Park jogger and were subsequently described by journalists covering the trial as a pack of wolves.

In "On the Subway," Olds extends and riffs off the tradition of such dehumanizing figuration by giving us a black man who has been skinned alive; the speaker realizes she bears his pelt on her shoulders:

> He is wearing
> red, like the inside of the body
> exposed. I am wearing dark fur, the
> whole skin of an animal taken and
> used. (5)

Olds is shrewd in conflating race and class and economic status by drawing the lines between the kinds of power each possesses, which is significantly unequal, historical, and imagined, accentuating more still the basis of her alarm. The speaker's power is one of privilege and class. She wears a fur coat, eats steak, and carries a briefcase. In contrast, his power is all brute force. "Alert under hooded lids" with his animal-like physical strength, he could easily take her life "and break [it] across his knee like a stick." The ease, swiftness, and indiscriminate nature of what he could possibly do to her are hallmarks of such violence and fear in American poetry. Olds, however, is not content to simply mark the boundaries of power that threaten and separate her from the young man across the subway aisle. Yes, they occupy different rungs of the social ladder, and public transportation puts them in proximity to each other. However, it is cunning, far-seeing, and useful to have the speaker recognize the advantages she enjoys at the expense of his subjugation.

Not only do black people possess animal-like and sexual energy in poems written by white poets, but black people also give agency for others to tap into their own carnal powers. As much as the black body is feared in American life, it is also desired. Dorianne Laux's poem "The Laundromat" situates a young woman who "gets off on words and gestures" in a Laundromat folding clothes. The speaker watches a flirtatious older woman eyeing a young man in silk shorts. The speaker is also aware of a man who waits for her to bend over. Everyone is "[c]aught in the crackle of static electricity." The scene is so sexually charged, one gets the feeling the room is poised for a group climax. The older woman voices an innuendo: "hot isn't it?" But then

> A long black jogger swings in off the street to
> splash his face in the sink and I watch the room
> become a sweet humid jungle. We crowd around
> the Amazon at the watering hole, twitching our noses
> like wildebeests or buffalo, snorting, rooting out
> mates in the heat. I want to hump every moving thing
> in this place. I want to lie down in the dry dung
> and dust and twist to scratch my back. I want to
> stretch and prowl and grow lazy in the shade. (32)

The poem's contextualized moment of stasis unapologetically leaps off into a writhing, anaphoristic admission of arousal and sexual craving. This is the burden black male and female bodies have had to shoulder since time immemorial: perceived hypersexual beings whose bodies conjure both fear and fantasy. However, does it mean white poets should not write about that perception and desire, even if the metaphoric propositions are unsettling?

So many poems written by white poets are undecided and do no more than give utterance to a personal exhaustion of race in public dialogue or, worse, to a seemingly interminable chasm between the races.

> We are stuck on
> opposite sides of the car, a couple of
> molecules stuck in a rod of light
> *Olds, "On the Subway," 5*

As the speaker in C. K. Williams's poem "The Singing" states:

> both of us
> knew just where we were
> in the duet we composed the equation we made
> the conventions to
> which we were condemned (5)

Although I bristle whenever I read Bishop's ekphrastic description of Osa and Martin Johnson's photograph of Africans in the *National Geographic*, I think "In the Waiting Room" a fine, exemplary poem which avoids the pessimism and doubt we associate with discussions of race. Although the poem participates in the colonial gaze and discourse about natives, primitivism, and Western civilization, as did the Kansan couple's films and books of exotic wildlife safaris, the poem goes beyond the Johnsons in imagining and representing a larger humanity. The poem does not glorify difference nor seek to create some sort of natural hierarchy in mankind, but asserts, albeit hesitantly, the unity of all human beings:

> Why should I be my aunt,
> or me, or anyone?
> What similarities—
> boots, hands, the family voice
> I felt in my throat, or even
> the *National Geographic*
> and those awful hanging breasts—
> held us all together
> or made us all just one? (7)

The moment is afforded even greater import as we realize the young lady in the poem begins to awaken to her own humanity, much to her wonderment and surprise. One wonders if Bishop attended the 1955 Museum of Modern Art exhibition of photographs *The Family of Man*, curated by Edward Steichen, who sought to give photographic expression to the universality of mankind. Needless to say, the politics of "In the Waiting Room" are obviously complicated—

> The waiting room was bright
> and too hot. It was sliding
> beneath a big black wave,
> another, and another. (7)

—but Bishop, unlike Robert Penn Warren, seems more naïve and less xenophobic, one who simply fell victim and subject to the reigning images of African peoples at that time. Even so, we are the better for her interpretation and artwork, for we have the privilege to access a fuller portrait of the woman and the times in which she was living.

Tony Hoagland is probably the most controversial white poet writing about race today. Poems such as "The Change," "Rap Music," and the aforementioned "Poem in Which I Make the Mistake of Comparing Billie Holiday to a Cosmic Washerwoman" have caused enough hubbub in poetry circles to prompt the Geraldine R. Dodge Foundation to organize a "conversation" at last year's poetry festival on the topic "Race & Poetry" which featured Lucille Clifton, Terrance Hayes, Tony Hoagland, and Linda Hogan in dialogue.

Hoagland's language in "The Change" is irreverent and sardonic—

> pitted against that big black girl from Alabama,
> cornrowed hair and Zulu bangles on her arms,
> some outrageous name like Vondella
> Aphrodite—
>
> .   .   .   .   .
>
> hitting the ball like she was driving the Emancipation Proclamation
> down Abraham Lincoln's throat (12)

—while in "Rap Music" he engages familiar constructions of fear and white alienation:

> I don't know what's going on inside that portable torture chamber,
> but I have a bad suspicion
> there's a lot of dead white people in there
>
> .   .   .   .
>
> and what I'm not supposed to say
> is that black for me is a country
> more foreign than China or Vagina
> more alarming than going down Niagara on Viagra
> And it makes me feel stupid when I get close
> like a little white dog on the edge of the big dark woods (49)

Most important, to my delight, he creates a space for us to discuss race, even if the poems are excessively self-justifying and make us uncomfortable. Lamentably, though, the poems seem too contrived in their constructed narrow-mindedness and too controlled in their attempt to court controversy. James Baldwin, in the classic *The Fire Next Time*, asserts that "the relatively conscious whites and the relatively conscious blacks . . . must, like lovers, insist on, or create, the consciousness of the others" (346). It is a beautiful utterance. Hoagland does not in the end eschew audience; his poems read as if he envisions a liberal-minded readership to willfully irritate, not seduce: he's not a lover, he's a fighter. But then, just as he begins to wrestle, he does an about-face, as if he knows he can push the envelope only so far, as if he knows what's at stake is the fragility of his own selfhood. (To do so would require him to interrogate not only the illusion of blackness but the whole systematic rhetorical structures constructed over time that equate whiteness with superiority, power, and even literacy and literary heritage à la the Fugitives.) This is when his endings reach too comfortably for the epiphanic, redemptive line that salvages Hoagland the Poet:

> this tangled roar
> which has to be shut off
> or blown away or sealed off
> or actually mentioned and entered
>   *"Rap Music,"* 49

> Poof, remember? It was the twentieth century almost gone,
> we were there,

> and when we went to put it back where it
> belonged,
> it was past us
> and we were changed.
>   *"The Change,"* 11

Yet I would rather have his failures than nothing at all. At least his poems announce him as introspective in a self-critical way on this topic. Self-censorship should never be an option for poets.

Writing about race has to be so much more than writing about race, and moreover, race in poetry is not a mere discussion between black and white peoples of the United States, or a visit to the Martin Luther King, Jr. National Historic Site, or some poeticized contraption set up to ensnare an overly sensitive group of readers who passionately believe in equity, justice, racial harmony, and change. It bears repeating again: for us to actualize as a country whose ideals and documents profess the value of a diverse ethnic and racial populace, we must begin to pen a body of poems that goes beyond our fears and surface projections of each other to a fuller account of the challenges and reaches of an ever-evolving democracy.

BIBLIOGRAPHY

Baldwin, James. *The Fire Next Time*. 1962. In *Collected Essays*, 291–347. New York: Library of America, 1998.

Bishop, Elizabeth. "In the Waiting Room." In *Geography III*, 4. New York: Farrar, Straus and Giroux, 2008.

Brown, Sterling A. Interview by Steven Jones. May 4, 1973. Transcript at Institute for the Arts & Humanities, Howard University.

Daniels, Jim, ed. *Letters to America: Contemporary American Poetry on Race*. Detroit: Wayne State University Press, 1995.

Dobler, Patricia. "Some Heretics." *Virginia Quarterly Review* 72, no. 2 (Spring 1996). vqronline .org/some-heretics.

Grimshaw, James A., Jr. *Understanding Robert Penn Warren*. Columbia: University of South Carolina Press, 2001.

Haggis, Paul. *Crash*. Lions Gate Films, 2004.

Hall, Donald. *Breakfast Served Any Time All Day: Essays on Poetry New and Selected*. Ann Arbor: University of Michigan Press, 2004.

Hannah, Barry. *Airships*. New York: Grove Press, 1994.

Hoagland, Tony. "The Change." In *What Narcissism Means to Me*, 12.

———. "Rap Music." In *What Narcissism Means to Me*, 49.

———. *What Narcissism Means to Me*. Minneapolis: Graywolf, 2003.

Laux, Dorianne. "The Laudromat." In *Awake*, 32. Pittsburgh: Carnegie Mellon University Press, 2013.

Maris, Kathryn. "I Am Not a Racist." In *The Book of Jobs*, 42–45. New York: Four Way Books, 2006.

Morrison, Toni. *Playing in the Dark: Whiteness and the Literary Imagination*. Cambridge, Mass.: Harvard University Press, 1992.

Olds, Sharon. "On the Subway." In *The Gold Cell*, 5. New York: Random House, 2012.

Pinsky, Robert. *Democracy, Culture, and the Voice of Poetry*. Princeton, N.J.: Princeton University Press, 2002.

Sanders, Mark A. "Sterling A. Brown and the Afro-Modern Moment." *African American Review* 31, no. 3 (1997): 393–97.

Steichen, Edward. *The Family of Man: The Greatest Photographic Exhibition of All Time—503 Pictures from 68 Countries*. New York: Museum of Modern Art/MACO Magazine Corp., 1955.

Taylor, Henry. "Landscape with Tractor." In *The Flying Change*, 3. Baton Rouge: Louisiana State University Press, 1985.

Warren, Robert Penn. "Pondy Woods." In *A Robert Penn Warren Reader*, 320–22. New York: Random House, 1987.

Williams, C. K. "The Singing." In *The Singing*, 4–5. New York: Farrar, Straus and Giroux, 2003.

Wright, James. "On a Phrase from Southern Ohio." In *Above the River: The Complete Poems*, 30. Farrar, Straus and Giroux, 1990.

18 ～ writing white

MARTHA COLLINS

Major Jackson's 2007 essay "A Mystifying Silence: Big and Black" did American poetry a great service by asking why there should be a "dearth of poems written by white poets that address racial issues" (141). Four years later, Claudia Rankine's open e-mail invitation to friends to share "some thoughts on writing about race" echoed Jackson's question by asking writers (of all races) to consider (among other possible subjects) why, if they hadn't written "consciously about race," they had "never felt compelled to do so," and whether, if fear was involved in their reluctance, they would address that. Of the nearly one hundred responses that were ultimately posted under "Open Letter Responses" on Rankine's website, over half came from white writers, a number of whom did indeed address those questions, which I'd like to consider in a general way here, occasionally referencing Jackson's essay.

A couple of years ago I heard Natasha Trethewey make a distinction between writing about race and writing from racialized experience. I think we go a long way toward understanding why white poets don't address racial issues more often when we acknowledge that it's almost impossible for poets of color *not* to write from racialized experience—whereas it at least *seems* to be very easy for white poets not to do so. "Seems," because of course we're all writing race whether we realize it or not: a writer of color will see the whiteness in my poems even if I don't. And for many years I did not: for me, as for many white people, race was—whether I would have phrased it this way or not—something others had: white was default, was *no* race. For many white poets, and certainly for myself for some time, to write race was to write "about" race: to consciously take on a "subject" which, like war or the environment or love or divorce, I could approach and then abandon until next time. And it was not something I did very often—precisely, or at least partly, because it was not "my" subject.

But if there are internal reasons for this avoidance (which I will return to), there are also external ones. Some years ago, race—along with culture, gender, and sexual preference—came to the fore as an "identity" issue. During that period I recall putting together a panel of writers for PEN New England called "Writing Across the Borders of Race, Gender, and Culture." Most of the participants were novelists (white and of color) writing in the voice of an Other; the one poet, Suzanne Gardinier, whose then-recent book *The New World* (1993) included sections in the voices of Harriet Jacobs and immigrants, spoke eloquently of the way that love can and must be the vehicle for such "border crossings." But the panel was quite controversial, with more audience resistance than I had anticipated. If "identity" had established the right of all voices to be heard, it had also brought to the fore the related idea of "appropriation." I remember teaching a literary translation workshop at Oberlin College in the late 1990s and having some students voice doubts about whether such translation was legitimate at all, since it was clearly an appropriative activity.

When race finally became central to my own writing in the book-length poem *Blue Front*, which focused on a lynching my father had witnessed as a child, the issue of appropriation came up in the responses of some readers and listeners who would ask, for instance, "How does it feel to be writing African American history as a white person?" That the question arose at all has a great deal to do with the reluctance of white poets to write about race, I think. In a wonderfully perceptive review of *Blue Front*, the African American poet Lynne Thompson importantly notes that "white America has to come to grips with the same legacy as do African Americans" (13), but she recognizes that the "subject of lynching is one over which some African American writers, artists, and musicians have exerted a proprietary claim by virtue of having been the historical victims of this most brutal of injustices" (12). Among the several answers that Major Jackson reports having received in answer to the question of "why the dearth" is the belief that writing about race "is not a white issue, but an issue for black people and other people of color" (144). That has no doubt been true, for many of us; but there is external pressure as well.

Deeper than the fear of appropriation, though, is another fear. If the culture creates a sense that race is somehow not white people's territory, that sense is reinforced by a fear of "getting it wrong" if we do enter the territory. On the external level, this may be due to what Jackson calls "the presence of a perceived hypercritical audience" (144). While praising the "few contemporary white poets" who "even at the risk of criticism from contrarian black poet-critics such as myself . . . are willing to take the risk of censure and disapproval" (145), Jackson provides exactly the criticism he mentions when he discusses those poets, and in the process puts a lot of ways of "getting it wrong" on the table. This is extremely useful: if white poets are to deal with race, we need to know our limitations and mistakes. But the fact that they may well be noted—whereas silence will not—is surely an important factor here.

Still deeper than the fear of external censure, though, is an internal fear of getting it wrong. Several poets on the Rankine website speak of this. Jan Clausen mentions, in passing, her "own uncomfortable awareness that I'm not 'right' on race in all the ways I'd like to be" (1); Sally Keith writes: "I can confess a fear of error. I can say that I want to be right. I also do not want to be spoken for, or to be misunderstood. All of this makes me pretty nervous" (2). Rachel Zucker goes deeper: "I feel unable to speak about race, afraid of making mistakes. How horrible to be called out as racist, to seem racist, to be racist" (6). To *be* racist: because of course, on some level, we all are.

How, then, do white poets get past these difficulties and enter the mine-filled territory of race? Recently and currently, a number of white poets have delved into the place where personal and public history converge. In a section of her 1994 book *The Flashboat* called "Family Stories"—which I later realized had given me a kind of license to explore my own family history—Jane Cooper ponders

> how to redress the past
> how to relish yet redress
> my sensuous, precious, upper-class,
> unjust white child's past. (190)

In subsequent poems Cooper explores "this complex shame" (208) and the legacy of her ancestors and their descendants, often using questions, as in "Being Southern": "Can any white person write this, whose ancestors once kept slaves?" (203).

In her "open letter," another possible topic Claudia Rankine poses is: "Do you believe race can be decontextualized, or in other words, can ideas of race be constructed separate from their history?" (2011). The implied "right" answer is of course no, and it seems telling, to me, that many of the white poets who have most explicitly and extensively racialized their writing have been ones (often women) who are able to call upon the racism in their family histories. Michelle Boisseau's *A Sunday in God-Years* (2009), Catherine Sasanov's *Had*

Slaves (2010), Tess Taylor's *The Forage House* (2013), and Susan Tichy's work-in-progress *Trafficke: An Autobiography* all have as their starting and continuing points their ancestors' involvement with slavery. White people do not all have that background, of course—as I do not, at least to my knowledge. But my first big shift away from the "occasional" poem about race to a central focus occurred when, prior to writing *Blue Front*, I saw an exhibit of lynching postcards and discovered that the "hanging" my father told me he'd witnessed as a boy was actually a lynching attended by ten thousand people, and that the primary victim was an African American man. It took me a year to begin delving into that powerful intersection of racist history with my own family: I too was afraid of "getting it wrong," and perhaps of "appropriation" as well. But if I hadn't written about that lynching, I don't think I could have gone on writing.

For some poets for whom race has become an important subject, more recent personal experience has been a factor. Growing up in the South has often been part of this, as in the important explorations of the civil rights movement in *A Murmuration of Starlings* (2008) and *Persons Unknown* (2010) by the late Jake Adam York, or in poems in Kate Daniels's *A Walk in Victoria's Secret* (2010); similarly, memories of the race riots in D.C. and L.A. figure in the poems of Ailish Hopper. Particularly stunning in York's work are the implicating ways he inserts himself into his poems, noting in *Persons Unknown*, for example, a "moment" when "I can mistake myself / for the redneck at the end of a joke" (13).

Not every white poet can easily find such connections, but almost everyone has stories. One of the things that most impressed me in reading through the "Open Letter Responses" was the number of white writers, some of whom had never written about race, who felt compelled to tell their own stories. These accounts suggest that race weighs heavily on many white Americans, whether we have written about it before or not, and are themselves an important reason for us to be grateful to Claudia Rankine for her invitation.

Another connecting factor, also prominent in York's work, is black music. Jackson notes that white poets' "most popular strategy of representing blackness is to write about black music or some popular musician, entertainer, or sports figure"; "rarely," he says, do such poems "feature black lawyers, political leaders, or eminent scientists" (147). True enough. But I would note that the connection with black music is often not a simple one for the (mostly male) white poets who explore it, including York, Kevin Coval, Bruce Smith, and Ira Sadoff: the poets' deep emotional involvement allows them to metaphorically and literally (though complexly and incompletely) cross (as Coval says) to the other "side of the city" (12). That Coval's composite character L-vis "is someone who uses *and misuses* Black cultural production, who is at times appropriate and *who appropriates*, who blurs the line and crosses it *carelessly*" (xi, italics mine) reflects a deeply important awareness that race is not just something that happens "out there"; it's deeply imbedded in all of us, for good and for ill.

Coval's composite character suggests the depth of this; an earlier example is the more controversial minstrel figure who appears as a kind of alter ego in John Berryman's *Dream Songs*. Another earlier instance occurs in, and between, two poems in Denise Levertov's *Relearning the Alphabet*, "The Gulf" and "The Gulf (II)." The first, written during the 1967 Detroit riots, depicts and then imagines a boy grabbing gladioli from a flower shop (15); the second begins with the first of two speakers saying: "My soul's a black boy with a long way to go, / a long way to know if black is beautiful" (50). The first poem is the sort that Jackson focuses on in his essay and that most people probably think of when they think of white poets writing about race: it depicts a person of color. In this case it does so with indisputably fine intentions, and it is not content simply to describe; by imagining, it attempts to understand. The second is a more difficult poem, incorporating the introjection that I think is one of the deeper ways in which race is a part of white American experience: somewhere in most of us white folk is very likely a figure that corresponds to that "black boy." A more conscious version of this Other appears in Kate Daniels's "Autobiography of a White Girl Raised in the South": "In any self-portrait from the '50s, you'd have to see the me / that was not me: the black girl trudging along the side of the road / while I whizzed past in my daddy's car" (7).

But of course there was *not* such a literal figure for many of us white poets— and there may not be, either, in our poems. Major Jackson states: "Many white contemporary poets do not have black friends. If they do . . . , those poems are not being written" (146). I remember reading this and thinking, yowsie, by those standards I have no friends at all: how many times have my friends appeared in my poems?

But he has a point. There are of course white poets whose friends and families include persons of color, and who have accessed these relationships in their work, as Fanny Howe has done in both poetry (*Tis of Thee*) and prose (introduction to *The Wedding Dress*). But for the rest of us, the absence of nonwhite people may be telling in other ways. In her "open letter" response, Joy Katz acknowledges that, prior to adopting a Vietnamese child, "I was nothing, no-race, neutral," and recalls how the adoption made her aware of her whiteness; still later, she realized that "my poem-people were white" and couldn't be revised to be anything else (1). Rachel Zucker's response begins with a similar statement: "All the people in my poems are white"—though Zucker goes on to say that "that's not true," that she "never say[s] otherwise" for fear "of seeming racist" (1). Recovering from my no-friends-at-all-in-my-poems defense, I consider Joy Katz's acknowledgment and realize that my own "poem-people"—who until the last ten years or so were often third-person stand-ins for myself or someone like me, "a woman" or "a man"—are also mostly white, or at least not recognizably anything else.

In fact, I have realized in the years since I published *Blue Front*, my life itself has been extremely white. While I was writing that book, I was think-ing mostly about my father, who became the imagined or questioned figure through whom I tried to observe the lynching. But at some point I began to consider what all of this had to do with me, a white woman living nearly a century later. Then the term "white papers" came into my consciousness and provided a title for what ultimately became a book of numbered but untitled poems that deal with race, particularly the issue of what it means to be white in a multiracial society still haunted by its deeply racist past. A number of the poems focus on my very white midwestern childhood; others involve historical explorations of the racial history of several places (all northern) where I have lived; still others examine the uses we make of the words we so inaccurately call ourselves, particularly "white." Ten years ago I would have said that I had very little "racial" history. In writing this recent book, I learned a great deal about the history of race, including the history of whiteness, and a great deal about myself. My own experience has become racialized, in a conscious way, and whether that awareness is apparent in my poems or not, it has changed the way I live my life and see the world.

As I've said more than once, in talking about this subject, "I know that I still miss the obvious, avoid the difficult, speak from ignorance." That will continue to be true, I am sure. But with every opportunity I have to explore this subject, I am drawn more deeply into it, and a little further away from the factual, tonal, and psychological errors and limitations that continue to be a significant part of who I am. As Ira Sadoff writes in response to Rankine's open letter: "I'm not sure I've succeeded in writing a really good poem about race yet. I see holes in the vision and I learn from them" (3). Or as Rachel Zucker says at the end of her deeply moving response: "This essay is one of the most uncomfortable things I've ever written. . . . I'm getting nowhere, I feel. Only making a spectacle of myself. Implicating myself, at least, for a start" (10).

Perhaps that is the place where all white poets need to start, and to keep starting, over and over, until we get it, if not right, at least a little less wrong.

BIBLIOGRAPHY

Boisseau, Michelle. *A Sunday in God-Years*. Fayetteville: University of Arkansas, 2009.

Clausen, Jan. Untitled. In "Open Letter Responses."

Collins, Martha. *Blue Front*. Minneapolis: Graywolf, 2006.

———. *White Papers*. Pittsburgh: University of Pittsburgh Press, 2012.

Cooper, Jane. *The Flashboat: Poems Collected and Reclaimed*. New York: Norton, 2000.

Coval, Kevin. *L-vis Lives! Racemusic Poems*. Chicago: Haymarket Books, 2011.

Daniels, Kate. *A Walk in Victoria's Secret*. Baton Rouge: Louisiana State University Press, 2010.

Gardinier, Suzanne. *The New World*. Pittsburgh: University of Pittsburgh Press, 1993.

Howe, Fanny. *Tis of Thee*. Berkeley, Calif.: Atelos, 2003.

———. *The Wedding Dress*. Berkeley: University of California Press, 2003.

Jackson, Major. 2007. "A Mystifying Silence: Big and Black." The in-text citations for this essay refer to the page numbers in this volume, 137–154. (First published in *American Poetry Review*, September/October 2007.)

Katz, Joy. Untitled. In "Open Letter Responses."

Keith, Sally. "Open Letter." In "Open Letter Responses."

Levertov, Denise. *Relearning the Alphabet*. New York: New Directions, 1970.

"Open Letter Responses." Claudia Rankine website, 2012. newmediapoets.com/claudia _rankine/home.html.

Rankine, Claudia. Open letter to "Friends," February 2011. Reprinted at therumpus.net/2011 /02/an-open-letter-from-claudia-rankine.

Sadoff, Ira. Untitled. In "Open Letter Responses."

Sasanov, Catherine. *Had Slaves*. Danbury, Conn.: Firewheel, 2010.

Smith, Bruce. "Devotion: Race Traitor." In *Devotions*, 75–76. Chicago: University of Chicago Press, 2011.

Taylor, Tess. *The Forage House*. Pasadena, Calif.: Red Hen, 2013.

Thompson, Lynne. Review of *Blue Front*, by Martha Collins. *Poetry International*, no. 12 (2008): 12–13.

York, Jake Adam. *A Murmuration of Starlings*. Carbondale: Southern Illinois University Press, 2008.

———. *Persons Unknown*. Carbondale: Southern Illinois University Press, 2010.

Zucker, Rachel. "Exempt, implicated." In "Open Letter Responses."

19 ∼ writing like a white guy

JASWINDER BOLINA

My father says I should use a pseudonym. "They won't publish you if they see your name. They'll know you're not one of them. They'll know you're one of us." This has never occurred to me, at least not in a serious way. "No publisher in America's going to reject my poems because I have a foreign name. Not in 2002," I reply. "These are educated people. My name won't be any impediment." Yet in spite of my faith in the egalitarian attitude of editors and the anonymity of book contests, I understand my father's angle on the issue.

With his beard shaved and his hair shorn, his turban undone and left behind in Bolina Doaba, Punjab—the town whose name we take as our own—he lands at Heathrow in 1965, a brown boy of eighteen become a Londoner. His circumstance then must seem at once exhilarating and also like drifting in a lifeboat: necessary, interminable. I imagine the English of the era sporting an especially muted and disdainful brand of racism toward my alien father, his brother and sister-in-law, toward his brother-in-law and sister, his nieces and nephews, and the other Indians they befriend on Nadine Street, Charlton, just east of Greenwich. The sense of exclusion arrives over every channel, dull and constant.

At least one realtor, a couple of bankers, and a few foremen must have a different attitude. One white supervisor at the industrial bakery my father labors in invites him home for dinner. The Brit wants to offer an introduction to his single daughters. He knows my father's a hard worker, a trait so commonly attributed to the immigrant it seems sometimes a nationality unto itself, and maybe the reticence of the nonnative speaker appeals to the man's sense of civility. As a result he finds my father humble, upstanding, his complexion a light beach sand indicative of a vigor exceeding that of the pale English suitors who come calling. In my imagination, my father's embarrassed and placid demeanor, his awkward formality in that setting, is charming to the bashful, giggly daughters, and this impresses the supervisor even further. But nothing much comes of that evening. My father never visits again. He marries my mother, Sikh Punjabi also, a few years later, but the event is evidence that one Englishman considered my father the man, not my father the "Paki."

When he moves to hodgepodge Chicago nine years after arriving in England, he becomes another denizen of the immigrant nation, the huddled masses. He might be forgiven for thinking he will not be excluded here, but he isn't so naïve. America in 1974 is its own version of the UK's insular empire, though the nature of its exclusion is different, is what we call institutional. He knows that in America nobody should be rejected, not unabashedly and without some counterfeit of a reason, but all my father's nearly three decades as a machinist at the hydraulics plant near the airport teach him is that economies boom and economies bust, and if your name isn't Bill or Earl or Frank Malone, you don't get promoted. You mind the machines. Bills and Earls supervise. Frank is the name the bosses go by, all of them hired after my dad but raised higher. So when my father suggests I use a pseudonym, he's only steadying my two-wheeler, only buying me a Popsicle from the cart at Foster Avenue Beach. This is only an extension of covering my tuition, of paying my room and board.

At the time, I'm only a year or so into an MFA. I stop by the office of a friend, an older white poet in my department. Publication to me feels impossible then, and the friend means to be encouraging when he says, "With a name like Jaswinder Bolina, you could publish plenty of poems right now if you wrote about the first-generation, minority stuff. What I admire is that you don't write that kind of poetry." He's right. I don't write "that kind" of poetry. To him, this is upstanding, correct, what a poet ought to do. It's indicative of a vigor exceeding that of other minority poets come calling. It turns out I'm a hard worker, too. I should be offended—if not for myself, then on behalf of writers who do take on the difficult subject of minority experience in their poetry—but I understand that my friend means no ill by it. To his mind, embracing my difference would open editorial inboxes, but knowing that I tend to eschew/exclude/deny "that kind" of subject in my poetry, he adds, "This'll make it harder for you." When, only a few months later, my father—who's never read my poems, whose fine but mostly functional knowledge of English makes the diction and syntax of my work difficult to follow, who doesn't know anything of the themes or subjects of my poetry—tells me to use another

name, he's encouraging also. He means: Let them think you're a white guy.
This will make it easier for you.

~

The one thing I least believe about race in America is that we can disregard it.
I'm nowhere close to alone in this, but the person I encounter far more often
than the racist—closeted or proud—is the one who believes race isn't an ac-
tive factor in her thinking, isn't an influence on his interaction with the racial
Other. Such blindness to race seems unlikely, but I suspect few of us entirely
understand why it's so improbable. I'm not certain either, but I've been given
some idea. At a panel discussion in 2004, a professor of political philosophy,
Caribbean-born with a doctorate from the University of Toronto, explains that
he never understood why the question in America is so often a question of
race. A scholar of Marxist thinking, he says in nearly every other industrialized
nation on earth, the first question is a question of class, and accordingly class
is the first conflict. He says it wasn't until he moved to the United States in the
early '70s—about the same time my father arrived—that he intellectually and
viscerally understood that America is a place where class historically coincides
with race. This, he says, is the heaviest legacy of slavery and segregation.

To many immigrants, the professor and my father included, this confla-
tion of success and skin color is a foreign one. In their native lands, where
there exists a relative homogeneity in the racial makeup of the population or
a pervasive mingling of races, the "minorities" of America are classed on the
basis of socioeconomic status derived from any number of factors, and race is
rarely, if ever, principal in these. You can look down on anybody even though
they share your skin color if you have land enough, wealth enough, caste and
education enough. It's only arriving in England that the Indian—who might
not even recognize the descriptor "Indian," preferring instead a regional or
religious identity to a national one—realizes anyone resembling him is subject
to the derision "coolie." It's only in America that such an immigrant discovers
any brown-skinned body can have "Camel fucker" or "Sand nigger" hurled
at him from a passing car—a bit of cognitive dissonance that's been directed
at me on more than one occasion. The racially African but ethnically Other
philosophy professor understands the oddness of this as well as anyone. He
explains that in the United States, as anywhere, the first question remains a
question of class, but the coincidence between class and color makes the first
American social conflict a conflict of race. Therefore, for the racial immigrant

and his offspring, racial difference need be mitigated whenever possible, if only to lubricate the cogs of class mobility: nearer to whiteness, nearer to wealth.

If the racial Other aspires to equal footing on the socioeconomic playing field, he is tasked with forcing his way out of the categorical cul-de-sac that his name and appearance otherwise squeeze him into. We call the process by which he does this "assimilation." Though the Latin root here—shared with the word "similar"—implies that the process is one of becoming absorbed or incorporated, it is a process that relies first on the negation of one identity in order to adopt another. In this sense, assimilation is a destructive rather than constructive process. It isn't a come-as-you-are proposition, a simple matter of being integrated into the American milieu because there exists a standing invitation to do so. Rather, assimilation first requires refuting assumptions the culture makes about the immigrant based on race, and in this sense assimilation requires the erasure of one's preexisting cultural identity even though that identity wasn't contingent upon race in the first place.

The first and perhaps essential step in assimilating into any culture is the successful adoption of the host country's language. What's unusual in America is that this is no different for the immigrant than for the native-born nonwhite. This is most obvious when I consider African Americans, whose language is variously described as "urban" (as in "of the slums of the inner city"), "street" (as in "of the gutter"), and "Ebonic" (as in "of ebony, of blackness"). These descriptors imply that, whatever it is, black vernacular isn't English. Rather, it's "broken English," which is of course what we also call the English of the nonnative speaker. I'm tempted to categorize "countrified" or "redneck" dialects similarly, except I remember that any number of recent U.S. presidents and presidential candidates capable in such a vernacular are regarded as more down-to-earth and likable rather than as less well-spoken or intelligent. It seems that white dialect serves as evidence of charisma, charm, and folksiness, not of ignorance.

In 2007 the eventual vice president campaigning in the primary election against the eventual president says, "I mean, you got the first mainstream African American who is articulate and bright and clean and a nice-looking guy. I mean, that's a storybook, man." The ensuing kerfuffle is almost entirely unsurprising. Though the white candidate believes he's merely describing the candidate of color and doing so with ample objectivity and perhaps even with generosity, the description implies that the black man's appearance and eloquence constitute an exception to his blackness, which is a function of genetics, which only further suggests that the black candidate is an exception to his basic nature. The implication is that he is being praised for his approximate whiteness. Not shockingly, this very conflation of his eloquence with white racial identity leads pundits in another context to ask the obnoxious question "But is he black enough?" The conundrum the candidate faces is that he need be an exceptional speaker and writer, but part of the "exceptional" here is the idea that he's an "exception" to his race. He has co-opted the language of whiteness. If he then neglects to take on the subject of race with that language, with the fierce urgency of now, he might further be accused of rejecting his own racial identity. Is he a candidate or a black candidate? If it's the former, he might not be "black enough." If it's the latter, he can't win.

In a country where class and race structurally overlap, what we call "standard" English reflexively becomes the English of whiteness rather than simply the English of the educated or privileged classes. When I adopt the language I'm taught in prep school, in university, and in graduate school, I'm adopting the English language, but in the States, that language is intrinsically associated with one race over any another. By contrast, in the England of history, the one prior to the more recent influx of immigrants from its imperial colonies, Oxford English is spoken by subjects as white as those who jabber in Cockney. Adeptness in language usage isn't a function, then, of melanin but of socioeconomic location. Color isn't the question; class is. Unlike the Cockney of England or the dialects of India, none of which is contingent upon racial difference, alternative dialects in American English are inherently racialized. Assimilation in America thus comes to mean the appropriation of a specific racial identity by way of language. The conundrum for the poet of color becomes no different from the one that faces the candidate of color: Am I a writer or a minority writer?

～

The day I'm born, my father engages in the American custom of handing out cigars to the Bills and Earls and Franks of the factory floor, even though he has never smoked in his life. Smoking is anathema to his Sikh Punjabi identity. Drinking, on the other hand, is most certainly not, and he gets gleefully and mercilessly drunk with his brothers at home. He boasts everywhere, "My son will be president." He believes it. Twenty-four years later, in 2002, when he counsels me to use a pseudonym, he knows I'm already adept in the language. I've been educated in it, and in spite of all his diligence and intelligence, this is a key he's never been given. I talk like them. I write like them. I'm an agile agent in the empire so long as nobody grows wise. He no longer expects a presidency, but he sees no limit to potential success in my chosen field, except for the limits placed on me by my racial difference from the dominant culture. He doesn't consider the possibility that I might write about race in my work, that I might want to embrace the subject, because he knows, like the candidate of black Kenyan and white Kansan bloodlines, I've been conditioned to resist making race the essential issue.

And it's true. The manner in which I avoid the subject of race in my first book is nearly dogmatic. Race is a subject I don't offer any attention to. To do so would seem only to underscore my Otherness, which would only result in the same sorts of requisite exclusions I experienced growing up in mostly white schools and neighborhoods. Assimilation in those circumstances isn't a choice so much political as necessary. Some remnant of a survival instinct kicks in, and one's best efforts are directed at joining rather than resisting the herd. To be racialized is to be marginalized. When another Asian kid joins the playground, we unwittingly vie to out-white each other. This tactic I learned from practice but also from my immigrant family. When your numbers are few, assimilation is the pragmatic gambit.

It's not something that we engage in without a queasy feeling. When my father suggests I Wite-Out my name, he's entirely aware that he's suggesting I relinquish the name he and my mother gave me. This isn't an easy thing, but growing up, I've never been kept from doing what the "American" kids do—though I'm born here and though my parents have long been citizens, "American" remains a descriptor my family uses to signify whiteness. Like the white kids, I join the Cub Scouts and play football at recess, I attend birthday parties at my American classmates' houses and go to junior high socials. In high school, after years of elementary school mockery, I attempt—not unlike the young Barry Obama—to anglicize my name, going by "Jason" instead, a stratagem that those who become my friends reject after only a few weeks. I go to the homecoming dance. I go to the prom. I stay out past curfew and grow my hair long. I insist that my mother close all the bedroom doors when she cooks so my clothes don't reek of cumin and turmeric. I resist any suggestion that I study the sciences in order to prepare for a career in medicine or engineering. I never meet an Indian girl; there aren't any in the philosophy and English departments I'm a member of anyway. My parents know I'm bereft of their culture. They must at times feel a lucid resentment, a sense of rejection and exclusion. Their son has become one of the English, as much a "Frank" or "Bill" to them as any American. But this, they know, is necessary. If the first generation is to succeed here, it's by resisting the ingrained cultural identity and mores of its immigrant forebears. If their son is to become president, my parents know it won't happen while he's wearing a turban. This is why they never keep me from engaging American culture, though it quickly comes to supplant their own. Assimilation is pragmatic, but pragmatism calls for concessions that compound and come to feel like a chronic ache.

～

It's because of the historical convergence of race and class in America that we conflate the language of the educated, ruling classes with the language of a particular racial identity. If I decouple the two, as I might be able to do in another nation, I realize that what's being described isn't the language of whiteness so much as the language of privilege. When I say "privilege" here, I mean the condition of not needing to consider what others are forced to consider. The privilege of whiteness in America—particularly male, heteronormative whiteness—is the privilege to speak from a blank slate, to not need to address questions of race, gender, sexuality, or class except by choice, to not need to acknowledge wherefrom one speaks. It's the position of no position, the voice from nowhere or from everywhere. In this it is godlike, and if nothing else, that's saying something.

To the poet, though, the first question isn't one of class or color. The first question is a question of language. Poetry—as Stéphane Mallarmé famously tells the painter and hapless would-be poet Edgar Degas—is made of words, not ideas. However, to the poet of color or the female poet, to the gay or transgendered writer in America, and even to the white male writer born outside of socioeconomic privilege, a difficult question arises: Whose language is it? Where the history of academic and cultural institutions is so dominated by white men of means, "high" language necessarily comes to mean the language of whiteness, and a largely wealthy, heteronormative maleness at that. The minority poet seeking entry into the academy and its canon finds that her language is deracialized/sexualized/gendered/classed at the outset. In trafficking in "high" English, writers other than educated, straight, white, male ones of privilege choose to become versed in a language that doesn't intrinsically or historically coincide with perceptions of their identities. It's true that minority poets are permitted to bring alternative vernaculars into our work. Poets from

William Wordsworth in the preface to *Lyrical Ballads* to Frank O'Hara in his "Personism: A Manifesto" demand as much by insisting that poetry incorporate language nearer to conversational speech than anything overly elevated. Such calls for expansions of literary language in conjunction with continuing experiments by recent generations of American poets are transforming the canon for sure, but this leaves me and perhaps others like me in a slightly awkward position. I don't possess a vernacular English that's significantly different from that of plain old midwestern English. It seems I'm able to write from a perspective that doesn't address certain realities about myself, and this makes me queasy as anything. The voice in my head is annoyed with the voice in my writing. The voice in my head says I'm disregarding difference, and this feels like a denial of self, of reality, of a basic truth.

It isn't exactly intentional. It's a product of being privileged. In the forty-six years since my father left Punjab, the forty or so years since my mother left also, my parents have clambered up the socioeconomic ladder with a fair amount of middle-class success. We're not exactly wealthy, but I do wind up in prep school instead of the public high school, which only isolates me further from those with a shared racial identity. Later I attend university, where I'm permitted by my parents' successes to study the subjects I want to study rather than those that might guarantee future wealth. I don't need to become a doctor or a lawyer to support the clan. I get to major in philosophy and later attend graduate school in creative writing. Through all of this, though I experience occasional instances of bigotry while walking down streets or in bars, and though I study in programs where I'm often one of only two or three students of color, my racial identity is generally overlooked or disregarded by those around me. I've become so adept in the language and culture of the academy that on more than one occasion when I bring up the fact of my race, colleagues reply with some variation of "I don't think of you as a minority." Or, as a cousin who's known me since infancy jokes, "You're not a minority. You're just a white guy with a tan." What she means is that my assimilation is complete. But she can't be correct. Race is simply too essential to the American experience to ever be entirely overlooked. I can't actually write like a white guy any more than I can revise my skin color. This, however, doesn't change the fact that if a reader were to encounter much of my work without knowing my name or having seen a photograph of me, she might not be faulted for incorrectly assigning the poems a white racial identity. This is a product of my language, which is a product of my education, which is a product of the socioeconomic privilege afforded by my parents' successes. The product of all those factors together is that the writing—this essay included—can't seem to help sounding *white*.

~

Recently I was invited to give a few poetry readings as part of a literary festival taking place in a rural part of the country. I borrow my father's compact SUV and let its GPS guide me for a few days on the road. I spend afternoons and evenings reading poems with local and visiting writers in front of small audiences at community centers and public libraries. The audiences are largely made up of kind, white-haired, white-skinned locals enthusiastic to hear us read from and speak about our work, even when they've never heard of most of us. They at least appreciate poetry, a rarity I'm grateful for. During the introductions that preface each event, even the organizers who've invited me have difficulty getting my name right, and in one school library, I enunciate it over and over again. I say, "*Jas* as in the first part of *justice*; *win* as in the opposite of defeat; *der*, which rhymes with *err*, meaning to be mistaken." I say, "JasWINder," lilting the second syllable, and smile as about a dozen audience members mouth each syllable along with me until they feel they have it right. When they do, they grin broadly. After each event I chat with them one or two at a time, and I do my best to reflect their warmth. They're complimentary about the work, and though I don't expect they're a demographic that'll especially like my poems—even when you write poems like a white guy, you might not be writing poems everyone will like—the compliments are earnest.

Still, in all this pleasantness, the awkward moment occurs more than once. It's some variation on a recurring question I get in town after town. The question usually comes up as a matter of small talk while I'm signing a book or shaking someone's hand. No one delivers it better, with so much beaming warmth and unwitting irony, than the woman who says she enjoyed my poems very much and follows this quickly with an admiring "You're so Americanized, what nationality are you?" She doesn't pick up on the oxymoron in her question. She doesn't hear the hint of tiredness in my reply. "I was born and raised in Chicago, but my parents are from northern India." Once more, I ought to be offended, but I'm not really. Hers is an expression of curiosity that's born of genuine interest rather than of sideshow spectacle. I'm the only nonwhite writer at the events I participate in. I'm the only one who gets this question. It makes me bristle, but I understand where it comes from.

After my brief tour is over, I make the five-hundred-mile trip to suburban Chicago to return the Toyota to my parents. I eat dinner at home, and after, my father drops me back in the city. Invariably the trip down the Kennedy Expressway toward the skyline makes him nostalgic for his early, underpaid days in small apartments on the North Side, his city long before it became my city. He tells a story or two, and we talk as usual about the news, politics, the latest way my uncle annoys him. He goes on a while before his attention returns to the moment, and he asks how my trip went. I tell him it went well. I say the audiences were kind and the drives were long. I say, out there, the country looks like a painting of itself. I don't mention what the woman asked, the recurring question echoed by others. "You're so Americanized, what nationality are you?" It won't matter that she asked it while eagerly shaking my hand. It won't matter that she asked while asking me also to sign a copy of my book for her. It won't matter that she offered her gratitude that I'd come all that way to read in her hamlet on the outskirts of America. Though she might have meant the opposite, he'll hear the question as the old door closing again. The doorway, then, is both welcome and departure, is border guard and border crossing, and though I'm not on the woman's side of it, I'm not entirely on my father's side either.

Perhaps for this reason, there's the continuing sense that I *ought* to write about race even as I resent that I need be troubled by the subject in the first place. After all, I should permit myself to be a poet first and a minority second, same as any male, white writer. But even as I attempt to ignore the issue altogether, I find myself thinking about it, and I realize now that this fact more than any other makes it so that I can't write like a white poet. Writing is as much the process of arriving at the point of composition as it is the act of composition itself. That my awareness of racial identity so often plays a part in my thinking about my writing makes it so that I can't engage in that writing without race being a live wire. Even one's evasions are born of one's fixations. More to the point, what appears to be an evasion might not be exactly that at all. John Ashbery doesn't make a subject matter of his sexuality, but this doesn't mean he's unable to inhabit the identity of a gay writer. Similarly, even though Mary Ruefle might not take on gender identity overtly in a given poem, it doesn't make that poem an adversary to the cause of feminism. I don't bring all this up to absolve myself exactly, though it's true I'm trying to figure out a way to alleviate a guilt I'm annoyed to feel in the first place. I imagine male, white poets will recognize this feeling. I bet any poet of conscience who doesn't actively write about sociopolitical subjects knows this feeling, but the poet is trying to write the original thing, and that originality might not take up orbit around a more obvious facet of a poet's identity. When any of us doesn't take on such a subject in our writing, it might not be because we neglected to do so. Rather, it might be that the subject informed every bit of our deciding to write about something else.

More important, when it comes to writing about difficult issues of identity, especially those with far-reaching political and cultural implications, maybe the choice needn't be a dichotomous one. Maybe I don't need to choose between being the brown guy writing like a white guy and the brown guy writing about being Othered. Instead, maybe I need only be a brown guy writing out his study of language and the self—the same as the Paterson doctor, the Hartford insurance executive, the lesbian expat in Paris, the gay Jew from New Jersey, the male white poet teaching at the University of Houston, or the straight black female professor reading her poem at the American president's inauguration. Though "high" English might be born of a culture once dominated by straight white men of privilege, each of us wields our English in ways those men might not have imagined. This is okay. Language, like a hammer, belongs to whoever picks it up to build or demolish. Whether we take language in hand to deconstruct itself, to confess a real experience or an imagined one, or to meditate upon the relationship between the individual and the political, social, historical, or cosmological, ownership of our language need not be bound up with the history of that language. Whether I choose to pound on the crooked nail of race or gender, self or Other, whether I decide on some obscure subject while forgoing the other obvious one, when I write, the hammer belongs to me.

20 ~ whiteness visible

TESS TAYLOR

I.

Over twenty years ago, in her groundbreaking *Playing in the Dark: Whiteness and the Literary Imagination* (1992), Toni Morrison looked forward to a time when it would be possible to study literature for insight into the processes of racialization. Her essays examined the role of American literature in mediating racial knowledge, analyzing key nineteenth-century texts for clues to the ways whiteness and blackness construct one another in the American literary imagination.

Here's one noteworthy totem Morrison uncovered: at the end of Edgar Allan Poe's *The Narrative of Arthur Gordon Pym*, immediately after a black man on Pym's boat dies, "a white giant rises up" (Morrison 32). Pym and Peters approach an opaque white fog and are showered by a white ashy substance. Morrison describes this terrifying white opacity as an uncannily frequent American literary presence, noting that "figurations of impenetrable whiteness" appear again and again "after the narrative has encountered blackness" (32). According to Morrison, literary figures of white opacity respond to sites of anxiety and violence: they appear "in conjunction with representations of black or Africanist people who are dead, impotent" or who have been subjected to violence at the hands of white forces (33). Indeed, by looking at how these figures of whiteness and blackness interrelate, Morrison proposes that suffocating white opacity emerges *in order* to veil racial trauma, thereby becoming a mechanism for whites to deny their own racial experience and to distance themselves from the painful knowledge of their complicity in the history of racism.

But Morrison is not only practicing literary criticism, she is also calling for new literatures. As Morrison reads Poe, she invites literary practitioners to begin to read the (possibly terrifying) fogs in which they find themselves. Reminding fellow writers that she is not only a critic, Morrison notes: "Writing and reading are not all that distinct for a writer" (xi). She implicitly invites white storytellers to more carefully read their own approaches to their own lives, histories, and racial contexts. White fog provides an apt figure to describe sites of trauma and violence, but it also corresponds to more ordinary forms of whiteness. It is worth noticing that the figure of blinding whiteness that follows traumatic violence shares a form with the more banal "experience of nonexperience" that polices the margins of literary inquiry, both critical and aesthetic, in which knowledge of such violence is shrouded, emptied, or denied.

Morrison points writers toward new questions, inviting literary practitioners to read the racial fogs in which they find themselves today. How might writers who have been discouraged or even disinvited from thinking about their racial experiences *as racial* begin to read and write those experiences? Which instincts toward silence or omission would such a writer have to overcome? What is at stake in naming spaces where race, racialization, and racism occur in white lives? If whiteness is partially maintained by strategies of not-saying, not-knowing, self-normalizing, what does it mean to craft art in which whiteness can be destabilized? In short, how does a subject take responsibility for moving from whiteness to witness?

Three contemporary poets—Jake Adam York, Rachel Richardson, and Martha Collins—have been remarkably successful at giving aesthetic form to these questions as they struggle to name and claim some of the paradoxes of inheriting white experience. How does each work against the "fog" that Morrison describes? How does each deploy, reveal, and break racial codes? How does each position the expression of racial knowledge, especially racial knowledge white writers have often failed to acknowledge or reveal? It's worth noting that merely examining and naming the white body *as white* is historically itself a charged act. Melville's Ishmael—the ultimate anonymous narrator—has historically been presumed white simply because he occupies the space of voyeur-reporter describing (other) racially marked bodies. In contrast, Collins, York, and Richardson self-examine and self-mark. They call attention to their own bodies, stories, and speech, attempting to read the uneasy codes that converge upon them. In doing so, each tries to make the occluding cloud somewhat less blinding—and to show a way through it.

2.

In *A Murmuration of Starlings* and *Persons Unknown*, two-thirds of a triptych written before his untimely death in 2012, Jake Adam York looks outward, backward, down. He travels the South, reading not texts but landscapes—cities, rivers, roads—for what they can and cannot reveal about racial violence. Revisiting martyrs of the civil rights era in Mississippi and Alabama nearly fifty years after church bombings in Mississippi killed four girls, York recalls a staggering number of crimes "No one sees" ("Murmuration" 56, 58). He wants to unsettle silences, to write hidden victims "back into history" ("Homochitto" 4). His person-by-person excavation of both victims and victimizers dramatizes a regional (and national) tendency toward amnesia—forgetfulness layered over failure to condemn.

If Poe's Pym disappeared into a white fog, York's poetry works to recover some of the trauma that the myth of "nonexperience" can veil. He examines strategies by which racial violence is minimized—both by a history that has disregarded victims and protected perpetrators and by a culture that would rather forget than recall. Following Morrison's injunction to overcome "every well-bred instinct . . . *against noticing*" (10), York visits sites with no overt monument, naming aloud what we "cannot hear." His poems speak requiem, and act as audible trace. "A city is a kind of memory," he writes of Jackson, Mississippi, but Jackson's plaques denote where Welty lived and not where Medgar Evers did. York speaks into and against this uneven silence: "City of Ghosts, / you can't abandon your history, / and it won't abandon you. / You watch each other, / you call each other's names" ("City of Grace" 59–60).

But in order to call names, York himself must name the absence. At the place where Mack Charles Parker's body was recovered from the Pearl River in 1959, York writes, "the rivers heal their quiet / . . . they fill their scars so perfectly / that remember feels like forget" ("Sensitivity" 10). York routinely finds that sites of civil rights era lynchings are unmarked, unmarkable. He resorts to writing in negations: "There are no answers. / There is no one to ask" ("Shore" 85). York's poems thus make maps of violent inequities in record, in history. At the now vacant lot where Joseph Thomas was murdered by a sniper in 1967, York expands his work

> for everyone who had a killing
> but not a killer,

> for everyone who simply disappeared,
> who walked out
>
> as if into air, taken
> into a fog's unknown hands,
>
> leaving nothing but a name,
> a date, and that fear,
>
> constant as water,
> that anyone could be next. ("Shore" 86)

Dying at the hands of fog: the surreal, otherworldly figure Morrison identified in Poe re-forms in York as the mist out of which anonymous racial violence is delivered. Yet "fog" here refers not only to anonymous acts of terror committed by unnamed, unprosecuted white people against black ones, but also to enabling forces that allow such violence to remain unseen, unsolved. The fog is not merely the violence, in other words, but also the failure to condemn it. Precisely because this violence has been committed by "no one," it dissipates, becomes normalized, functions as if enacted by all. This poem depicts spaces where threat lurks. York expands Morrison's trope, showing what the "nothingness" of a white fog can do, what the silence surrounding it is for.

But York does not stop at merely examining the unevenness in public space and record. He also tracks the ways a racist society reads him as he moves through public space. As he travels looking for Medgar Evers, Emmett Till, and Reverend James Reeb, York reflects on how his outward appearance renders him safe, neutral, invisible. Large, white, and bald, the body he travels in disguises him from those who might take offense at his motives. His body protects him.

Yet this disguise comes at a cost. York's bodily form feels like a mask, turning him into a "person unknown" to himself. Walking, he will "catch that curve / in a window or a windshield / that wrecks my face / so for a moment / I can mistake myself / for the redneck at the end of a joke" ("Darkly" 13). The active voice in "I can" is no accident: York acknowledges how he can, when he needs to, disappear from scrutiny or threat behind the opacity of his bodily form, and the ways he (even unknowingly) participates in what he calls "a conspiracy of color" ("Second Person" 75).

What is troubling is how often the active form of "I can" slips into a more passive "you"—and how often York is asked to join this conspiracy. More than once York's presence elicits racist remarks from people who believe he'll agree with them. In "The Second Person," York visits a southern history museum and speaks with a woman who says of a neighboring town: "I just love it / you know—there are no darkies there" (75). The second-person "you" objectifies York's whiteness. York describes the conversation as "an echo the heat or the history / in our voices draws us into— / someone else's version of ourselves" (75). In the space of the poem, York is able to reflect how his seemingly neutral white male body crafts him as a character separate from his wishes, intentions, and self. Skin, voice, and place inscribe him into a historical hegemony that private reflections cannot will away. At such moments, the "I" York prefers to know colludes with forces larger than the self. York strains, imperfectly, within his disguise.

Rachel Richardson's *Copperhead* also explores the stickiness of racialized experience, mining the dimensions of coming to racial knowledge within the thorny context of family inheritance. The word "copperhead" indicates both Civil War slang for a northern sympathizer with the secessionist South and a deadly snake. Richardson, a white descendant of Louisiana planters, sees these roots as flickering and forked. Yet—as if she were a northern sympathizer—Richardson explores how her engagement with her family history separates her from a culture that would rather take its norms (and silences) for granted. Returning from elsewhere, Richardson drives on the wide Natchez Trace path: "the world keeps its silence" and "No one blames me for a thing" ("Natchez Trace" 15).

In order to read her past—to decode it—Richardson tells private family stories. She depicts this act as fragile, as opening both her history and herself to blame. By contrast, the horses, she feels, "have no debt to anyone" ("Horses" 80). This fragility is not merely self-protection. It also helps Richardson show how "secession" from something as enormous as "racism" is not simple or unilateral. Racism is a slippery institution. Our worlds, identities, and inheritances are sticky. Richardson often struggles to reread already learned codes— an act that attempts to exorcise even as it shows connection. Richardson's work is poignant because she has already learned to love a world she partially condemns, and because she knows she does not have a neutral place from which to tell her stories. About that world she writes, "The swamps and the silver coffee tray I loved with equal passion" ("Scale" 22) and "For years no one lured me away" ("Note" 36).

How does a speaker disentangle herself from racist legacies? If York's body was made strange in a plate-glass window, Richardson depicts intimate experiences she must herself try to reinterpret. She is also flawed, and despite her best efforts, some of her own most deeply held stories remain illegible, even to her. Richardson retraces an early childhood moment when her grandmother's black maid tried to show her how to eat a fig, an instant her grandmother forcefully interrupted. Some code or knowledge was transmitted. Richardson depicts it this way: "I never remember / what was said, only the look of her in the doorway, // the eyes . . . / . . . I won't recall gestures, or // the way Lola looked," she writes ("Refrain" 16). The choice of the word "won't" instead of "can't" speaks volumes. Some force beyond Richardson's own willing has policed—even veiled—her memory, denying her access to this moment's central divisive trauma. But the poem's title, "The Refrain," suggests that precisely because it is veiled, the moment snags and eddies. Because Richardson cannot remember the code's content but only its forceful implication, the event spins in her mind, retaining its uneasy power.

Richardson the storyteller re-crafts these memories in order to find the tangled center of this potent memory. But at the same time, Richardson knows she cannot imagine perfectly. At times her project is as dreamlike as the assembled snake that she "conjured" as a child. In the poem "Snakebit," Richardson the writer admits she's "inventing the snake / inventing the venom" (18). Again and again Richardson hints at violence she cannot see. "My grandmother is not hurting anyone," writes Richardson ("Field Notes" 39), and yet her poems are written in the full awareness of historical damage. For Richardson, the venom of inherited racism is at once both real and imaginary, present and strangely absent from sites where she would try to find it. In the poem "Relic," Richardson discovers a white Ku Klux Klan robe in an attic. Like the grandmother "not hurting anyone," this object is now surrounded by calm, even vulnerability: "frail white folds / softened, demure. No burn." In fact it "sat, silent, like any other contents / of any other box: photographs / of the dead, heirloom jewels" (26). The silence surrounding the artifact unsettles. What is Richardson's duty to this familial and also unsettling object? What history does it conceal? What would she be told now if she asked about it? Entangled in these questions is Richardson's dual sense of belonging and not belonging to places and ancestors she uncovers.

Morrison reminds us that a writer's combinations of "intentions, blindness, and sight [are] part of the imaginative activity" (xii). By making the margins of her knowledge visible, Richardson raises important questions. Does she turn away too quickly from difficult knowledge, veiling access to something like truth, or does her writing—full of absences—dramatize places where family loyalties, speech codes, and mental geographies betray her? Something like blame hangs in the balance: our desire to find the venom, to extract it.

Is Richardson to blame for what she has inherited? It is possible to blame Richardson for being from the family with the heirloom jewels, boxes, and white cape. It is of note that one might move toward blame just at the moment Richardson explores marks (class, wealth, history) that the umbrella category "whiteness" exists partially to obscure. Meanwhile, in her writing, present-day racism and racist legacies reappear in slippery shape-shifting ways. The Klu Klux Klan robe seems temporarily impotent and boxed, but Richardson, noting the way Britney Spears poses both as "a symbol of the New South" ("Portrait" 20) and as "a slave" (21), traces a morphing essence, a series of tropes that have disappeared in one place only to re-form elsewhere.

Richardson's poems do leave her open to blame. But in exploring the highly personal transmissions of inheritance, they are also humble. In one, a child-Richardson poses with her grandmother's longtime servant and not-ever-quite friend: "And in this picture— // my grandmother must have taken it— / you're smiling, probably because / we've been told to. And I'm smiling, too, / fierce with new teeth" ("Photograph" 79). Richardson sifts through rubble that is poisoned, conjured. The care with which she attempts rescue, but also depicts entanglement, is its own literary reward.

Like Richardson and York, Martha Collins explores the impossibility of separating herself from racist legacy. The untitled poems of her recent *White Papers* reveals her knowledge of the way race is bound up in daily transaction, unconscious judgment, and embedded assumption. White readers (or perhaps any readers) will find it hard to read *White Papers* without finding themselves implicated in the charged codes of daily racial knowledge. Here, for example, Collins describes the town where she grew up: "Because mostly they rarely spoke / of or noticed or even whispered / about and did not of course . . ." (1). Did not of course—what? Befriend? Know? Fall in love with? Collins's sentences are full of pronominal dividing lines, calling attention to the unseen gap separating "us" from "them."

Her sentences are also full of ellipses. Her language reenacts silences and divisions that force us to encounter and articulate painful divisions we already know. Collins crafts many poems in the first person plural, assuming a collective presence that another "we"—we who read—must grapple with. Both the "we" and the silence in the poems imply collective knowledge, knowledge so basic it need not be spoken. We (any one of us of any race) may say we do not know what a white code is, Collins argues, but we recognize it when we see it.

If York and Richardson explore their unease at being called to be conspirators, either of space, voice, or inheritance, Collins's sentences actually enact conspiracy, dramatizing the ways racial knowledge creeps up on speakers and subjects and appears where we least expect it—in the grammar of everyday life. Yet Collins also deftly uses this grammar against itself, calling on her readers to contend with the implications of the divisive, painful, uncomfortable knowledge her poems make plain. She often writes in folded sentences: "we saw them mostly saw / ourselves what did // we didn't know / where we were living" (3). In its use of duplicity and excision, Collins poses a telling question: "what did we didn't know." Quoting A. S. Byatt, Morrison describes situations where "a sense that the text has appeared to be wholly new, never before seen, is followed, almost immediately, by the sense that it was *always there*, that we, the readers, knew it was always there, and have *always known* it was as it was, though we have now for the first time recognised, become fully cognisant of, our knowledge" (xi–xii, quoting Byatt 516). Collins prompts such cognition, playing with assumptions that readers may not openly acknowledge but, in her poems, are called upon to recognize as their own. Collins's poems force us each, whoever we are, to examine complicities and to name dividing lines that border our lives.

Indeed, Collins uses fragmented, charged language to represent the flawed process of coming to racial knowledge at all. She recalls her childhood: "white, as Jesus was white" (14) and "My heart was black with sin" (29). Collins bristles at these memories, and, in particular, at the moment when she wrote in school about *Brown v. Board of Education* "Yes but not yet" (1).

But yet. Collins cannot stop there. Her poems read the racial codes not just of her past but also of her present. We see her attempting to name and decode racism in her own life, thoughts, and language, a process of active watching and sometimes falling short. One poem lists the privileges her (white-skinned) life has afforded:

> could get a credit card loan car
> come and got without a never had
> to think about a school work job
> to open doors to buy a rent a nice
> place (41)

This poem may embody the most banal white code of all. Rather than write in the "we" of group privilege, Collins has crafted a poem where the first person is absent, or rather assumes itself. This privileged but absent entity takes so much for granted, it need not articulate its own presence. Collins depicts the base state of "just normal, just white"—of being allowed to pass, unremarked.

How should poets talk about race? Is it enough to trace violence, to explore embeddedness and inheritance, to reveal coded sites of racial knowledge? None of these things necessarily makes a poem successful. York, Richardson, and Collins each struggle to see through the fog of racial amnesia. By giving spoken forms to often unspoken racial knowledge, these poets expose themselves, owning up to their complicity without fully escaping it. They also provide models for other writers, white or not, to think about their own racial entanglements; they begin to map uneasy racial codes without promising redemption or absolution. That is the project Collins calls "this un- / learning untying" (64). As they chart new aesthetic paths, they offer new paths of utterance and understanding. Twenty-some years ago, Morrison called on her readers to examine the literature of whiteness, the ways whiteness figures to create blackness, and also to begin documenting the white experience itself. She writes that, yes, studies of African American experiences and colonialisms have proliferated, but this "well-established study should be joined with another, equally important one: the impact of racism on those who perpetuate it" (11). What is that impact? We are still learning to name it.

BIBLIOGRAPHY

Byatt, A. S. *Possession: A Romance*. New York: Random House, 1990.

Collins, Martha. *White Papers*. Pittsburgh: University of Pittsburgh Press, 2012.

Morrison, Toni. *Playing in the Dark: Whiteness and the Literary Imagination*. Cambridge, Mass.: Harvard University Press, 1992.

Richardson, Rachel. *Copperhead*. Pittsburgh: Carnegie Mellon University Press, 2011.

———. "Field Notes." In *Copperhead*, 39–41.

———. "The Horses." In *Copperhead*, 80.

———. "Natchez Trace, Southbound." In *Copperhead*, 15.

———. "Note, upon Learning That Jimmie Davis Did Not Compose 'You Are My Sunshine.'" In *Copperhead*, 35–36.

———. "Photograph, 1983." In *Copperhead*, 79.

———. "Portrait of Britney Spears, Kentwood, 1996." In *Copperhead*, 20–21.

———. "The Refrain." In *Copperhead*, 16.

———. "Relic." In *Copperhead*, 26.

———. "The Scale." In *Copperhead*, 22–23.

———. "Snakebit." In *Copperhead*, 18–19.

York, Jake Adam. "City of Grace." In *Persons Unknown*, 57–60.

————. "Darkly." In *Persons Unknown*, 11–16.

————. "Homochitto." In *Persons Unknown*, 3–6.

————. "A Murmuration of Starlings." In *A Murmuration of Starlings*, 52–61. Carbondale: Southern Illinois University Press, 2008.

————. *Persons Unknown*. Carbondale: Southern Illinois University Press, 2010.

————. "The Second Person." In *Persons Unknown*, 73–77.

————. "Sensitivity." In *Persons Unknown*, 9–10.

————. "Shore." In *Persons Unknown*, 82–87.

21 ～ the gentle art of making enemies

AILISH HOPPER

I. The Past That Won't Stay Past

To talk about race in America is, unfortunately, to often feel caught in a game of racial "gotcha," as we step around closed spaces in the present, kept that way by racial codes. And so it's not surprising that many will do anything to avoid speaking, or writing, freely about race—or, when and if they do, to feel resigned and exhausted by it. Many of us are concerned about being pigeon-holed as one or another racial "type," or feeling like, as John L. Jackson calls it, a "racial sinner" (93). As poets, how is it that we will use the same language that has run the errands of race to depict (and pick) the lock of being free? And how not to bring the diamond-headed needle of our attention into the dusty groove of, as Toni Morrison in *Jazz* characterized our past, an "abused record with no chance but to repeat itself?" (120).

Because race in America is just like bad fiction, with one-dimensional characters, predictable plotlines, passive verbs, subjectless sentences. Even our remedy-stories constrain, or can, if they too become more narratives to be race-patrolled; stories of heroism or helplessness, identities that become narrow containers. Yet it is possible to rewrite, meaning not merely "revise," but write poems that neither ignore racial codes nor give over their power to them. Poems that, like all good art, expand our vision of ourselves—all that we are, all that we are not—to introduce the "another world," as Paul Eluard suppos-edly put it, that's "in this one."

In practice this concept can feel a little like an enigma. What, really, do emancipated bodies and language look like? Partly, they look like us. They take what is real—our real experiences, our real bodies, and the real encountered world—and use that to show what is here but hidden, by codes, from our view.

In Elizabeth Alexander's poem "Race," an "ivory spouse" looks at "pencil markings in a ledger book" as she "is learning / her husband's caesuras." Like the couple, many in America look at our relations around race and can "see silent spaces / but not what they signify" (22). For many—often, especially, white readers, and editors, publishers—the gate to these closed spaces is elegy; it's the gesture of reaching out or into these caesuras, not only in the past but in the present. In his "Elegy," Jake Adam York points to the mechanics of this resonant elision:

> the Greeks
> always cut something from their lines,
>   a syllable or two, to create a silence
> or a place to hear it
>
> . . . .
>
>   as if to say
> even memory can forget itself
>   and be written into another history
> while everyone is looking at something else. (96)

This is the kind of past that does not stay past. Like Morrison's title character in *Beloved*, these kinds of events and memories "ha[ve] claim but [are] not claimed," and thus infiltrate—permeate, at times—a present that is, for some of us, ineffably tinged with "bottomless longing" (58). The body of American society is revealed to be missing some of its limbs, is like the man who is missing his legs, as Natasha Trethewey notes, "bother[ing] / the space for knees, shins, scratching air / as—years later—I'd itch for what's not there" (30). And while each of us is affected in profoundly different ways, these painful events of history are nevertheless a shared seam.

However closed they may be, these spaces nevertheless transmit scripts and performances—encrypted, made invisible by euphemism—into each now. Many of us feel them as we pass through, many others of us see their contents in plain sight. Kevin Young's "For the Confederate Dead" describes this sense of these spaces, "below sea- / and eye-level" where "a mural runs / the wall, flaking, a plantation / scene most do not see—" so that we, instead, are left "digging beside the monument / (that giant anchor) / . . . / fighting the sleep-walking air" (97).

Challenge the codes, however, and you will be punished by their enforcers—who may be black or white. This protective border serves what James C.

Scott calls the "public transcript," which justifies and prosecutes "rules" that are by nature hidden. They can only be expressed in codes, euphemisms, and other forms of disguise, which appear as simply agreed-upon, unanimous. Meanwhile there exists a "hidden transcript," the things that are said away from the gaze of the racial codes and their enforcers (45). As in the rest of the world's activities, poetry, publishing, and criticism numbingly and brutally reflect this dynamic, what Marcel Cornis-Pope calls "narratives of containment" (xii).

A fine example of this enforcement appeared in the review of Rita Dove's poetry anthology by Helen Vendler, who uses "multiculturalism" as a euphemism for aesthetic inferiority in order to patrol a status quo. Done under the guise of a dichotomy that's "merely" aesthetic, the critique—while it may have had other, insightful things to say, and not that I am at pains to support Dove's (or Penguin's) particular project—nevertheless reveals the public script of whiteness. "Twentieth-century American poetry," Vendler writes, "has been one of the glories of modern literature . . . names and texts . . . known worldwide," but she complains of Dove's "introducing more black poets and giving them significant amounts of space, . . . in some cases for their representative themes rather than their style. Dove is at pains to include angry outbursts as well as artistically ambitious meditations." Here the public transcript, whiteness, punishes Dove for breaking its "rules," such as challenging white definitions of and allowances for "diversity" (Vendler begrudges not the fact of these poets being included but the "significant amounts of space" they are given); attempting to ruin white achievements (its "glories") for their own emotional needs (her Manichean gesture comparing "artistically ambitious" work with "angry outbursts"). White poetry: known worldwide as valuable, stylish, artistically ambitious; black poetry: of unproven value, concerned with content over craft, filled with angry outbursts.

There is also a third kind of transcript, Scott says, in which the narrative of containment is ruptured, a space is opened between onstage and backstage. This is the space of rewriting. Poems that do this can use any number of techniques; what qualifies them as rewriting race is that, rather than seeking to "pretend . . . racelessness," as Major Jackson put it (142), they seek to be race-real. With rewriting, though we are still by the terms of society raced, we are awake inside of race, and awake inside of our art. From here, real choice begins.

II. Scenes of Instruction

Of course, not everyone has a choice about whether or not to be awake to race. When we say "white privilege," we mean those allowed by social structures and codes to be "asleep," not subject to what Paul Mooney calls "nigger wakeup calls," or, as Henry Louis Gates calls them, "scenes of instruction," which viciously initiate one to the physical and existential costs of being in one's particular skin (Touré 125). Any "we" is thus subject to scrutiny, as a likely euphemization of race, as Tracy K. Smith shows:

> There is a *We* in this poem
> To which everyone belongs.
>
> As in: *We the people—*
> *In order to form a more perfect Union—*
>
> And: *We were objects of much curiosity*
> *To the Indians*
>
> *We* has swallowed *Us* and *Them*. (20)

Julie Agoos in her book *Property* borrows the form of a court transcript to show this *We*'s most common disguise: a narrative in which someone is "merely" in power and someone else, who "just happens" to be there, argues or pleads:

> Q: Unless you want to claim the black man's skin
>   In evidence—made him one to fear—
>
> AttD: Objection!
>
> Q:—caused harm
>   To the boy—
>
> . . . . . .
>
> AttD: Your honor—
>
> Q: against the law. (76)

The American racial imagination is quite taken with this, the de jure aspect of race, where there are clear victories and losses, so Agoos's poem partly feels like a familiar scene, whether from the imaginary frames of *To Kill a Mockingbird* or newsreels of twentieth-century headlines. In addition to de jure racism and de facto racism (overt, unacceptable to mainstream, national social norms), there is the harder-to-see *de cardio* racism, the ways that all of us, in whatever different ways, reflect and internalize race narratives (J. Jackson 160). In this way, race narratives, in our perception, transform how we look into who we feel we are. Evie Shockley's "You Can't Deny It" displays the way that this gives all identity a quality of performance:

cast of characters

speaker	an african american woman		
you	an african american woman	→	*roster of emotions*
			pride
			puzzlement
			connection
setting:	dinner, early 21st century		defensiveness
			pleasure
			understanding

(54)

Here two African American women encounter not only each other but each other's racialized experiences. A "selected bibliography" describes three works of American literature that serve as shared touchstones as they move from "puzzlement" or "defensiveness" to "pleasure" and "understanding." The authors of the books listed are also African American; thus, to discuss the works is possibly, no matter one's race, to wonder from which perspective of race/class—possibly even before literary or personal taste—each other will come. The poem describes two women not only negotiating relationship but doing so in the dimly lit minefield of identity performance. It reflects the constraints of, on one hand, reaching for the gifts of the world (educational access, wine, literature) but, possibly on the other, still needing to be "black enough" lest one be cast out, left in the land of being not-black, not-white. Importantly, this racial negotiation, however black-specific Shockley's poem may be, also mirrors numerous other racialized experiences, including those with racial privilege. People who challenge racial norms, if they go far enough, will all be threatened with some form of social death.

This protective and threatening script is embodied in Douglas Kearney's poem "Swimchant for Nigger Mer-Folk (An Aquaboogie Set in Lapis)," which channels the voice of each player on the stage of the public transcript, for instance an enforcer who announces:

ATTENTION: NIGGER MERMAIDS & MERNINNIES
CHAINED LIKE HOOKED AND SINKED SARDINNIES:
DO NOT BLEED IN THE SEA. THE STAINS WON'T WASH
OUT. WE AIN'TNT RESPONSIBLE FOR YOUR MESS.
MUCH OBILGED, THEE MANAGEMENT

Kearney's poem shows us the color line, the scripts of power that enforce it, or order to "mess with" it, to—as all acts of naming do—amplify the danger, so that it loses power. The references and signifyin' that Kearney performs on the public transcript are too numerous to fully address here. The message, anyway, is clear: black folk are "chained" and "hooked" and ultimately "sunked"—and this is an act for which the white perpetrators, or anyone in "management," says they "ain'tnt responsible" (62).

III. A Tyranny of Elegy

Yet our remedy narratives, too, are familiar and are their own constraint, whether the quasi-transcendence of "we are one" or the disempowerment of the "suffering black body" on "the stage of sufferance" (D. Brooks 28). Elegy can be its own tyranny; hero(ism) can permanently detain(ee) us. It's hard but necessary, says Toni Morrison, to see the way we can become captive to our own attachments—can "live in a redesigned racial house and . . . call it diversity or multiculturalism as a way of calling it home" ("Home" 8).

This asks us to de-transcendentalize our most familiar and replied-upon approaches to racial pain and difference. Jane Cooper, for instance, looks squarely at white guilt, the edifice at which most white exploration stops, asking: "When is memory transforming? when, a form of real estate?" (23). Likewise, here is Martha Collins, trying to look past the edifice of racial code constraint:

> and if I look at your face at your hands your
> triumphant or suffering body and do not
>
> see . . .
>
> *who wasn't us*
> who isn't us
> who isn't there
> (49)

James Baldwin in "Everybody's Protest Novel" critiques predictable moral-
ity narratives, "neatly framed . . . incontestable . . . terrified of the darkness,
striving mightily for the light" (11). In "Ode to My Blackness" Evie Shockley
likewise presses on this complexity, and constraint, acknowledging the ways
that blackness is her "shelter from the storm" and, at the same time, "the
storm"; her "anchor // and the troubled sea" (30).

Even hope, precious hope, might be a false remedy. Tyrone Williams in
"I Am Not Proud to Be Black" describes this place, free from racial codes, as
standing where "Hope ends and thinking breaks out." This hope, if it is hope,
is "disfigured"; to Williams, we are sitting at a "table" that,

> already broken,
> Dysfunctional, is finally institutionalized
>
> . . . .
>
> Another country cobbled out of continents
> Extant and not: February, Juneteenth, Kwanzaa . . .
>
> . . . .
>
> Or we throw our hands in the air like we just
>
> Don't care, nobodies or nations, the false dilemma. (60)

Here Williams points to the symbolic taxes we each pay to our identities, such
as "February, Juneteenth, Kwanzaa," safe houses of African American identity.
None of these symbols lives outside the racial narratives' border patrol. The
existential basis of this constraint—of resistance and remedy—is beautifully
reflected in Thomas Sayers Ellis's poem "Or," in which the narratives, if not
quite being more of the same, are clearly also not yet outside the (either/) "Or"
dimension.

> or
> Other
>
> or theory or discourse
> or oral territory.
> Oregon or Georgia
> or Florida Zora (4)

Ellis unites theoretical spaces ("Other" and "theory" and "discourse") with
physical ones, which are encoded as white ("Oregon") or black ("Georgia"), or
as sites of resistance ("Florida Zora," i.e., Hurston).

Or Moor.
Or a Noir Orpheus
or Senghor

or

Diaspora (5)

Even symbols of strength, tragic heroes like Shakespeare's Othello ("Moor");
the literary and intellectual hero Léopold Senghor; the millennial, heroic over-
tones of "Diaspora" and, later in the poem, of roots ("Yoruba"); a U.S. African
American symbol of unity, the Black Church ("Worship"); and the ethos of
survival ("Neighbor")—all are here mere empty, if "important," "ports" (5).

IV. A Cold Shower

Elizabeth Alexander's "Race" shows us another important gesture of rewriting,
in which the poet turns toward the audience, breaking the fourth wall, to say:
"Many others have told, and not told, this tale" (22). She candidly reveals her
awareness that it is a "tale," a story and performance, and not reality, and she
thus keeps us as readers from pretending, either.

This step in rewriting, what Bertolt Brecht called the "alienation effect"
or a "cold shower" (12), is the least understood, and most necessary, step:
the gesture, on the part of a poem, toward the script and the stage of racial
codes—the gesture that flaunts its freedom in front of the enforcers. As its
name suggests, this can thus make us readers feel like the poem is messing with
us. Because it is. Brecht calls this process "liberating the spectator," or bringing
the audience into the work of art by acknowledging not only the script and
the stage but all of the context—the backstage of history, the scripts of privi-
lege's euphemisms—all of the elephants in the room (D. Brooks 28). For, as
Major Jackson pointed out, part of the problem with racism in America is that
discussing it is a "spectator sport" (141). Here rewriting asks us all to acknowl-
edge that, in the stage play of white power and its forms of domination, there
are no spectators. And whoever challenges the script, whether as "spectator" or
performer, will indeed be punished.

Thus, in this dramaturgy of power, anger is a particularly forbidden emo-
tion, depicted—and delegitimized—as nothing more than the property of
conspiracy-theorists, or people who let emotion get in the way of their think-
ing. For the artist, this will be expressed in charges of aesthetic inferiority
(sometimes coded as accusations of being "experimental") or, more often, di-

dacticism. In Ross Gay's poem "Within Two Weeks the African-American Poet Ross Gay Is Mistaken for Both the African-American Poet Terrance Hayes and the African-American Poet Kyle Dargan. Not One of Whom Looks Anything Like the Others," the title alone begins the cold shower, calling out white readers for the effects of their racialized experience, in this case a white person who asks Gay to sign someone else's book, "whispering, / *but that's not you?*" Gay's response is "I do not / feel sorry for you. No" (30).

This fierceness, however, is a nuanced one, familiar in some ways from Gwendolyn Brooks, who in "The Womanhood" urged, "First fight. Then fiddle. . . . / . . . muzzle the note / With hurting love; the music that they wrote" (54). Though we must "first fight," the "muzzling" of "their" note is always done "with hurting love." Likewise, Gay goes on:

> I think only that when a man
> is a concept he will tell you about the smell
> of smoke . . . the distance
> between heartbreak and rage. (30)

Thus the fierceness of rewriting, aimed at protecting the body, is rarely far from kindness, the nurturer of all bodies. Here the poem makes clear the cost to one person—being, literally, not seen—of another's complicity in the public transcript. Gay highlights the difference between the two racialized experiences. As someone who appears black, and subjected to the resulting slights, fights, and existential horror, the speaker attempts with the poem to puncture the public transcript, the white racialized narrative encoded to deny its presence, to highlight the person's refusal to own their own speaking-as, expressed so vividly in the white person's assumption that her actions were innocent, an accident, and not by a design, even if that design is far larger than herself.

Gay's poem, especially the "No." here, reflects the fact that, again, within the scripts of race, anger has a special and dangerous role. Harryette Mullen, in "We Are Not Responsible," articulates how much of white ideology relies on striking out at even the appearance of anger. Borrowing the form of legal disclaimers, the poem embodies the physical and emotional distance that are characteristic of the denial: "We do not endorse the causes or claims of people begging for handouts. . . . Before taking off, please extinguish all smoldering resentments. . . . In the event of loss, you'd better look out for yourself. Your insurance was cancelled because we can no longer handle your frightful claims" (77). Mullen ingeniously characterizes the white cultural body as a bureaucrat waving away someone who has filled out a form incorrectly, illuminating the

way that anger and "angry people," no matter their racial identity, are sym-
bolically no longer privileged or white, the mask of obliviousness covering an
attempt to morally justify white power's own refusal.

This suspect gesture, anger, is equally distorted across the racial spectrum.
For white poets, for instance, pain is visible only in its neurotic forms, such
as "white guilt," which is merely another version of white refusal. Real ac-
countability, naming the stage and the script we all stand on and speak from,
is thus an important rupture. Martha Collins acknowledges: "a few years after
Brown / v. Board of Education I wrote a paper / that took the position *Yes but
not yet*" (1), not adding a narrative of remedy, despair, or even hope. She simply
opens this closed space in history and lets stand her naked complicity. This
poetics is thus a cold shower not only on history but on our readerly desire to
be soothed or to find sympathetic understanding.

Rewriting aims to disrupt what Brecht called a "hypnosis" that can happen
between poem and reader, if it is based on stable, but false, notions of our own,
and others', identities (12). Inside this hypnosis, all manner of racial codes can
safely be transmitted, with the reader unaware. The disruption, since language
is so complicit, too, is well assisted by visual language or actual images. Claudia
Rankine, in *Don't Let Me Be Lonely*, pairs a poem with an illustration by John
Lucas that makes material the social internalization of "toxic" racialization:

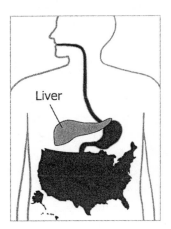

Above it the speaker says, "Be happy you can't read their thoughts, I want to
say to / him. I smile into the rearview mirror instead" (90). This is thus also
a poetics of self-alienation, with speakers expelling our national poisons, the
visceral and embodied decrepitude hidden in these closed spaces, from their
bodies by reciting a litany of the Real.

In this way, rewriting introduces the "unthinkable," as Pierre Bourdieu defined it: "that which one cannot conceive . . . because it defies the terms under which the questions are raised" (Trouillot 85). The policing racial codes neatly define what can and cannot be raised, as well as the ways it can be introduced. Thus Thomas Sayers Ellis's "Pronoun-Vowel Reparations Song" (103–19)—which brings up the sine qua non of racially taboo subjects, reparations for slavery—dislocates nearly every formal convention of language using colossal font and single-letter homophone code, not only signifyin' but embodying in language how unthinkable to us are any new, restorative and relational, race narratives.

Importantly, Ellis begins with the public transcript, the vowel song, including the "alternate" vowel *y*, whose homonym is, of course, "why." Ending the line "A E I O U" on the poem's first page (105), its questioning sound rings out: why? By the next page Ellis begins to rewrite, exposing the hidden transcript that lies beneath:

I   O   U,

and asking, again:

Y

The larger font size of "Y"/"why" presses the poem's reach beyond the page and the racial stage, so that there is no longer a performer/audience dichotomy; every spectator must play a part. In response to his own question, he asserts:

I

Followed by:

B E F O R E   U

B E F O R E
U

It is difficult to imagine a more confrontational move than this reversal. A colder shower for power. It aims neither at persuasion nor at sympathetic understanding; it aims to disrupt:

A   E   U   O   ME

At one level, this is a poem simply making a demand. And I can imagine the patrolling racial euphemisms, accusing it of aesthetic inferiority or didacticism. Indeed, the poem's radical choices clearly provoke exactly this. But Ellis, who describes these as "identity-repair poems," deploys far more than mere demand. While obviously discarding the usual tools of lyricism and mimesis, having sacrificed them to alienation, the poem does still move, playfully "singing" this most unthinkable thought, with "U O ME" hyphenating and repeating the different "syllables" ("AAA—EEE UUU—OOO M—EEEE), alternating regular type with italics as if fluctuating between notes ("OOOO / U—OOO / U—OOO"). The song and the speaker's aims are ambiguous, lying somewhere between a taunt and a playful dance with the white-power race police. Ellis riffs again with a children's grammar rhyme ("U A-F-T-E-R Q"), which he disrupts and displaces ("F-I-X"), and finally resolves ("E Q U A L S") with the poem's end:

A   P   O
L   O   G
I   Z   E

Jamming the signals of narrative, the poem still theorizes, proposes a "fix." In its semantically stark landscape we are left with Ellis's basic message, which is evident not only in its content but in the means he uses to get there: that, for the story to change, everyone, not only the "bad guys" in our race narratives, needs to give something up, whether it is sympathy, comfort, money, or power. Like the world created in Ellis's profoundly original poem, we have to be willing to enter a landscape that we don't at first recognize and yet already live in. By breaking from mainstream linguistic, typographic, and prosodic norms, he signifies on them, which is to say that he, playfully and freely, undermines their hold. Ellis shows that: 1) power lives inside our language; 2) we can take hold of and change things via language; 3) only if we're open to a radical change, not only in language, but in how we think and be.

V. Patterned, Wild, and Free

The freedom of this language project is a "playful ontological instability" (D. Brooks 22), although, like all freedoms, it comes with a price. Because we're not really talking about race, or writing about it, if the abyss, the absurd, or some form of social death isn't somehow on the line. If not, we risk writing about, and for, white power. The poet rewriting race not only disrupts; she is willing to be disrupted, as well.

Rewriting thus demands complexity; we become traitors to our racialized experience, which we acknowledge freely. In rewriting, poets from across the racial identity spectrum can and must negotiate some kind of alterity. Language is an important site of that, for language gestures are social gestures. And, though it is hard to feel or believe, "since language *is* community, if the cognitive ecology of a language is altered, so is the community" (Morrison, "Home" 8). Dawn Lundy Martin's book *Discipline* beautifully embodies this:

> We walk backward
> into a room because we want to restate our thoughts. All the
> brown skins are glowing in this light and no one is afraid we're
> all joyous but it's difficult to tell if the joy is real or if
> it's just lack of fear. What kind of understanding will sink
> into the body?
> . . . when it feels something it really does. It changes, though,
> and it grows up and looks completely different in the face. (47)

Thus the goal of alienation—of, for a moment, making enemies—is not to divide but to connect. A poet who rewrites, however, insists that there is no connectedness possible if it is done while trying to *dissolve* difference. Instead, we must hold difference and particularity—boldly, fearlessly, lovingly—in view. Stand fully in our own shoes, and in one another's, without regressing to mere universalism, a blurry, overdetermined picture of "we are one."

Here rewriting can be seen as a poetics of existential vulnerability, in which we are willing to somehow step from behind our racial masks. Douglas Kearney in "The Black Automaton in de Despair ub Existence #3: How Can I Be Down?" shows us that any real encounter with the limits of race is at least partly an existential encounter, as he asks, "to be / or not . . . Toby:"

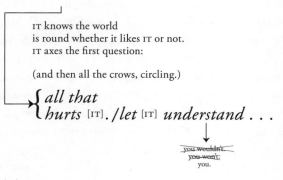

(16)

Kearney's partly retracted but nevertheless active assertion "understand . . . / you wouldn't / you won't" shows how this poetics also asks us, thus, to reckon with trust. The myriad suspicions that get raised in response to acts of rewriting are the echo in our head of the race narratives' "insistence," as Baldwin said, "that it is [our] categorization alone which is real and . . . cannot be transcended" (18). The public show, and the hidden realities—the things that whites don't say in front of blacks, the things that blacks don't say in front of whites—all of these, if disrupted, can, even temporarily, come "to an end, and the necessity of actively choosing one's orientation among them" can begin (Bakhtin 296, qtd. in Hale 454). We can fall into "plain talk," outside of, and even playing on, the careful codes that we would otherwise rely on.

There is no plain talk possible, however, if we do not do the real work: for each of us, especially white people, to look and see our own racialized experience, our own internalization of the structures and power of race. Martha Collins, in the last "White Paper" of her book, links her family's experience to societal patterns, showing how what seemed to be "just" her life was in fact a mirror of larger structural agendas, how her "yes but" response when presented with an agenda of change likewise reflects the public transcript, and so must be rewritten, reimagined:

> I'm still learning this un-
>
> learning untying
> the knot of *Yes but* re-
> writing this   *Yes*   Yes (2012, 64)

Stuttering the syntax and extracting punctuation so that both visually and musically the discursive admixture can run freely through a reader's own experience, the real force in this poem is still its use of alienation: the courage of its embodied complicity with the structures that it names, and yet, through that sense of accounting, its solidarity with the forces that seek possibility and change.

As Gwendolyn Brooks described and these poems remind, only if they mess with us, if they "first fight," do poems clear a space around what would "fog out [our] identity" ("Sundays" 16), so that rewriting, too, urges us to "First . . . civilize a space / Wherein to play your violin with grace" ("Womanhood" 54).

These are a range of gestures and aesthetics, which can be read as "formal" or "experimental," as "conciliatory" or "aggressive," but in all of these cases what makes them rewriting is that, paradoxically, even while they aim to destabilize, these acts of "messing with" are acts of re-membering or making whole. In Remica L. Bingham's "Simmie Knox Paints Bill Clinton for the White House," she sees deeply both the individual in his full complexity ("When he mentioned never knowing his father— / killed three months before his birth—I put my camera / down") and her own ("I thought of my own fading mother"), as well as the larger patterns that connect ("*We both know what it's like to be deprived of things*"). Only then is she able to "s[ee] him clearly. His face creased and stained as any other / human face." And then, only then, she says, "I picked up my brush" (25).

BIBLIOGRAPHY

Agoos, Julie. *Property*. Keene, N.Y.: Ausable, 2008.

Alexander, Elizabeth. "Race." In *Antebellum Dream Book*, 22. Saint Paul, Minn.: Graywolf, 2001.

Bakhtin, M. M. *The Dialogic Imagination: Four Essays*. Edited by Michael Holquist. Translated by Caryl Emerson and Michael Holquist. Austin: University of Texas Press, 1981.

Baldwin, James. "Everybody's Protest Novel." In *Collected Essays*, 11–18. New York: Library of America, 1998.

Bingham, Remica L. "Simmie Knox Paints Bill Clinton for the White House." In *The Ringing Ear: Black Poets Lean South*, edited by Nikky Finney, 25–26. Athens: University of Georgia Press, 2007.

Brecht, Bertolt. "On the Experimental Theatre." *Tulane Drama Review* 6, no. 1 (September 1961): 2–17.

Brooks, Daphne A. *Bodies in Dissent: Spectacular Performances of Race and Freedom, 1850–1910*. Durham, N.C.: Duke University Press, 2006.

Brooks, Gwendolyn. *Selected Poems*. New York: Harper & Row, 1963.

———. "The Sundays of Satin-Legs Smith." In *Selected Poems*, 12–18.

———. "The Womanhood." In *Selected Poems*, 52–66.

Collins, Martha. *White Papers*. Pittsburgh: University of Pittsburgh Press, 2012.

Cooper, Jane. *The Flashboat: Poems Collected and Reclaimed*. New York: W. W. Norton, 2000.

Cornis-Pope, Marcel. *Narrative Innovation and Cultural Rewriting in the Cold War Era and After*. New York: Palgrave Macmillan, 2001.

Ellis, Thomas Sayers. *Skin, Inc*. Saint Paul, Minn.: Graywolf, 2010.

Gay, Ross. *Bringing the Shovel Down*. Pittsburgh: University of Pittsburgh Press, 2011.

Hale, Dorothy J. "Bakhtin in African-American Literary Theory." *ELH* 61, no. 2 (Summer 1994): 445–71.

Jackson, John L., Jr. *Racial Paranoia: The Unintended Consequences of Political Correctness*. New York: Basic Civitas, 2008.

Jackson, Major. "A Mystifying Silence: Big and Black." The in-text citations for this essay refer to the page numbers in this volume, 137–154. (First published in *American Poetry Review*, September/October 2007).

Kearney, Douglas. *The Black Automaton*. Albany, N.Y.: Fence, 2009.

Martin, Dawn Lundy. 2011. *Discipline*. Calicoon, N.Y.: Nightboat.

Morrison, Toni. *Beloved*. New York: Knopf, 1997.

———. "Home." In *The House That Race Built*, edited by Wahneema Lubiano, 3–12. New York: Pantheon, 1997.

———. *Jazz*. New York: Knopf, 1992.

Mullen, Harryette. *Sleeping with the Dictionary*. Berkeley: University of California Press, 2002.

Rankine, Claudia. *Don't Let Me Be Lonely*. Saint Paul, Minn.: Graywolf, 2004.

Scott, James C. *Domination and the Arts of Resistance*. New Haven, Conn.: Yale University Press, 1990.

Shockley, Evie. *The New Black*. Middletown, Conn.: Wesleyan University Press, 2011.

Smith, Tracy K. *Duende*. Saint Paul, Minn.: Graywolf, 2007.

Touré. *Who's Afraid of Post-Blackness? What It Means to Be Black Now*. New York: Free Press, 2011.

Trethewey, Natasha. *Domestic Work*. Saint Paul, Minn.: Graywolf, 2000.

Trouillot, Michel-Rolph. *Silencing the Past: Power and the Production of History*. Boston: Beacon Press, 1995.

Vendler, Helen. "Are These the Poems to Remember?" Review of *The Penguin Anthology of Twentieth-Century American Poetry*, edited by Rita Dove. *New York Review of Books*, November 24, 2011.

Williams, Tyrone. *On Spec*. Richmond, Calif.: Omnidawn, 2008.

York, Jake Adam. "Elegy." In *Persons Unknown*, 95–97. Carbondale: Southern Illinois University Press, 2010.

Young, Kevin. *For the Confederate Dead*. New York: Knopf, 2007.

Race, Poetry, and Humor

TONY HOAGLAND

At a 2011 commemoration of the National Book Awards' fiftieth anniversary, in the half-full auditorium of the New School in New York City, a panel met to discuss, in public, the aesthetic "track record" of the NBA poetry awards. The panel included Susan Stewart, James Longenbach, Stephen Burt, Elizabeth Alexander, and Maureen McClane.

In some ways the event was an occasion of justified self-celebration; over those fifty years, a surprising number of groundbreaking collections of American poetry had been selected by the NBA, choices that represented the insight and sometimes even the daring of past NBA committees. Winners have included Adrienne Rich's *Diving into the Wreck*, Robert Bly's *The Light Around the Body*, books by William Bronk and Lucille Clifton, none of them obvious candidates for establishment approval, but special, perhaps even crucial books in the progress of American poetry.

Alexander, the first speaker of the night, opened her remarks with a rueful and witty preface: "Apparently I have been put on earth to count colored heads; when they are there and when they are not. It is tiresome at times, but in fact it is a habit which is an ethical practice: count and name; mark absence; herald presence; keep silent."

It was a droll beginning, self-consciously wry about the unenviable duty of monitoring racial equity in culture. Alexander went on to observe the disproportionately large number of white males in the NBA roll books, and the comparatively very few women and minorities represented.

"In looking through the list that we were given of winners of the NBA for tonight, the headline for my five minutes was clear: there were no black winners of the National Book Award for poetry from 1950 until 1999. Numbers don't lie," she said. "No Hispanic, no women—two black women in fifty years. No Gwendolyn Brooks," Alexander continued. "No Robert Hayden, no Amiri Baraka, no Jay Wright. No Michael Harper. No Sonia Sanchez. No Yusef Komunyaaka. No Rita Dove."

Now Alexander's tone became less wry and more aggrieved, as she read what seemed to be presented as a list of injustices. "I wish," said Alexander, "that poetry were much different than the Oscars, in how cultural capital is doled out to people of color. In the conferring of materiality, it matters. Who gets the prizes matters."

Then—in a bold move, considering the occasion—Alexander told an unpleasant anecdote from the annals of the past, drawn from a biography of Wallace Stevens. It happened in 1952, during a meeting of the NBA poetry committee. While waiting for an absent member, the committee, which included Stevens, passed the time by looking at photographs of previous committees. Stevens, on seeing a photo in which Gwendolyn Brooks appeared, remarked, "Who's the coon?"

What was the motive—and what was the effect—of Alexander's choice to publicly remind panelists and audience of the not-so-distant, not-so-pretty past? Stevens's racism is quietly well-known, and it is a fact that complicates, if not the stature of his poems, at least the canonization of the person who made them. Like American racism at large, such complicating facts should not be swept under the rug. Indisputably, someone must keep pulling back the curtain on the historical backstage. And of course our collective historical memory, our *hauntedness*, is one ongoing source of our humanity, of our often inadequate attempts to improve ourselves. Some memories must be reawakened. Or, as one of Michael Harper's best-known poems says, "In nightmare begins responsibility."

Compared to Stevens's recorded remark, Alexander's remarks were a model of diplomatic gentility. Nonetheless, there was a quality to Alexander's action that felt like "outing" Stevens—and, by proxy, "outing" the National Book Awards.

There is nothing particularly unusual about this episode of contemporary literary culture. In fact, the proceedings of the evening offer an opportunity for insight because of their cultural familiarity. From such episodes we can measure our rating on the race-spectrometer. First, we can observe that it is as difficult as ever not to take matters of race and privilege personally. Second, we can see that nothing marks the conversation about race more than humorlessness and compulsion. These compulsions are laced and laden with subtexts that are meant to stay hidden.

"Compulsion" is a strong word, but appropriate to the conversation of American race. What it implies is the agency of subterranean as well as aboveground motives in our choices, tone, and behavior. In matters of race, unconscious forces always seem to be actively coexistent with those explicable by rationality.

White writers, for their part, are caught in the double—or triple—bind of power, apology, and hazard. As a result, they feel mostly compelled to say nothing, at least nothing remotely controversial, on the subject of race and aesthetics. White literary approbation, or disagreement, is registered in silence. On the evening in question, the white poets performed their roles in the customary manner: gazing abstractedly into space as Alexander spoke, or smiling and nodding in agreement. Yet in this white performance there is something so passive as to be unsatisfying. At most, the silent acquiescence seems to signify "I might agree with you" or "I consent to be powerless, that is, remain silent, in this conversation."

Alexander felt compelled, that evening, to remind the community at large about the formative racism of our past. This is a crummy but important responsibility. It is important and valuable that a self-elected individual (not an institution) gallantly perform that role for the community. As Alexander's preface acknowledged, "Tonight, I shall be the Watchkeeper of Memory."

As for subtexts, one subtext pretty much shared by both black and liberal white persons in the American zeitgeist is that the historical oppressor must be transformed into a Penitent before equity can be achieved. Compensation, if not economic, then at least psychological, must be offered. A humbling—like the one Alexander administered to Stevens and the NBA—must be ritually enacted as a form of reparations. As a corollary, the increased elevation of the historically victimized class is another kind of ritual equity. As Alexander said, emphatically, "Prizes matter—they matter."

Such subtexts underlie our racial conversations at every level, from the very political and very public to the very private. "What is it our responsibility to say?" we ask ourselves. Then, "What do we really think and feel?" Then, "What are we allowed to say?" Where do truth, courtesy, frankness, aesthetics, history, and justice coexist, and where do they contradict or interfere with each other? For, after all, our racial stories and our psychic fabrications around race are as complex and layered as the long narrative of our individual bodies, as secret as our family stories, or our sexual histories.

~

The accepted contemporary subtexts of American literary whiteness include the whole long shadow of American racial injustice, first of slavery and secondly of ongoing economic and social inequality—haunting realities. We stand indefinitely, and anxiously, in their shadows.

Another part of the shadow is ongoing white privilege, and the natural instinct to retain advantage. Take myself as an example. On the one hand, I'll acknowledge my privilege readily; on the other hand, I hope not to be inconvenienced. Secretly too, my ego will privately continue to believe that whatever success I have experienced has been legitimate, is appropriate, and has been earned by my individual talent and hard work.

These are called subtexts for a reason; I will never say this openly, because of the hazard that accompanies frank expression in the public forum on the topic of race. The topic itself, everyone knows, has become the territorial property of persons of color. Thus the frank, exploratory, spontaneous speech that our shared reality requires can easily end in blame or disgrace. I won't ever disagree, openly, with the consensual liberal parameters of the racial conversation. I will be a yes-person. Occasionally, in a marginal way, among my liberal white friends, I will ironically acknowledge that the machinery of affirmative action is at work in the cultureplace. This calculation of equity (counting heads) is the price of repairing history. I consent to the machinery, and though I would personally prefer not to pay the disadvantageous price of it—oh well, it's not about me.

My main public obligation is to appear unconflicted. Whether I feel good about it or not, to be conflicted about race would, in itself, be an admission of confusion about these labyrinthine American matters. Confusion is suspect.

The gap between these two unconscious positions—the position of historical plaintiff, played that evening by Alexander, and the position of uneasy but secure self-righteous possessors of privilege, played by myself—is substantial and, so far, mostly unbridged. Both positions seem a little petrified or fossilized. Our consensual silence—the particular silence of white liberals—on the subject of race is, paradoxically, ultimately an obstacle to acknowledging the present and moving into the future. It's not hard to see that we—both white and black poets—are still breathing through straws.

Brothers and sisters—am I allowed to say that?—we are haunted. One question is: Can a conscious poetry help bridge it?

Humor

It is too bad that our collective superego, our tragedy of consciousness and history, demands our utter seriousness on this subject. Because humor is, in all of our affairs, a way to let the cats and the dogs out of the bag. Humor makes the ugly bearable, the truth audible. Humor releases resentments, truth, misunderstanding, and our relief simultaneously. It also embodies our ambivalences and our contradictory understandings. In a way, in fact, our ability to joke is some basic testament of freedom.

Here's the poet Paul Beatty, from the preface to his novel *The White Boy Shuffle*:

> In the quest for equality, black folks have tried everything. We've begged, revolted, entertained, intermarried, and are still treated like shit. Nothing works, so why suffer the slow deaths of toxic addiction and the American work ethic when the immediate gratification of suicide awaits? In glorious defiance of the survival instinct, Negros stream into Hillside, California, like lemmings. Every day they wishfully look heavenward, peering into the California sky for a metallic gray atomic dot that will gradually expand until it explodes some one thousand feet over our natural and processed heads. It will be the Emancipation Disintegration; Lunch counters, bus seats, and executive washrooms be damned; our mass suicide will be the ultimate sit-in.

Paul Beatty is still my favorite poet, black or white, on American race. Even though he does not write poetry anymore—he is now a novelist—his two books of poems describe the gamesmanship, insanity, and suffering of race with an acrobatic freedom I have found in no one else's work. No one comes close to passages like this:

> Me and angry sister x
> Would read our poems over breakfast
> They were fresh
> Smelt of incense and just crushed hummus
>
> Garbanzo beans are the seeds of freedom
> I couldn't wait till my dreads tickled the tips of my ears

We figured going to hear this established poet
Might promote our hairgrowth

A poet whose description under his picture read

the author is a demolitions expert an accomplished marksman
    philosopher
black belt voodoo witch doctor lobbyist who lives in a thatch hut in
    Rwanda
And is at present trying to get congress to pass the james bond act
law that permits black folk to drink martinis with a straight face
and to kill white folks with impunity

. . . .

we sat and listened in a white church

but this poet had on a pressed starched collared shirt

. . . .

he was missing
his mutton chop hate whitey sideburns
And read long monotone poems

. . . .

after we left we realized he never said black   not once
                                    maybe we'd missed something

. . . .

who turned the magic fire hose on his dashiki
and turned it into one of them
irish spring soap commercial prep school sweaters

. . . .

fuck the elephant's graveyard
i want to know where the revolutionary spirit go to die
("About the Author," in *Joker, Joker, Deuce* 52–54)

Beatty has sardonic fun, and he makes fun—even against a context of consider-
able sorrow. In particular, Beatty's poetic genius is how adroitly he plays with
clashing layers of idiom and stereotype which cross-fertilize and cross-examine
both sides of the street, whiteness and blackness. He makes fun of the myth of
equal opportunity and the fact of social liability, of overcompensating white
guilt, and fantasizing welfare moms. He ventriloquizes both white- and black-
inflected speech.

Why do I find his work so reassuring? Because, for all its tones—empathy, anger, corrosive sarcasm—the poems in *Joker, Joker, Deuce* are neither overly idealistic nor especially complaining. Beatty really is not promoting anything but the comedic carnival of realism. Vast injustices of tragic proportions are part of that carnival. To me, there's more truth, reality, insight, and dark acrobatic freedom about race in Beatty's work than in a slew of sincere collections of poetry that take on the subject. And freedom of speech is a marvelous kind of freedom.

Thomas Sayers Ellis is another young poet who fights the historical race battle with humorous fists. In his recent book *Skin, Inc.: Identity Repair Poems*, Ellis has a section called "Society for the Friends of Former Property." Ellis's funny is a grim-funny, but its tone illustrates a kind of coming-out and is emotionally refreshing because it seems more real than the sanctimony and reverence of much other work. Here is a passage from Ellis's poem "The Obama Hour":

> Finally, one of us is properly
> positioned to run. By "us" I mean Black,
> by "positioned" I mean White
> and by "run" I mean Race and its varied speeds of darkness,
>
> . . . .
>
> including the difficult qualifying times
> between the theft of our arrival and all hate crimes. (60)

The twisty compressions of a passage like this create a greater-than-usual intimacy between the writer and readers, either white or black, through their frankness—frank aggression—and playful anger. Ellis's sincere jabbing is compactly thoughtful and verbally adroit in the way that humor is swift. It makes fun of the explanations it skips over, and it reformulates history as a mode of discussing it ("by 'run' I mean Race and its varied speeds of darkness"). Elsewhere, in the poem "No Easy Task," Ellis's speaker says, "The problem / with American poetry / is there's not enough Africa / in it; bling-bling has more / rhythm and imagery / than all of Ashbery" (62).

Moving at this speed, the speed of jabbing humor, one might get somewhere in the racial dialogue, somewhere beyond mere rehashings of the historical positions, assuming the politically correct postures of our time, one more time.

What humor brings into the racial conversation is flexibility and resilience, the freedom to play against codes rather than be imprisoned by categories.

Laughter directed at the self as well as the other, at the unsaid as well as the unsayable, is a freedom that releases the pressures of identity, and maybe even points the way to revelation. In humor, boundaries are loosened, not fortified. This is a lot to ask from individuals and groups who have been punished by category (poets of color)—and likewise of other people who have been protected by category (uncolored poets)—and yet such self-exposé is what is needed, and such linguistic-psychological performances are something that poetry is uniquely well suited to deliver.

What White Poets Haven't Done

If African American poets, generationally, are beginning to write over the lines and into the cracks of racial self-protectionism, white poets have not really stepped up to the same challenge. Poetry by white poets is largely barricaded into a kind of ivory tower of niceness, or a cul-de-sac of political correctness. Most often, the poems of white writers simply practice omission. White poets, always sincere, always politically correct, often perceptive, are largely petrified when it comes to working creatively with the more fictitious, performative aspects of race. I don't know many poems about race by white poets that are not boring.

The cautiousness—and muteness—of white poets on American race is understandable, even appropriate. Because of our history of unshared power, racial humor in white mouths is legitimately suspect. It is easy for a white writer to get it wrong, to thoughtlessly evoke the history of oppression just by opening his mouth. It is one thing for Chris Rock to make a joke about watermelon; it would be another thing for a white comedian. We could say that the price tag is still on that joke—and that black Americans have already bought and paid for it. A haunted sea of grief underlies Billie Holiday's singing "Strange Fruit," but the song becomes something different sung by Diana Krall.

Nonetheless, race is a huge presence in American life; we are saturated in its tensions and confusions, guilts, resentments, and hallucinations, its curiosities and passions; it is, finally, artistically and politically unavoidable. Inevitable, too, that we shall make progress in our permissiveness to speak, our efforts to deploy art's powers toward the thawing of traumatized, frightened, and self-protective discourse. The poems of grievance and testimony written by poets of color will become tiresome unless they innovate their own consciousness. "Identity poetics," says Reginald Shepherd, is boring, giving back the already known, in an endless and endlessly self-righteous confirmation of things as they are [but] . . . The greatest literature has always engaged in the generation of new realities, not the reiteration of the same old given reality. (42–43)

And it is time for white poets to interrogate and publicly explore our own layered consciousness in walking around in a world colored by the history of color. It is time for grace, daring, and courage in the presence of the Other, in the interests of open discourse.

Until white writers are as open and frank and funny about their own anxieties, blindnesses, and feelings about race—whiteness and brownness—as black poets and comedians are now, until those imaginary poems of the future are written, stiffness, reserve, suspicion and jealousy, formality and distrust, and silence rather than equity will be the ghost in the room in our communities and our art. Fortunately, not just our hauntedness but our powerful mutual curiosity about race litigates in favor of openness.

Return to the Scene

Meanwhile, back at the NBA auditorium, later that same evening, another memorable, racially contorted interchange occurred. Stephen Burt had just praised Terrance Hayes's new collection, *Lighthead,* which had been awarded the 2010 National Book Award, as an exceptional book which unified and represented the best in American poetics of our moment. Burt, a white poet, naturally did not mention, though it was implicit, the fact that the book was written by an African American poet. Burt's subtext, of course, was that this book, and its recognition, should satisfy both the high aesthetic tradition of the National Book Awards audience and the desire, expressed earlier by Alexander, for more equitable racial distribution of cultural recognition.

In the Q-and-A that followed, an elderly lady in the audience raised her skinny pale arm. "Why didn't Major Jackson"—like Hayes a youngish African American male poet—"win the award," she asked, "instead of Terrance Hayes?"

Duh-oh. It was a poignant, awkward, and deeply discouraging moment. For, after all, the lady's unconscious assumption—that one black poet was as good as another when it came to prizewinning—confirmed our worst suspicions about categorical imperatives, about the blindness to individuality fostered by racialized vision.

If any doubt existed about the veracity of Alexander's critique, about arrested development of perception at the cultural level, that point was made.

Yet the moment also represented the aesthetic myopia that comes from head-counting. After all, Alexander and the lady from Dubuque both were counting heads of color. "Numbers don't lie." "Awards matter." But numbers can lie. It is worth noting that Alexander fielded the woman's question with grace and kindness.

Add one more episode. The next night, as a counterpart to the panel discussion of NBA history by talking heads, a brief poetry reading was held elsewhere in the city. The poet-critics of the NBA poetry panel discussion were invited to read a poem or two of their own, plus a poem by one of the NBA Poetry Prize winners of the past. Five poets read work that evening; of the five, two chose to read poems by Wallace Stevens. Maybe it is mere speculation what compulsions and subtextual motives underlay those choices, but it is quite possible that the readers who chose Stevens poems were marshaling a kind of defense of Stevens's poetry—not the man, but the poetry—in response to Alexander's attack of the night before.

White apologetic liberalism gets us only so far. Nor, appearances suggest, do finger-wagging demands for cultural reparations have a great record of success. The poem confessing complicity, playing the violin of historical guilt, the poem that asserts solidarity with the oppressed in a ringing tone of self-righteousness, how often these can seem like hollow gestures.

In an ironic way, the sophistication and familiarity of our discourse about race has made us less able to speak authentically; our public conversation has made us as polite and clumsy as people playing catch while wearing oven mittens.

We would like for the narrative to end with justice, but for the time being, that outcome seems unlikely. It might be better to aim for mercy, or at least greater honesty. The humility that comes from self-knowledge and the acceptance of our imperfect, tragic, mutually entangled circumstances is the place where we must stand. In our ignorant, denying, confounded, decade-after-decade grapplings with race, our ignorance has to be out in the open, visible to both white and black speakers, to offer any hope of progress.

Say your arm is broken in a dream, and in that dream you are driving around a big city looking for first aid. It is late at night in the dream and raining. Block after block you drive, through intersections, past warehouses and gymnasiums. You go past township after township. The neon glow of tilted pink martini glasses, the fluorescent glare of all-night drugstores and shopping malls with their acres of empty parking lot—you keep going. You have seen several signs saying Mercy Clinic, Mercy Emergency Care, but you keep on going. You need a hospital, but you are looking for the one you heard about, the one called Justice. That's the situation all of us are in.

BIBLIOGRAPHY

Beatty, Paul. *Joker, Joker, Deuce*. New York: Penguin, 1994.
———. *The White Boy Shuffle*. Boston: Houghton Mifflin, 1996.
Ellis, Thomas Sayers. *Skin, Inc.: Identity Repair Poems*. Minneapolis: Graywolf Press, 2010.
Shepherd, Reginald. *Orpheus in the Bronx: Essays on Identity, Politics, and the Freedom of Poetry*.
   Ann Arbor: University of Michigan Press, 2008.

23 ～ the unfinished politics of nathaniel mackey's *splay anthem*

PATRICK S. LAWRENCE

Little critical work has been done on Nathaniel Mackey's *Splay Anthem* (2006), a collection of installments of his two serial poems *Song of the Andoumboulou* and *"Mu."* However, because other sections of the two poems have appeared over the past several years in venues such as *Callaloo*, *African American Review*, *Chicago Review*, and the *Nation*, there is a body of critical writing on the on-going concerns of the portions of the poems appearing outside the collection that can shed light on how they are worked out in *Splay Anthem*, which won Mackey the 2006 National Book Award for poetry. As Mackey has continued to explore certain themes throughout the life of the poems, we gain added value from returning to this prizewinning collection and reassessing the poems' significance in a changing world. Though *Song* and *"Mu"* were begun in the later part of the twentieth century, they take on new meaning in the context of the events that have occurred contemporaneously with their continued publication. Thus a more complete focus on the poems and their modern-ist/postmodernist techniques can shed light on the developing relationship between experimentation and politics, a relationship that has been fraught since the 1960s at least. *Splay Anthem*'s indirect political project acknowledges that the work of striving for equality and community is ever incomplete, but provides a tentative foundation for this effort.

Splay Anthem is a weave of several themes and recurrent experimental forms. Jarring enjambment causes lines to read both with those that came before and those that follow with ambiguity, while often refusing to signify concretely. This is in keeping with the effect of the variations-on-a-theme style of polysemy used throughout the poems, in which words are exploited for their double (or multiple) meanings, often with plural meanings suspended simultaneously, refusing to resolve in clear reference. Mackey's use of the word "rung," for example, signifies simultaneously both the past tense of "to ring" and the lateral crosspieces of a ladder. Additionally, words often appear in alienated forms, used repeatedly with slight changes to spelling but retaining just an echo of their other forms. The themes that emerge amid this weave are complex and epic, following an incomplete but continuously striving humanity as it searches for a communal, global identity. This process is difficult and often painful. It is evinced by Mackey in his preface, where he explains what he means when he uses the name Andoumboulou: "The song of the Andoumboulou is one of striving, strain, abrasion, an all but asthmatic song of aspiration. Lost ground, lost twinness, lost union and other losses variably inflect that aspiration, a wish, among others, to be we, . . . that of some larger collectivity an anthem would celebrate" (xi). Mackey's evocation of the need for collectivity and the pain of its alienation resonates with the collection's title. This text, then, strives to be an anthem, a song for a new nation, but a nation born of misdirection, of splayed—that is shuttling, sideways, crooked—movement toward the realization of its identity.

Like much experimental work, *Splay Anthem* has been criticized by reviewers for sacrificing transparency to technical ostentation. For example, Brian Phillips, reviewing the book for *Poetry*, derides Mackey's writing as "technical accomplishment rather than a sign of real mythic power" and "skill rather than vision" (236). Similarly, Phillips is suspicious of the text's opacity, and indicts *Splay Anthem* for "us[ing] its atmosphere of complexity to put you in a position of ignorance, from which its merely ambiguous elements will seem more profound than they actually are" (237). For Phillips, formal complexity obscures and in some ways causes the failure of Mackey's project: "Mackey's essentially Romantic, Blakean enterprise of forging an individual mythology (here drawn from Islam, Africa, literary theory, and jazz) gets knocked a little out of focus by his postmodern retreat from definite meaning. . . . It covets the prestige, or at least the high tone, of the mythic, while leaving behind the possibility of actual belief" (236). Not everyone would agree that Mackey's project is Romantic; this contention is contradicted by Matt Sandler, who counts Mackey's work among "the disparate array of experimental poetries broken off from the Romantic idea of artistic progress at the turn of the twentieth century" (1378–79). Still, Phillips rightly identifies the book's project as one of seeking a mythology appropriate for a skeptical postmodern moment; he is simply unconvinced of Mackey's success.

What keeps the project from realizing its goal, Phillips contends, is its excessive awareness of the foreclosure of reference and meaning. However, Mackey's project is as ambitious as Phillips's comments suggest, as the text attempts to bridge the gap between a "retreat from definite meaning" and the metaphysical fulfillment of the epic mode. John Palattella points to this possibility, arguing that the poems do not "seek to restore a lost paradise that transcends history's confines. Instead, they dramatize the search for an imperfect remedy for lives and lands bruised and broken by history. . . . *Splay Anthem* is the most delicate and delirious installment of Mackey's epic song of salvage" (41). Thus Palattella sees the poem not as a failure of foundation—an imperfect epic—but as a chronicle of the search for a foundation placed out of reach by postmodern philosophy and alienation. The poems do not fail; rather, they are a meditation on failure.

The formal characteristics that some see as a deficiency thus become the hallmark of a new epic for a more skeptical time. Norman Finkelstein notes that the poems' theme of the elusiveness of fulfillment resonates with their broken aesthetic, which seems unable to faithfully conform to poetic conventions that might take for granted the wholeness of the speaking subject (166). Moreover, the poems' brokenness signals the important relationship between Mackey's poetry and the politics that are seldom more than implicit in his work. As Finkelstein notes, "In Mackey's work, this aesthetic and spiritual resistance also implies resistance to dominant cultural narratives, and therefore has a political dimension as well" (166). Finkelstein draws our attention to how Mackey's poetry dramatizes the inability to speak clearly, to write conventionally, something that is construed in the poems as a result of the disconnect between word and meaning. Because the speaker of *Splay Anthem* cannot believe in the unity of being, his existence in the world is unstable, directionless. But, as Finkelstein argues, it is when this instability erupts into the form of the poems that we begin to see its political valence. By disrupting poetic conventions—by being difficult—*Splay Anthem* resists the ideological structures that such conventions support and becomes a resistance to aesthetic hegemony. It is a song of sadness in otherness, in other-where-ness, and this lament signals the profound brokenness—of the psyche, of identity, of affect, of language— that has been the terrible price of the complex and insidious structures that maintain an unequal distribution of power in the world.

The argument that Mackey's aesthetic has this broadly political valence will come as a surprise to some and an apologia to others; Mackey's poetry can be and has been read as both resisting *and enacting* dominant discourses. On the one hand, reviewers and critics alike—and Mackey himself—often note the influence that earlier writers, including modernists and postmodernists now colossi of the Western canon, have had on Mackey's poetry. For example, Sandler mentions Poe and Pound, as well as Charles Olson and even Flaubert (provocatively, Sandler's reference to Flaubert is to *Salammbô*, an Orientalist vision of North Africa, a location that is the source of some of the material for *Splay Anthem*) (1379). Palattella invokes Pound and Beckett (41, 44). The invocation of Beckett comes in a description of Mackey's aesthetic of "creak" alluding to a famous passage from Beckett's *Worstward Ho*: "Try again. Fail again. Fail better" (Beckett 89). This reference highlights the poems' aesthetic that pairs incompleteness with striving, but also underlines the modernist context for Mackey's work. Additionally, as we saw above, Phillips asserts that Mackey's project is "Blakean," and even Mackey himself invoked William Carlos Williams in the speech he gave accepting the National Book Award. This mention of Williams was the only part of Mackey's acceptance mentioned by Bob Thompson in his *Washington Post* write-up of the awards ceremony, indicating not only the familiarity of Williams for a general readership but also his resonance for readers of Mackey's poetry.

Multiple thematic vectors support such comparisons, particularly those pointing to modernists who looked to Asia and Africa for refreshment of their technical repertoires. Still, *Splay Anthem* is suggestive of a sensibility we associate more readily with postmodernism: the sampling of a global source text. As Megan Simpson notes in discussing Mackey's earlier work: "The various musical, poetic, and cultural elements that find their way into Mackey's sequence [*Song of the Andoumboulou*] include West African myth (Yorubá and Dogon in particular), Haitian deities, voudoun, flamenco, Moroccan and Andalusian influences, Arabic and Islamic traditions, Gnosticism, reggae, jazz, and blues" (37). What is produced is a multi-origin text that weaves together a variety of traditions from around the world. Still, no matter the specific borrowing, the affiliation with high modernists and dominant-voice authors threatens to class Mackey's work among those that fail to advance a liberatory aesthetic, though perhaps not with those that advance a repressive one.

However, to attempt to nuance the overly restrictive idea that poetry that fails to adhere to certain conventions or that does not directly address material conditions can have no activist function, it is useful to turn to Timothy Yu's work on Asian American experimental poetry and the avant-garde. Yu argues that the avant-garde in poetry is always political and that cultural artifacts are a palimpsest on which can be read the signs of histories of racial exclusion, identity formation, and disenfranchisement. Tracing specific movements, Yu demonstrates that race is the implicit context for avant-garde movements in the United States. He argues that coming together as a group to elaborate a coherent aesthetic always takes place with knowledge of racial politics, either adopting a specific platform or pointedly refusing to do so (1–18). In such an environment, refusing or neglecting to comment on or address racial politics becomes a political act in itself.

Yu reminds us that race has been this implicit and explicit context stretching back at least as far as the modernists frequently mentioned as precursors of Mackey's work: "Race and the avant-garde have been linked since the dawn of the twentieth century, when avant-garde artists such as Picasso, Ezra Pound, and Gertrude Stein found inspiration in African masks, African American culture, and Asian literature" (1). However, Yu goes on to demonstrate the Orientalism of this gesture:

> For these white European and American avant-gardists, racial others offered an escape from Western aesthetics, serving as a source for the revolutionary break-throughs that have characterized the twentieth-century avant-garde. But such non-Western sources remained largely in the realm of folk culture or ancient tradition. For much of the century, white avant-gardists rarely felt the need to acknowledge the presence of nonwhite artists as peers and contemporaries. (1)

The similarity between the project of early modernists and Mackey, then, brings to light the importance of considering the possibilities and complications of an experimental poetics appropriate to resisting the dominant discourses of Orientalism and whiteness. Experimentalism of this form seems to develop the same techniques as more complicit or historically problematic texts, but its goal is more inclusive. Whether it can accomplish that goal remains unclear—put in doubt as much by Mackey's poems as by any theoretical discourse.

Yu argues for the inextricable imbrication of avant-garde aesthetics and the racial politics of the twentieth century, contributing to an understanding of the role of experimental or high-aesthetic texts in the struggle for racial and ethnic equality. In a similar vein, Aldon Lynn Nielsen argues for the importance of literary theory for African American culture. Nielsen finds himself resisting a false binary that opposes postmodern philosophy to African American experience and thought. In discussing Mackey's having received the National

Book Award for *Splay Anthem*, Nielsen finds proof of an overlap between the fields that suggests the profound reshaping of culture that Mackey's poetry might represent or aspire to:

> [I]f Mackey's acceptance of the award staged a renewed recognition of the African American intellectual and experimentalist, it also staged a convergence of critical and aesthetic modalities that had seldom been thought of together within the larger American literary and critical environment. For in Mackey we see and read a poet/critic equally well-versed in Lévi-Strauss and Ogotemmêli; one as conversant with the historiography of Ivan van Sertima as with Hayden White; one who has studied Janheinz Jahn's *Muntu* as well as he has studied Roland Barthes's *S/Z*. (21)

Nielsen's description of Mackey pointedly pairs heavyweights of European thought, including structuralists and poststructuralists, with those who offered narratives counter to Eurocentric epistemologies. Tracing alternate origins of European knowledge and redrawing the lines of influence to include African cultures, these groupings mimic *Splay Anthem*'s creation of a global culture. Nielsen's intent, and perhaps *Splay Anthem*'s effect, is to remind us of the interconnection of global cultures, of the millennia-old intercourse and spreading of knowledge across what are later imagined to be firm boundaries and the danger of making distinctions between particular intellectual pursuits and specific political projects.

The poems of *Splay Anthem* themselves complicate a discussion of theory and experimentalism that would rely too readily on such binaries. It is almost a cliché that all art is political; August Wilson said as much in 1999, crediting it as a lesson he learned from Amiri Baraka. Yet when we turn to Mackey's work, we find both this cliché and a nuancing of it. In a passage important enough to cap the collection and that Mackey himself found significant enough to quote in his acceptance speech for the National Book Award, we read:

> nothing
>
>   wasn't
>
>   politics we'd say. Wanting our want to
>   be called otherwise, kept at bay though
>   we were
>
>   .   .   .   .   .
>
>   A
>   mystic march they'd have said it was,

        acknowledging politics kept us at

bay,   everything was mystical

they'd say. Wanting our want to be

                    so

     named; kept at bay as we were,

                      what

    the matter was wasn't a question, no

                         ques-

tion what

it was (125)

We find circling in these sections of the final passage of the book, "Song of the Andoumboulou: 60," two concepts that become complementary but that we have seen opposed in the discourse surrounding experimentalism: material politics and deferred linguistic meaning.

    On the one hand, the poem tells us "nothing / wasn't / politics," implying a total-political project that encompasses everything. According to this reading, we interpret the line to mean [there was] nothing / [that] wasn't / politics," or that every action has a political valence, something in keeping with a reading of activist impulses and culture in which even choosing to remain apolitical is a (negatively construed) political act. This insistence on positive action is supported by the other meaning suspended in this same line, a reading that could be evoked by restating the line to emphasize that *the concept of nothingness* was not political ("nothing[ness] / wasn't / politics"). In either case, what is being evoked is the sense in which activism informs or ought to inform every action, every aesthetics and theory, and perhaps pointedly also informs theories that explore or espouse nihilistic or relativistic positions. However, the following words bracket this concept: "we'd say" is a phrase that locates this opinion in the past and shifts the emphasis from material politics to the subjectivity of the activist epistemology. The idea that everything is political is only a viewpoint here—something we said, not a truth that the poem accepts.

    As the passage that follows shows, Mackey is concerned with how that discourse of activism was a way to address—and keep at bay—the "wants" of oppressed people. In typical Mackey fashion, several things are unclear in this passage. Who are the political actors whose wants are being kept at bay? Are these "wants" goals or lacks? Who are those who would oppress them and use the claim of "politics" to rename and therefore mistake and erase their "wants"? Ultimately, the historical context cannot be fixed, something that both obscures the poems' message and, paradoxically, constitutes it. An earlier poem in the book suggests a contemporary situation for *Splay Anthem*. In section 18 of *"Mu"* we read, "Bullets flew, bombs fell / outside, century's end as / andoumboulouous as / ever" (17). The combination of war and the end of the century suggests a contemporary context—perhaps the September 11 terrorist attacks, the Persian Gulf War, or the wars in Iraq and Afghanistan—and the phrase "andoumboulouous as / ever" cements our sense that history is a process of successive imperfect reiterations. In addition, the ambiguity of the "we" in the later poem and the projection of the scene into an indeterminate past suggest activism against material injustice of many kinds and in many eras. Perhaps it is this lack of specificity, compensated only by an indeterminate seeking ("our want"), that supports claims that experimental poetry such as this is insufficiently invested in material change, but the poem suggests that our understanding of one era is important to our understanding of another, that history's struggles are iterations in a series, rather than distinct events. A demand for historical specificity, then, would miss the mark, as the poems suggest that history echoes itself by speaking in tones that resonate with multiple periods.

Again, we should view the polysemy—the simultaneity of two or more referential vectors—of *Splay Anthem* as a marker of a successful project rather than a failed one. The poems do not by accident happen to insufficiently evoke *either* historical or more contemporary concerns; they succeed in highlighting the similarities between many periods of striving. In the poem "Sound and Cerement" (section 38 of *"Mu"*), a particular passage brings the two together:

> In a hot room haunted by
> snow, the intractable two
>
> in
>
> disarray . . . Borne away by who
> knows what. Were it a bus, relegated
> to the back of the bus . . . A politics
> articulate of late of late let go, a
> pool of remorse we fell into (117)

The explicit reference to Jim Crow in this passage suggests that racial politics are the specific subject of the poem and the civil rights era its historical context. However, what follows is the indication that we are somehow coming after that moment of ideological clarity, as we read of "A politics / articulate of late of late let go." The politics of the past was clearly expressed ("articulate of late") but has been discarded ("of late let go"). Thus what the poem expresses is an apolitical atmosphere of sadness and dejection in a post-civil-rights era. (In a gesture typical of Mackey's poems, we are only a single space away from the opposite reading: replacing the phrase "A politics" with the word "apolitics" suggests that it is not politics but apolitical attitudes that have been discarded.) The suspension of multiple meanings and invocation of disparate times is part of the aesthetics and thematics of the poems in this volume. The echoing of one era with another is a constant concern in the collection, and it should be no surprise that both the excitement and the frustration of the 1960s and 1970s should be found to resonate with those same feelings in the early twenty-first century. Ultimately, what is at stake is a thematics of seriality and deferral, where a given utterance or act never takes its full meaning from a single historical event, but instead accrues or accretes meaning as it is reworked or relived in successive generations.

That *Splay Anthem* engages contemporary conditions in the United States seems evident and is underscored by Mackey in his preface (xv). However, the stakes of that engagement are perhaps ambivalent—indicating the speaker's feelings about a post-9/11, post-racial society (understanding both those terms to be bracketed). As Sandler notes, "the social critique in the poetry itself remains largely implicit" (1379). From this vantage, the poems seem engaged but lack a specific project. Instead, Sandler remarks, Mackey seems to be shooting for "a sort of post-racial aesthetic" (1380), a utopic vision of global community. Simpson notes the same impulse in earlier installments of *Song*, describing the desire evinced by the poems to make possible "a cross-cultural identity, neither essentialist nor assimilationist, but improvisational" (39). This vision is, again, only indirectly political, as we have to remember that this utopia is envisioned as always receding, viewed through the lens of history but focused on the unfinished-ness evoked by the poems' lack of closure. For Sandler, "The post-avant politics of what [Mackey] calls, following Duke Ellington, his 'blutopia,' are fundamentally wandering, as much projection as protest" (1379–80). The poems are bound (and unbound, perhaps) by their seriality. While they extend the promise of greater fulfillment in the future, they also bear the burden of never being complete. Proposing a way of living under such conditions is useful, as it is perhaps undeniable, if unwelcome, that the postmodern

challenging of traditional epistemologies has left us in a world where we feel
pointedly the lack of mythical models and the impossibility of their return.

Thus it is that readers find the politics of *Splay Anthem* to be secondary
to its eclecticism, its mythopoetic epic imaginary, to the play of sounds and
images. Megan Snyder-Camp, for example, in her write-up of the book for
the National Book Foundation suggests, "For all the social relevance and ur-
gency his work contains, the best way to read Mackey is to take it in the way
you would listen to one of the eclectic radio shows he DJs from his home in
Santa Cruz—sit back and let the sounds carry you." However, it is these very
apolitical impulses that represent the profound politics of *Splay Anthem*. Eclec-
ticism is always a motivated borrowing; mythologizing is an effort to retrieve
or found particular cultural formations; linguistic and phonetic playfulness
puts in question the terminology of activism and the effectiveness of artistic
resistance. Nonetheless, these elements of Mackey's poems represent an effort
to engage and overcome the problematics of the postmodern political milieu,
not a flight from material concerns. In answer to our current world—broken,
alienated, contingent—*Splay Anthem* proposes an alternative one: broken,
alienated, contingent, *but striving*.

BIBLIOGRAPHY

Beckett, Samuel. *Worstward Ho*. 1983. In *Nohow On*, 87–116. New York: Grove, 1996.
Finkelstein, Norman. "Nathaniel Mackey: Monophysite in Spite of Himself." Review of *Splay
  Anthem* and *Paracritical Hinge*, by Nathaniel Mackey. *Talisman*, nos. 32–33 (2006): 166–71.
Mackey, Nathaniel. *Splay Anthem*. New York: New Directions, 2006.
Nielsen, Aldon Lynn. "Now That We Know . . ." *MELUS* 35, no. 2 (2010): 19–35.
Palattella, John. "Poetry, From Noun to Verb." Review of *Splay Anthem*, by Nathaniel Mackey.
  Nation, September 18, 2006, 41–44.
Phillips, Brian. "Eight Takes." Review of *The End of the Poem: Oxford Lectures* and *Horse
  Latitudes*, by Paul Muldoon; *Scar Tissue*, by Charles Wright; *Splay Anthem*, by Nathaniel
  Mackey; *The Wilds*, by Mark Levin; *Hoops*, by Major Jackson; *Funny*, by Jennifer Michael
  Hecht; and *Collected Poems: With Notes toward the Memoirs*, by Djuna Barnes. *Poetry*,
  December 2006, 232–43.
Sandler, Matt. Review of *Splay Anthem*, by Nathaniel Mackey. *Callaloo* 32, no. 4 (2009):
  1378–80.
Simpson, Megan. "Trickster Poetics: Multiculturalism and Collectivity in Nathaniel Mackey's
  Song of the Andoumboulou." *MELUS* 28, no. 4 (2003): 35–54.
Snyder-Camp, Megan. Review of *Splay Anthem*, by Nathaniel Mackey. *National Book Founda-
  tion*, April 27, 2011. nbapoetryblog.squarespace.com/journal/2011/4/27/2006.html.

Thompson, Bob. "National Book Awards Honor 'Echo Maker,' 'Worst Hard Time.'" *Washington Post*, November 16, 2006.

Wilson, August. "August Wilson, The Art of Theater No. 14." Interview by Bonnie Lyons and George Plimpton. *Paris Review*, no. 153 (Winter 1999). theparisreview.org/interviews/839/the-art-of-theater-no-14-august-wilson.

Yu, Timothy. *Race and the Avant-Garde: Experimental and Asian American Poetry since 1965.* Stanford, Calif.: Stanford University Press, 2009.

IV. SELF AS CENTER

Sonics, Code Switching, Culture, Clarity

Mihaela Moscaliuc begins this section with a sharp ear for the bilingualism and multilingualism in poetry in her essay "Code Switching, Multilanguaging, and Language Alterity." The next essay takes on sound and sense in a different way, and as this project was completing around the time of the poet Amiri Baraka's death, Adebe DeRango-Adem's essay "New Living the Old in a New Way: The Jazz Idiom as Post-Soul Continuum" took on extra resonance. Gerald Maa's consideration of forms and structure and race legacies in "Arthur Sze's Tesselated Poems" suggests how the fragmentation can lead to reassemblage and a new kind of thinking regarding wholeness. Multiplicities continue as a focus in Randall Horton's "Ed Roberson and the Magic Hour" where construction, deconstruction, distraction, and re-reaction are managed with poetic intentionality. David Mura's personal and provocative essay "Asian Americans: The Front and Back of the Bus" explores poetry and the struggles for centrality, which can be seen, finally, as not about centrality at all, in a contrapuntal vision of what might be possible. The ways in which, even within identity communities, marginalization can be found are linguistically drawn in Charles H. Lynch's fascinating essay, "One Migh Could Heah They Voice: Conjuring African American Dialect Poems." And the closing two essays, both resolving this section and bringing the anthology to a close, Kazim Ali's and Rafael Campo's essays, which both appeared on the Poetry Society of America's site dedicated to exploring the idea of American poetics, give us first, in Ali's "What's American about American Poetry," a rangy, kinetic, deeply felt and thoroughly considered essay, an Instagram of intersections in poetry, and then, in Campo's "What It Means to Be an American Poet," a more personal effort by the poet to locate himself in the confluence of racial, sexual, and poetic lineage, and moving beyond (or between and through) to a wider view that perhaps Edward Said would agree with: that beyond the identity markers, indeed beyond the efforts to query, quarrel, and consider, or maybe because of them, one might find there is love, healing, and empathy.

24 ~ code switching, multilanguaging, and language alterity

A cartoon by Matthew Diffee published in the August 5, 2002, issue of the *New Yorker* shows a man answering the phone. "I'm sorry—you have the wrong language," the caption reads. You may have guessed: the man is white, casually elegant, presumably an intellectual, or at least a reader, if we are to go by the usual stereotypes: thick glasses and a thick tome he has bookmarked with his finger. Someone has interrupted his reading. Someone has assaulted his ears with foreign sounds. This someone needs to be put in his/her place: my way or the highway. This someone either owns the wrong tongue or has reached, by accident, a tongue (English) for which he/she is "wrong"—unsuitable. Either way, the non-English speaker needs to be reminded of the unassailable right of the English language to be the "right" language. The man's genteel, if perfunctory, "I'm sorry" and his mismatching facial expression (perhaps offended, perhaps repulsed) capture the tenor of some of the prevalent concerns about the future of the American national language. Today, the anxiety stamped on the man's face would be exacerbated by ongoing debates on bilingualism/multilingualism and on the potential of immigration reforms to forestall, decelerate, or accelerate transformations within dominant national discourses.

Poets often use "wrong" languages to exert their right, as bilingual or multilingual and exophonic Americans, to write out of and about experiences that do not fully translate into English or that deal with and/or address their complicated relationship with the English language. Through the use of code switching, multi- or trans-languaging, and fusing, these poets engage in linguistic and cultural practices that transmute and revitalize American poetics. Talking about bilingual writers, Sylvia Molloy says:

> One always writes from an absence, the choice of a language automatically signify-
> ing the postponement of another. . . . The absence of what is postponed continues
> to work, obscurely, on the chosen language, suffusing it, even better, contaminating
> it, with an *autrement dit* that brings it unexpected eloquence. That alterity, or altera-
> tion, also disturbs the reading habits of the bilingual subject. (74)

Alterity also disturbs, in important ways, the reading habits of the monolin-
gual subject, and instead of "unexpected eloquence," it often produces fertile
"messes" and ruptures.

What happens when, in the middle of a line or sentence, we slip momen-
tarily into another language, or onto other foreign-sounding or foreign-feeling
ground? Take, for instance, Barbara Jane Reyes's "she heard a noise / lipad
maya dagat araw mar y sol shouting rocks and wind" (88), Gloria Anzaldúa's
"my black *Angelos*, / *la bruja con las uñas largas*, / I hear her at the door" (184),
or Eduardo C. Corral's "Dolar / store cologne. / La pinche migra at every
pinche corner" (*Slow* 35).

I often ask students with various degrees of proficiency in another language
to describe how they experience the non-English "intrusions" as they read or
hear them in poems by trans-lingual Chicano/a, Nuyorican, Cuban American,
or Filipino American poets. The answers reveal a broad range of excitements,
fears, confusions, and various shades of indifference, often in some sort of
combination. Overall, they are versions of these: These "intrusions" interrupt
meaning and linear readings; they add exoticism; they smack of pretentious-
ness; they make you trip or skip and send you on detours, demanding shifts
in attention that often result in erasures; they defamiliarize and raise all kind
of questions about context (e.g., Why use this other language if what is said is
translatable in English? Why lose readers to the need to impress/make a state-
ment?). They induce frustration, shame, or anxiety; the languages "closer to
home" and to politics, such as Spanish, seem to produce more complex and
often conflicted responses, whereas languages with which students are not fa-
miliar, as is often the case with Filipino, Vietnamese, or Japanese, elicit briefer
and more favorable responses, often related to the way visuals (as in Kimiko
Hahn's use of kanji in "The Izu Dancer") or sonics contribute to conversations
between form and content.

As we enter a poem involved in multi-languaging, we enter a process of
cultural exchange and emerge, always, with *something*. If unfamiliar with the
other language, we may not know what this something is and might not even

recognize the moment as a cultural encounter, though the very awareness of the need for translation marks it as one. This something might translate into nothing more than a moment of disorientation similar to the one experienced by the speaker of R. Zamora Linmark's "Da Kind, My Da Kind," who complains to the poet, "The symbolism of the missing / i-twins in 'Hawa' disoriented me at first" (42). What will reorient this speaker, it seems, is further disorientation and blurring. (As he returns to the sinuous English of his tome, Diffee's cartoon man will need to readjust his ears and eyes and relocate himself linguistically and spatially.) To feel disoriented on native ground can be healthy, if not productive. If nothing else, one is forced to step back and scrutinize the original points of reference. Occasionally, more than that happens. When points of reference shift, even momentarily, we reenter the familiar with new eyes and a more acute sense of unexplored possibilities. The process is akin, perhaps, to the one experienced by exophonic writers of English—writers for whom English is not the first/native language. Novelist and essayist Nancy Huston suggests that those foreign to a language can be "far more conscious of phonetical rubbings and rhyming than native speakers" (63). While she refers here to exophonic writers, the same could be said of native speakers approaching the "other" languages of their co-nationals.

Some brief illustrations of poems in which the use of non-English functions slightly differently, and to different effect: in Dominican American Rhina Espaillat's "Bilingual/Bilingüe," for instance, Spanish supplements and is appended to the dominant English; in Cuban American Pablo Medina's "Perro en Tres Partes/Lady with the Dog," Spanish provides balance and counterpoint to its English twin; and Nuyorican Tato Laviera's "My Graduation Speech" reads as an example of recombinant poetics that performs the tension between languages and sociolects and seeks to legitimize hybrid speech.

In Rhina Espaillat's "Bilingual/Bilingüe," starting with the title, the poem instructs by providing Spanish equivalencies for some of the English words, such as "one there / one here (*allá y aquí*)"; "his daughter's heart / (*el corazón*)"; "his name / (*su nombre*)"; and "the world / the word (*mundo y palabra*)" (60). In sampling the Spanish, we experience it as supplement or alternative reading with different aural and sensual qualities. Placed outside the main utterance, within parentheses, the Spanish is also experienced as aside, as incidental or ancillary to English. These strategies call attention to translation as a mediating act.

The poem asserts itself as an act of mediation, a timid yet strategic deployment of private and public enunciations that recount the assimilative powers of English. Espaillat brings the intergenerational tensions ever present in immigration literature into eloquent, meticulously crafted articulation: the father, though proud of his daughter's poems and secretly in love with their English, wants to keep the native Spanish and the adoptive English separate. The native tongue, the tongue of intimacy, needs to protect those familial spaces that may disappear in the process of Americanization. The father's attitude is typical of many immigrants who see in their children's acculturation and loss of native language both an absolute necessity and a curse. As Espaillat recalls in the afterword to her 1998 collection *Where Horizons Go*, the Spanish of the "inside" had to be "pure, grammatical, unadulterated" (67). The exiled father's fear of what the convergence of the two languages might engender—perhaps a hybrid identity to which he would have no access, no "key" (60)—replicates, to an extent, common American fears about the contamination of the national language; such fears, however, have more complicated origins.

A poem about the impossibility of being bilingual in her father's house, "Bilingual/Bilingüe" appears to preserve the neat separation of spaces and languages and thus the father's command. At least on the surface, the poem dances to his beat: conscientious and cautious, it keeps the Spanish inside (in the enclosure of parentheses) and the English outside. The speaker's acquiescence is reflected in other formal gestures as well: the couplets that soften the tension with their perfect end-rhymes, each fifteen syllables long; the clear division enacted by the first enjambment ("one there / one here") appending the one in the poet's desire/psyche; and the caesuras in couplets 4, 5, and 7 that split—as per father's request—though the speaker knows that "still the heart was one" (60).

Certain gestures, however, show Espaillat circumventing the father's interdiction and its binary dialectic: the unevenness of the stanzaic structure (nine couplets) and of the syllabic count (fifteen syllables per line), the disarticulated Spanish of the "inside," and the two instances of Spanish that escape parentheses and stray into public discourse ("y basta" and "mis versos," one in her father's voice, the other in the speaker's). The two languages attempt to coalesce in other surreptitious ways. Espaillat notes in the aforementioned afterword that "a poem in Spanish may have more in common with a poem in English . . . than with a grocery list, say, or a piece of technical writing that happens to use Spanish words" (70). Indeed, in contrast with poet and fiction writer Julia Alvarez, with whom she shares a native country and native tongue, and who claims to "write . . . Spanish in English" (218), Espaillat effects transpositions in which English and Spanish build collaboratively the poem's alliterative and assonant soundscape (world-word-mundo; lengua-learned; said-basta).

Espaillat's poem is perhaps as daring as it can be, given its context. As an elegy for the father, it cannot let itself fulfill the balance promised in the title "Bilingual/Bilingüe"; in other words, it problematizes and exemplifies bilingualism but does not perform it.

Cuban American poet Pablo Medina's 2005 collection *Points of Balance/ Puntos de Apoyo* comprises monolingual poems paired bilingually: an English "fulcrum" and a Spanish "fulcro" on facing pages. Medina prefaces the collection with an explanation of the fulcrum/*fulcro* as an invented form consisting of six lines of unrhymed couplets with a syntactic/semantic shift in the middle stanza. The fulcrums "combine the dialectic of the sonnet with the imagistic power of the haiku, but are free of either tradition." He adds that the poems "are not translations but, rather, reflections of each other," and that the collection lends itself to multiple readings: in Spanish, in English, "or, ideally, as it was written, concurrently in both languages" (n.p.). For instance, the poem "Perro en Tres Partes," which starts, "Primero, la cola metrónoma, / andante con brío" (8), inflects the paired one, "Lady with a Dog," which begins, "When the strange dog came / to her I knew I" (9), but is not a hypothetical translation of it, as one might anticipate. As it enters the English poem, the "strange dog"—honey-colored and flea-ridden, sad-faced and anxious in the Spanish fulcro—carries forward the emotional, assonant metronome it has established in Spanish, triggering an analogy that becomes pivotal to the emotional argument of the English poem: upon seeing the dog approach the lady, the speaker knows he wants her "as much," his skin "a snow field / on fire" (9).

Medina's monolinguals build semantic and sonic dialogues while maintaining boundaries and seeking, as the collection's title suggests, balance. The paired poems recall Ana Celia Zentella's description of bilingual speakers as "two monolinguals stuck at the neck" (qtd. in Stavans 135). As Medina notes in an interview in *Redivider*, to a large extent each language chose its poem, or rather the poem arrived in its language of choice—the "highly vocalic Spanish" or the "sculptural" English. The act of mediation/translation is presented as an asymmetrical process, with the two languages sufficient in themselves and generating their own poetic text, but also dependent on each other for the production of a "concurrent" reading. One may experience the compartmentalization of English and Spanish as a version of Espaillat's strategy of containment, but at the same time Medina's insistence on the autonomy of each language in which he has created an authorial identity as a Cuban American may be read as a fairly radical gesture—one that demands a reading process that involves sustained code-switching and insists that equal attention be paid the dominant/English and the non-dominant/minority/Spanish languages. In an essay included in *Stories in the Stepmother Tongue*, fiction writer and poet Ha Jin mentions that in abandoning Chinese he had to change his task as a writer. "In English," he observes, "we writers whose mother tongues are not English face a different kind of tradition and task" (79). The "balance" of Medina's title translates, in this case, into a subtle yet forceful argument for a bilingual poetics, a poetics that gives its practitioners permission to live simultaneously within languages and the cultures that inhabit them, without having to constantly negotiate and shifts "tasks." As a poetic commentary on both the power and the impossibility of translation, *Points of Balance/Puntos de Apoyo* counters the notion of translation as a lesser act, an act whose outcome depends for validation on a preexistent "original" text.

Nuyorican Tato Laviera's poem "My Graduation Speech," from *La Carreta Makes a U-Turn*, responds obliquely to *La Carreta*, a 1953 play by René Marqués, about a Puerto Rican family returning from the South Bronx to the slums of San Juan. Laviera's 1992 collection, about Nuyoricans who start heading back home but make a U-turn and remain on the mainland, dramatizes the many spaces of in-betweenness his subjects occupy in the United States and within the English language.

Though distinct from the "mestiza language" of Gloria Anzaldúa's *Borderlands = La Frontera*, Laviera's hybrid diction shares its performative qualities. The poem reads as a linguistic and semantic instantiation of the complications that arise when the site of articulation is experienced as a site of historical and political frictions. Standard and vernacular English, Puerto Rican Spanish, East Harlem Spanglish, and other sociolects fuse and cross-pollinate. It is worth remembering that both poles of Puerto Rico's bilingual range are colonial dialects, the result of four centuries of Spanish and American colonialism. Puerto Rican Spanish draws on Andalucian and Canarian Spanish, Taino Amerindian, and African tongues. To this, add the fact that the language of El Barrio/East Harlem, which is home to the largest and oldest Puerto Rican community in New York, has been perceived, even among bilingual educators, as objectionable pidgin, a neither-here-nor-there that is the by-product of an undesirable inbreeding between corrupted (read "urban, street") English and

Puerto Rican Spanish. This skewed view persists, although linguistic studies on speech patterns in Nuyorican communities show that sentences that use both Spanish and English are grammatical, that the switching occurs only when structures are congruent. As these studies point out, more often than not, code switchings signal an expansion of communicative and expressive potential, not a means of compensating for lack of monolingual fluency.

As a rhetorical text engaging publicly with the dominant culture, "My Graduation Speech" performs its relationship with the institutions that it represents (and more specifically with the educational institution that has "graduated" the speaker) as well as with the language (English) that shapes its official narrative(s). Thus the poem may be read both as an implicit interrogation of the educational system responsible for the speaker's presumed inarticulateness and as a strategy for legitimizing non-assimilated, hybrid dictions. In an earlier poem, "English," from Laviera's 1985 collection *AmeRícan*, the speaker remarks on the discordant demands the dominant culture places on immigrants' dreams. To be granted the opportunity to desire, they have to "re-define / ambitions / in-your-language" (23).

Although "My Graduation Speech" opens by acknowledging an irreconcilable split—the speaker thinks in Spanish though he writes in English—the diction of these first lines, all English, is "obedient," compliant. However, lacking a language that can facilitate both thought and utterance, the poem quickly implodes; languages clash, intertwine, and fuse. The "speech" act, playful and witty, enacts its own engendering via code switching, paronomasia, and various inter- and intra-lingual translational processes such as transliteration and homophonic transposition. Languages bleed into each other and into the fissures created by linguistic and political conflict, dramatizing the making of pidgin as a language of cultural and poetic survival. "Digo" morphs into "I dig" ("now, dig this: / hablo lo ingles matao"; "si me dicen caviar, i digo, / 'a new pair of converse sneakers'"), "hablam" into "Abraham" ("abraham in español / abraham in english"), and the Spanish "tato" into the English "taro" and into the "tonto" (dumb) of "both languages." The "AmeRícan" language of "My Graduation Speech" works toward creating what I call a recombinant poetics—that is, a poetics that makes *something* out of the states of "in-betweenness" and linguistic and cultural hybridity occupied by bi-/multi-/trans-lingual minorities, and that alters "genetically" the dominant discourse. The linguistic registers of Laviera's poetics reflect an ethos inseparable from history, identity politics, and interrogations of power. The language of his poem dramatizes the experiences of Puerto Ricans living on "unincorporated" American territory (Puerto Rico) and on the mainland (particularly in New York), and especially the tensions of living in a number of languages, socio-dialects, and cultural traditions at once, especially when relationships among them are fraught.

This recombinant poetics—which is, by nature, a poetics that politicizes aesthetics—extends to "borderlands" writings as well, especially as conceptualized by Gloria Anzaldúa in her *Borderlands = La Frontera*. The "border" thinking, border crossings, border contestations of Anzaldúa's and other Chicano/a poets' writings involve, inevitably, all kinds of language crossings and language contestations. Therefore, the mestiza language that emerges through the collisions, morphings, and cross-pollination of English, Castillian Spanish, Tex-Mex, Nahuatl, and other components of Chicano Spanish, asserts itself as a language that needs to reflect the historical and political circumstances that engendered it. As Korean American poet Myung Mi Kim aptly observes, "Part of the meaning of being a historical subject" is "to engage in how to . . . refigure and reinvent and reoccupy the manner of telling" (Morrison 80).

In his 2012 collection *Slow Lightning*, Eduardo Corral captures the tensions of border politics between Mexico and the United States and "reoccup[ies] the manner of telling." The permeable English of poems such as "Border Tryptic," "Variation on a Theme by José Montoya," and "Caballero" absorbs Spanish into its textures and re-creates the multi-vocality of the borderlands. Suggestively, the diction of borders powers the heart of the collection, through its centerpiece "Variation on a Theme by José Montoya." Here Corral's code switching takes place between languages and forms, white and nonwhite literary legacies, textual and oral traditions, legitimate and "illegitimate" voices. As Corral points out in his notes, the poem interweaves language from Robert Hayden's "Runagate, Runagate" and from two *corridos* or border songs (75). An earlier note in *Beloit Poetry Journal* points to the poem's indebtedness to José Montoya's "El Louie," an "elegy for a pachuco and Korean War veteran" that blends seamlessly and unapologetically English, Spanish, and caló (37). Corral's piece takes off in Spanish with "Hoy enterraron al Monchie" and then slips in and out of English and Spanish, often within the same breath—"La pinche migra at every pinche corner" (35); "his cuates poured" (40)—with the ease of a serpent that explores while also demarcating its territory. When the Spanish goes almost solo, as in the section that begins "Qué chido his chistes. Qué / chido his tocayo. Qué / chido his peso-colored balas. Qué"

(38), the music is sinuous and obsessive, the "how cool" of "Qué chido" both celebratory and grievous. We segue into the next section with "Marooned in salmon- / *morning*" (39), marooned in the cadences of Spanish.

The linguistic "border triptych" that becomes Corral's diction—English, Spanish, and collocations of English and Spanish—is imprinted with stories of border crossings and their human cost, and with stories of resilience and unassailable desires. The border checkpoints that police the crossings-over depicted in the triangulating sonnets of "Border Triptych" (one in the voice of an almost-retired patrol officer and the other two in the voices of illegal migrants, one Mexican, one Native American) also police the entrance of Spanish into English. In the first section Jorge, who has been crossing back and forth for fifteen years and usually "doesn't say a damn thing" when searched, replies in English, at the officer's prodding and promise to keep his lips tight, "I smuggle bikes" (12). The violations that conclude the second sonnet—"I was one of ten women. Our mouths were taped. / I was spit on. I was slapped. The other women were raped" (13)—shatter the English, forcing open its borders. The Spanish spills into the third sonnet, about two "Indios" who, like many others, will take their chance. They bury the "forked tongue" of a cascabel so "for one night [their] names won't flower / in the devil's throat" (14). The forked tongue does bloom, but in a different way: in the sonnet's diction, in the polysemic punning of the concluding couplet, "Sapo shits behind a cluster of nopales, / & shouts out our favorite joke, No tengo papeles!" (14). As Carl Phillips observes in the foreword to Corral's collection, "The conflation (another form of code-switching), in the sonnet sequence 'Border Triptych,' of Chicano material and traditional English (i.e., white) prosody is at once an argument for (enactment of) reconciliation and a reminder of the differences, historically, between two cultures" (xiii).

We know that American English has always been, and continues to be, a language-in-the-making, regardless of our chronic fears of contamination, but we do not know, of course, the extent to which the non-English languages of the nation will (be able/allowed to) participate in such processes of transformation. We do know, however, that the recombinant dictions of Nuyorican, "borderlands," and Chicano poets—those mentioned here as well as others such as Victor Hernández Cruz, Giannina Braschi, and Guillermo Gómez-Peña—have the potential of exacting change. Moreover, these poets are not alone in recalcitrating against the ethnocentrism of English. Others, such as Kimiko Hahn in "The Izu Dancer," Barbara Jane Reyes in *Poeta in San Francisco*, and

R. Zamora Linmark in *The Evolution of a Sigh* and other works, make visible in their poems the dialogues and clashes between languages and cultures and unsettle, in the process, various hierarchies of values upheld by the dominant culture. Their use of Spanish, Japanese, Chinese, Tagalog, Filipino English (Taglish), or Hawaiʻi creole, and direct engagements with issues of translatability, interrupt and disturb—productively, I would argue—normative reading practices. Perhaps in time these poets will alter reading expectations as well, making us less likely to respond with "Sorry—you have the wrong language."

BIBLIOGRAPHY

Alvarez, Julia. Introduction to "Joe." In Novakovich and Shapard, *Stories in the Stepmother Tongue*, 218–33.

Anzaldúa, Gloria. *Borderlands: The New Mestiza = La Frontera.* 3rd ed. San Francisco: Aunt Lute, 2007.

Corral, Eduardo C. *Slow Lightning.* New Haven, Conn.: Yale University Press, 2012.

———. "Variation on a Theme by José Montoya." *Beloit Poetry Journal* 34 (2011): 32–37.

de Courtivron, Isabelle, ed. *Lives in Translation: Bilingual Writers on Identity and Creativity.* New York: Palgrave Macmillan, 2003.

Espaillat, Rhina P. *Where Horizons Go.* Kirksville, Mo.: New Odyssey Press, 1998.

Hahn, Kimiko. "The Izu Dancer." In *Earshot*, 87–93. Brooklyn, N.Y.: Hanging Loose Press, 1992.

Huston, Nancy. "The Mask and the Pen." In de Courtivron, *Lives in Translation*, 55–68.

Jin, Ha. Introduction to "Saboteur." In Novakovich and Shapard, *Stories in the Stepmother Tongue*, 78–90.

Laviera, Tato. *AmeRícan.* Houston: Arte Publico Press, 1985.

———. *La Carreta Made a U-Turn.* 2nd ed. Houston: Arte Publico Press, 1992.

Linmark, R. Zamora. *The Evolution of a Sigh.* Brooklyn, N.Y.: Hanging Loose Press, 2008.

Medina, Pablo. Interview with MD. *Redivider: A Journal of New Literature and Art.* July 15, 2008. redividerjournal.org/interview-with-pablo-medina-2.

———. *Points of Balance/Puntos de Apoyo.* New York: Four Way Books, 2005.

Molloy, Sylvia. "Bilingualism, Writing, and the Feeling of Not Quite Being There." In de Courtivron, *Lives in Translation*, 69–77.

Morrison, Yedda. "Generosity as Method: Excerpts from a Conversation with Myung Mi Kim." *Tripwire: A Journal of Poetics* 1 (Fall 2000): 75–85.

Novakovich, Josip, and Robert Shapard, eds. *Stories in the Stepmother Tongue.* Buffalo, N.Y.: White Pine Press, 2000.

Reyes, Barbara Jane. *Poeta en San Francisco.* Kaneʻohe, Hawaiʻi: Tinfish Press, 2005.

Stavans, Ilan. "My Love Affair with Spanglish." In Novakovich and Shapard, *Stories in the Stepmother Tongue*, 129–46.

25 ～ new living the old in a new way

The Jazz Idiom as Post-Soul Continuum

ADEBE DERANGO-ADEM

To write in the jazz poetry style, rooted as it is in a particular aesthetic attributed to African American cultural history, is to pick up on the dialects, rhythms, intonations, and poetic diction unique to black vernacular speech and music. Two poets for whom typographic representations of the jazz idiom play an important role in poetic practice are Amiri Baraka and Elizabeth Alexander, writers who share particular stylistic and performative aspects even as they stand for separate jazz poetry communities. Jazz poetry can be said to be a central expression and representation of African American musical genius, hailing from the blues' dialectics of slavery and freedom, evolving into a synthetic, though dissonant, musical form and hybrid site of vernacular influence. Baraka and Alexander, in establishing their own stances toward jazz at different historical moments, both establish and thwart the cultural politics associated with their cultural moments—for Baraka the Black Power movement, for Alexander the rise of post-soul—and, in doing so, subvert the notion that a black aesthetic can ever be fulfilled or should. In keeping with Tony Bolden's premise that "the poetic score constitutes the most radical formal experiment of the Black Arts movement" (30), it is my interest to read the jazz poetries of both poets in light of their use of music as a poetic diction in itself. In a comparative analysis of the Coltrane poems of Amiri Baraka and Elizabeth Alexander, this essay charts a dialectics of jazz influence in their work, paying attention to the visual and aural strategies they employ to illustrate the relevance and reverence of jazz in the current "post-soul" era—an era reflective of "the political, social, and cultural experiences of the African-American community since the end of the civil rights and Black Power movements" (Neal 3). In considering the two poets' Coltrane poems, I shall trace the contours of what a black aesthetic looks like now, as a re-signification of ontological meanings inherent in black music, as well as the conditions of emergence for this aesthetic against the notion of the post-soul paradigm and its new cultural politics of difference.

The jazz literary aesthetic is a necessarily shifting paradigm of sound and text best symbolically embodied in the Coltrane poem—Coltrane being a figure integral to the jazz tradition not merely as musician but as spiritual agent of the powerless in his championed genre of bebop. Bebop arose in the early 1940s as a response to the highly commercialized swing era by embracing the creative expression of individual band members, all in an effort to encourage unpredictable polyrhythms. Marked by conflicting changes, sudden nuances, sharp interjections, broken rhythms, and passages punctuated by breaks and distortions—what one could read as the aesthetic effects of a sociohistorical struggle to demand presence—bebop is also a kind of meditation on living against the odds and through what Fred Moten in *In the Break* calls "an ongoing performance of encounter: rupture, collision, and passionate response" (2). Bebop is in many ways a climactic expression of the trajectory of African American music, and a people's spirit of resistance, aestheticized and politicized in the moment, whereby one must contend with what Baraka calls "a terrifying freedom" (*Blues People* 227). Jazz offered a new, self-authored politicized aesthetic and clarity of vision for black artists who had been forced to see themselves through a distorted perspective.

Amiri Baraka is well known not only for illustrating the poetics of black power but for producing a poetry that embodies black expressive culture as a performative mode of resistance, to be mused upon but also used to challenge white supremacy. In dialogue with the Black Power and Black Arts movements of the 1960s and 1970s of which he was a lead figure, Baraka's poetry explores the politics of artistic production while making an art of political engagement using the blues and jazz idioms. Coltrane was one of the more emblematic figures in the Black Arts era, known for his bebop compositions that doubled as political statement around the freedom of black art. Baraka's "AM/TRAK" introduces Coltrane's legacy by calling up his early career, responding to the hostile reactions to his innovative style, and finally presenting Coltrane as an ever-present inspiration to whom Baraka turned while in jail in 1967 following the summer of the Newark riots—also the year that Coltrane died. The poet concludes with the profoundly felt desire to approximate, in his life and art, the commitment, discipline, and beauty of Coltrane's musical sense. Instead of waiting for the reader to spiritually connect to the music, Baraka's jazz poetics is reminiscent of his own self-styled musicianship as a blues historian and political agitator. Sascha Feinstein notes how, as "Baraka interprets Coltrane's music in this light, [he links] the direct, aggressive sound of Coltrane's tenor with the political temperament of the time" (120).

In this way, "AM/TRAK" is a poem about jazz whose internal jazz structure transforms the written word into verbal artifact, complete with its own particular rhythm, emphasis, pitch, energy, and spirit suggestive of the masculinist nature of the Black Power movement. Rather than pure praise, Baraka's poem concludes with the profoundly felt desire to approximate, in his life and art, the commitment, discipline, and beauty of Coltrane's musical genius. The translation of jazz instrumentation into written form is brought into clarity with "AM/TRAK," a poem whose visual rhythm and visible fragmentation represent an aura of jazz meant to leap off the "white" page and be "heard" by the eyes in aural syncopation.

The poem is structured in five parts, with each section longer than the one before and the lines in each section also lengthening the farther one reads down, leading up to the fifth and most climactic section, which ends not with a whimper but a bang. The first section loosens up Baraka's voice as he invokes Coltrane's name in an almost locomotive breath, repeating "Trane" as a mantra to get the poem moving. By section 2 we actually hear Coltrane "blow / love, history" (lines 2.11–12), and soon enough fellow jazz musician Miles Davis appears on the scene. Davis, however, never owns up Trane who, as the third section describes,

> clawed at the limits of cool
> slandered sanity
> with his tryin to be born
> raging
> shit (lines 3.11–15)

Baraka goes on to call upon Coltrane as a spiritual guide crowned by the clear raw materials of his music: "hot vowels escaped the metal clone of his soul / fucking saxophone / tell us shit tell us tell us!" (lines 3.30–32). In section 4 Thelonious Monk enters the scene. It becomes clear that, for Baraka, praise of a single musician is not enough; in order to do justice to jazz, one has to address other major musicians with whom Coltrane worked closely. Describing Coltrane's dynamic collaborations with Monk, Baraka writes:

> There was nothing left to do but
> be where monk cd find him
> that crazy
> mother fucker
>   duh duh-duh duh-duh duh
>   duh duh
>   duh duh-duh duh-duh duh
>   duh duh
>   duh duh-duh duh-duh duh
>   duh duh
>   duh Duuuuuuuuuhhhhhh
> Can you play this shit? (Life asks
> Come by and listen (lines 4.1–13)

In Baraka's representation of Monk's unorthodox melodies, the alternating individual "duhs" and hyphenated "duh-duhs" when spoken aloud produce a strangely harmonious, almost symmetrical effect—one difficult to discern in the visually jagged appearance of the poem. The colloquialism "duh" implies a kind of nonsense interrogated parodically when "Life" asks, "Can you play this shit?" While seemingly mad, jazz has a method, and one that Baraka believes should be taught.

In section 5 Baraka appeals to his own recognition, as a jazz and blues historian and poet, to remain steadfast to the music itself, to overdose on its "free" kick of reality rather than give in to the drugging effects of the status quo:

> capitalism beats our ass
> dope & juice wont change it
> Trane, blow, oh scream
> yeh, anyway. (lines 5.3–6)

"AM/TRAK" finally reaches a climactic point with the arrival of Charlie Parker, described as the

> *black blower of the now*
> The vectors from all sources—slavery, renaissance
> bop charlie parker,
> nigger absolute super-sane screams against reality
> course through him
> AS SOUND! (lines 5.11–16)

The climactic point in Baraka's poem is the direct invocation of sound, both visually and in the potential aural power of reading the capitalized phrase aloud. This is the section where jazz becomes "Convulsive multi orgasmic / Art / Protest" (lines 5.25–27) in what seems to be a sea of influences—musical and even political—converging fluidly on the same stage:

> Trane was the spirit of the 60s
> He was Malcolm X in New Super Bop Fire
> Baaahhhhh
> Wheeeeeee . . . Black Art!!! (lines 5.44–47)

Notable in the diction of "AM/TRAK" is its attempt to depict Coltrane's scream in a protraction of vowels and consonants that lead the ear acoustically upward. The end of the section refrains from crescendo, remaining in upward ascension as the music of Parker or Coltrane might, while also recognizing this music to be part of Baraka's own interiority: "Trane / my knowledge heartbeat" (lines 5.69–70). We are left with an image of Baraka in jail, listening for guidance to Coltrane's 1965 collection *Meditations*, an album that tells him to simply live and organize his "shit / as rightly / burning!" (lines 5.80–82). "AM/TRAK" sets up a disruptive, dialogic, interrogative pattern that is less a pure celebration of the liveliness of jazz than of living against the odds.

Published in 1990, Elizabeth Alexander's poem "John Col" elaborates an aesthetic "continuum" for the Coltrane poem even as it signifies its reverence differently. The poem's emotional minimalism—in terms of visible emotion, in any case—stands in contrast to Baraka's rapid-fire prose, instead influenced by jazz in its more quiet nuances, its subtle rhythms, near-invisible rhymes, and well-timed line breaks that seem spontaneous in one turn and restrained in the next. The lack of punctuation seems to borrow from the Black Arts aesthetic, while presenting an overall picture of stoic composure. This is a poem influenced by the same cultural content as Baraka's without declaring itself to be an authentically black portrait of jazz musicianship. Alexander's truncation of Coltrane's surname in the title "John Col" suggests an intimacy with the musician, while paradoxically also effecting a psychic distance or ambivalence. If one follows the logic that "unlike the blues poem, the jazz poem is without form," one could approach the poem as a jazz poem encased in a blues structure—a fittingly dialectical outcome given that jazz, as Baraka the music historian would say, was born from the blues (Jemie 56–57). The last three stanzas, or second half of the poem, illustrate and elaborate this dialectical movement, as they perform a melancholic "chang-ing same":

> the bloody foot-
> lights cup the dark
> where red and black
> are beautiful
>
> a terrible beau-
> ty a terrible
> beauty a terrible
> beauty a horn
>
> And this brass heart-
> beat this red
> sob   this   this
> John Coltrane Col-
> trane song (lines 13–25)

Alexander's description of a dimly lit jazz club's stage in the fourth stanza evokes the Black Power slogan "Black Is Beautiful" while highlighting the per-formative aura of such a phrase. The breaking apart of "footlights" also paints a suggestively Christic picture: Coltrane as a Christ figure bathed in light while enacting a personal crucifixion. In the Coltrane poem we are asked to move with him from a political to a spiritual place, a place where elegy effectively outlives fervent praise.

Alexander's poem performs a specifically post-soul ethos. Metrical features and textual arrangements mimic the features of jazz by seeming to be spon-taneous but in fact exhibiting great syntactical restraint. The relatively short poem is characterized by a precise count of words per line, what Meta DuEwa Jones—through a rigorous study of its syllabic arrangements—defines as "the tapestry of a skillfully executed jazz solo" (108). The poem is literally located "in the break" between the Black Power and post-soul moment, in that it can be both elegy and experimentation, can speak both quietly and loudly. The poem contains no punctuation to indicate pauses and instead uses spaces and fragmented words to achieve its syncopated beat. Alexander is engaged in a formalistic jazz approach, and in this way exemplifies the impulse of the post-soul aesthetic—to thwart the notion that black aesthetic is synonymous with a radical, recalcitrant, oppositional stance. In fact, Alexander's poem stands in contrast with Baraka's especially for its muted structure and restrained form, which seem to demand a skillful execution as opposed to the visible aggression that was a central feature of Black Arts poetry. "John Col" is more elegy than rapturous praise, forwarding a steady rhythm in which line breaks and silence do some of the talking. Both Baraka and Alexander use jazz improvisation and syncopation as thematic and idiomatic structures in their Coltrane poems, thereby revising the preexisting poetics of African American literature and also contributing to the emergence of an Afrocentric poetics. The difference with Alexander's piece lies in its offering of alterity rather than identification; Alexander never provides biographical information as Baraka does in "AM/ TRAK." Instead, Coltrane's personal story and music become metonymies for the musical black consciousness that function as subtext throughout the poem, citing Coltrane as a figure of transhistorical influence. In this way, "John Col" is still "soul" in that it still cites music as a vehicle of transcendence.

To inhabit a post-soul moment is not to effect a radical separation from the past but to remain in tension with it in a kind of spiritual struggle, a struggle symbolic of the emergence of new modes of understanding what blackness is supposed to mean or how it's supposed to sound through the jazz idiom. As Alexander writes in her essay collection *The Black Interior*, an ethical analysis of black literature must always strive to create a complex picture of blackness, one that can shed light on the possibility that an "authentic" black aesthetic of any kind may only exist insofar as one reckons with the reality that black artists have "selves that go far, far beyond the limited expectations and definitions of what black is, isn't, or should be" (5). Vying for a vast intimacy with what is/was black, the post-soul aesthetic, the black artistic community Alexander is a part of is in fact one that refuses to be institutionalized *as* black. I read the jazz poetry of Amiri Baraka and Elizabeth Alexander as exemplary works representative of the shift from soul to post-soul, in the treatment of the jazz idiom in general and in the way they elaborate—albeit in differing ways—the search for a usable and empowered black past that can offer new amplifications of identity both within and on the outskirts of "difference."

Indeed, to approach the concept of post-soul, one needs to think differently about difference; that is, about the multiple dimensions of blackness at work within the notion of modern black aesthetics, which can be both strategic political engagement dating back to the civil rights era and artistic practice looking to the future. Yet the futurity of black aesthetics leaves one with more questions than answers: Can the "post" be productive if it infinitely defers the meaning of the term it describes? What are the relationships between the post- and traditional markers of racial allegiance and authenticity? What is the putative promise/commitment of the black aesthetic now, against claims of a post-racial future? Does the concept of post-black open up the "text" of blackness, so to speak, or does it merely close the book on what the Black Power movement worked so hard to establish? In signaling to a future place instead of a sustained effort to recognize blackness in the present and *as* presence, it seems as though there are not only aesthetic but spiritual implications of a post-soul blackness as well. Yet such a term also seeks to strategically de-essentialize blackness while accounting for a more nuanced understanding of what a black aesthetic today should look or sound like—an imperative that must still account for the ongoing politics surrounding black identity as both a "with" and an "against."

The problematic of the post-soul aesthetic centers around the notion that one can reconcile the need to interrogate the idea of a more freeing notion of black aesthetics against a cultural moment that has been termed not only post-civil-rights but post-struggle-for-freedom. Who the post-soul artists are, and how they might be able to speak truth to power especially if they've come of age after the civil rights era, is central to the issue of what and how a post-soul aesthetic works. In one sense, black aesthetics is always a product of a past, present conditions, and potentiality; but a specifically post-soul designation can seem less prophetic than abandoning, just as what Bertram Ashe calls "a palpable tension between freedom—as artists—and the struggle for freedom—as black people" (619) continues to get played out at the heart of black aesthetics. Post-soul represents the will of each generation of black artists to reinvent themselves both against what Trey Ellis, author of the seminal 1989 essay "The New Black Aesthetic," has termed a "Stalinism of Soul"—an aesthetic encompassing traditional expectations for black artistic and cultural production—and toward an aesthetic that rejects such expectations. The core issue at stake is how the "pains, pleasures, and problems of race in the post–Civil Rights movement United States" can reconcile the notion of a post-black, post-soul moment with the need to claim a black aesthetic both self-determined and wholly undetermined by white cultural influence or a need to perform blackness "correctly."

Thus the potential of the post-soul aesthetic is not merely a gesture toward a generation of black artists secure enough about citing what is nonblack as part of their cultural inheritance, it is a gesture toward the elaboration of an aesthetic tradition that can be comfortable existing "out of time" and in a future space outside of all aesthetic conventions. The post-soul matrix is reflective of a set of practices still committed to the civil rights era; reflective as a rearview mirror to visualizing emancipation from one's antecedents and a practice of throwing all notions of monolithic blackness into indeterminacy, forwarding not an erasure but a redrawing of black aesthetic signification. Questions of who the arbiters and audience members of the post-soul black aesthetic are or should be remain open for debate, a debate that merits further exploration of how the transformation of black art and identity away from appeals to authenticity still requires critical engagement with how to assess the new black cultural phenomena associated with a moment beyond soul. Post-civil-rights art might be post-soul, but not all black artists who came of age in the post-civil–rights era can be easily named post-soul artists. An emergent body of theoretical work on post-soul aesthetics must recognize or reckon with the fact that its generational contingent is itself rooted in contingency. Post-soul artists can maintain allegiance to the black community while noting the unstable bedrock upon which such a community might be founded. The post-soul matrix is one that encompasses a history of various movements that together demanded different kinds of coherence, definitions, and relations to freedom at different times, even if such movements were united by similar ends—namely, justice.

Ultimately, Baraka and Alexander converge in their mutual belief in the redemptive power of jazz as a way to challenge the social order, renegotiate black subjectivity, and explore how the self gets rooted (or uprooted) in sound. Jazz speaks to how, in Moten's terms, blackness becomes "the extended movement of a specific upheaval, an ongoing irruption that anarranges every line" (1). To grasp the cultural tradition of jazz at the heart of jazz poetry is to let go of the notion that every turn in poetry—genre, style, mode, criticism—is anchored to or must be influenced by a set of fixed referents. It is rather to visualize or hear its impact and transformative potential as a ritual performance at once historically motivated, spontaneously present, and future-oriented— like jazz. Indeed, jazz is the divine fire of spiritual and political transformation, and both Baraka and Alexander embody the jazz influence not only in their reactions to the sound but in their praise of the transformative potential of its reverberations. Jazz is the soul of the post-soul moment, the literary force of inventiveness made into sound (or sound of inventiveness made into literature). So too do jazz poets know their program must be left radically unfinished as an inventive play between unity and dissonance, a multiplicity of discursive routes and citations, and an idiom whose roots are rhizomes growing scattershot into the ages, confounding all attempts to essentialize it.

BIBLIOGRAPHY

Alexander, Elizabeth. *The Black Interior: Essays*. Saint Paul, Minn.: Graywolf Press, 2004.

———. "John Col." In *The Venus Hottentot*, 32–33. Charlottesville: University Press of Virginia, 1990.

Ashe, Bertram D. "Theorizing the Post-Soul Aesthetic: An Introduction." *African American Review* 41 (2007): 609–23.

Baraka, Amiri. "AM/TRAK." In Feinstein and Komunyakaa, *The Jazz Poetry Anthology*, 2–7.

———. *The Autobiography of Leroi Jones*. New York: Freundlich, 1984.

———. *Black Music*. New York: William Morrow, 1967.

———. *Blues People: Negro Music in White America*. New York: William Morrow, 1963.

Baraka, Amiri, and Amina Baraka. *The Music: Reflections on Jazz and Blues*. New York: William Morrow, 1987.

Bolden, Tony. *Afro-Blue: Improvisations in African American Poetry and Culture*. Urbana: University of Illinois Press, 2004.

Ellis, Trey. "The New Black Aesthetic." *Callaloo* 12, no. 1 (1989): 233–43.

Feinstein, Sascha. "From 'Alabama' to 'A Love Supreme': The Evolution of the John Coltrane Poem." *Southern Review* 32, no. 2 (1996): 315–27.

Feinstein, Sascha, and Yusef Komunyakaa, eds. *The Jazz Poetry Anthology*. Bloomington: Indiana University Press, 1991.

Jemie, Onwuchekwa. *Langston Hughes: An Introduction to the Poetry*. New York: Columbia University Press, 1976.

Jones, Meta DuEwa. *The Muse Is Music: Jazz Poetry from the Harlem Renaissance to Spoken Word*. Urbana: University of Illinois Press, 2011.

Lacey, Henry. "Baraka's 'AM/TRAK': Everybody's Coltrane Poem." *Obsidian II: Black Literature in Review* 1, nos. 1–2 (1986): 12–21.

Moten, Fred. *In the Break: The Aesthetics of the Black Radical Tradition*. Minneapolis: University of Minnesota Press, 2003.

Neal, Mark Anthony. *Soul Babies: Black Popular Culture and the Post-Soul Aesthetic*. New York: Routledge, 2002.

26 ~ arthur sze's tesselated poems

GERALD MAA

In what is now midcareer, Arthur Sze has found a form that has quickly become the most prominent one in his most recent books. His first long sequence poem, "The Leaves of a Dream Are the Leaves of an Onion," starts off his fourth book, *River River*. Since then, not only have long sequence poems been the pillars of each subsequent book, each volume's eponymous poem has also been a poem of four or more enumerated parts. As seems the case with anything written about Sze, Dana Levin's recent review of Sze's 2009 book *The Ginkgo Light* ultimately focuses on his sequence poems. David Baker, too, was drawn to this form in a 2010 interview of Sze for the *Kenyon Review*. In considering what Sze's poetry can reveal about the racial and cultural politics of contemporary America, one must focus first and most persistently on this form most distinctly his.

At a reading at the Folger Shakespeare Library years ago, I distinctly remember Sze answering a question about his poetic practice with the word "tessellation." At the Poetry International Festival in Rotterdam in 2007, he used that same word when the poets were each asked their favorite word. "Tesselation," Sze said when I interviewed him in 2011, "is the word for using bits of mosaic and putting pieces together to create that large image, that large picture" (139). When we closely consider tessellation as a poetic practice, we will see that "tessellation" elucidates and particularizes so much of Arthur Sze's distinct style that one could see him absolutely successful at having this word be the banner for his mature poetic practice. With tessellation, the primacy of the long sequence poem makes sense, since each enumerated section can be a piece within the larger image. Additionally, in Sze's sequence poems the juxtaposition and simultaneity at the root of tessellation occur *within* each section—from image to image, vignette to vignette, phrase to phrase, even word to word—enacting the characteristic and idiosyncratic leaps of imagination remarked on so often in reviews, essays, and interviews about his poetry. Granted, many, if not most, of the short poems in and after his 1995 volume *Archipelago* work with these leaps, and Sze has started to experiment with employing his tessellated poetics in long poems *not* parsed into sections. However, the long sequence poem is the principal form for the maturation of Sze's poetic expression. That each of the books gets its name from one of these poems should be evidence enough. Moreover, each of these nominating poems is clearly an attempt— each a brilliant one—to discover a figure for tessellation's expansive multeity: an archipelago; the redshifting web, one of many "galaxies [that] appear to be simultaneously redshifting / in all directions" (*Web* 277); a quipu, "a device made of a main cord with smaller varicolored cords attached and knotted and used by the ancient Peruvians (as for calculating)" (quoted in *Quipu* 3); and the ginkgo leaf, with its dichotomous venation.

Tessellation is first and foremost a pattern built from juxtaposition, most often a pattern that can be infinitely repeated. At the most basic level, each poem's composition of four or more sections sets the foundation for the ever-expansive sense, for, as the *Tao Te Ching* says, "one begets two; two begets three; three begets all." The expansive sense enacted by the sheer number of sections resists binary and triangulated readings we have been conditioned to seek, naturally, from our poems. This quantitative fact builds the resistance to poetic closure into the poetic practice at hand.

An ostensible interchangeability is another defining feature of tessellation. In the *Kenyon Review* interview, Sze mentions how he regularly arranges and rearranges language and ideas on scraps of paper before writing a poem. The initial sense of the interchangeability of the parts actually allows the author to clearly display the artful deliberation with arrangement, much like the famous case with Stevens and "Sunday Morning." With tessellation the inevitability of the order is determined primarily by aesthetics, since narrative cohesion is subordinate to other concerns.

Before moving on, I would like to underscore the fact that tessellation is a practice, not a heuristic; a compass needle, not an instruction manual. In addition to the figures from his nominating sequence poems, Sze in the *Kenyon Review* interview offers a multitude of other models: astronomy, the ancient game of go, ekphrasis, and Native American ceremony. This proliferation of images shows that although tessellation is a formalist's practice, it is a protean one.

~

One would be hard pressed to find someone who can claim without quali-fication that Arthur Sze's poetry primarily engages with matters of race and politics. This doesn't mean that his poems don't have a particularly insightful capacity to lay bare the nuances of race in America, especially since race is a fundamentally *seen* phenomenon. Claude Lévi-Strauss starts off his seminal essay "Race and Culture" by foregrounding the visible nature of race: "The variable genetic blends, to which the man in the street refers in speaking of races, all involve highly visible characteristics: size, skin color, shape of skull, hair type, et cetera" (4). Homi Bhabha builds upon this observation for *his* seminal essay, a work as influential as the French anthropologist's. In "Inter-rogating Identity," Bhabha circles around the point that racism is predicated on the impulse to see and then to know conclusively and spontaneously (64). Étienne Balibar, one of the world's foremost living Marxist thinkers, concurs with Bhabha in a more forthright and caustic turn of language. In "Is There a 'Neo-Racism'?" Balibar notes that "theories of academic racism . . . mimic the way in which scientific discursivity articulates 'visible facts' to 'hidden causes' and thus connect up with a spontaneous process of theorization inherent in the racism of the masses." He continues, "I shall therefore venture the idea that the racist complex inextricably combines a crucial function of *misrecognition* (without which the violence would not be tolerable to the very people engag-ing in it) and a 'will to know', a violent *desire for* immediate *knowledge* of social relations" (19; italics in original).

With this understanding of present-day racism, tessellation arises as a privi-leged practice to upend racial misrecognition, because tessellation is one of the main sources for optical illusions. (I would point readers to Raymond Pat-terson's underappreciated masterpiece "26 Ways of Looking at a Black Man" as an example of a tessellated poem that foregrounds a racial consciousness.) To see the optical illusions of tessellation at work, we can look at the open-ing note to "Spectral Lines," the central poem of Sze's most recent book, *The Ginkgo Light*. The poem's first section shuttles back and forth between the speaker's current experience around a ceremonial Native American building and his memory of a moment within an ancient Chinese space. I use the word "current" provisionally, because, in effect, both the occurrence within the Native American setting and the one within the memory about the ancient Chinese environment are happening at the same time. This is the simultaneity characteristic of Sze's tessellated poems. Condensing the two into a temporal and spatial simultaneity, this section is a camera obscura that projects into the current realm of Native American architecture a memory of a classical Chinese funereal space. Here is the section in toto:

> Who passes through the gates of the four directions?
> Robin coughs as she tightens a girth, adjusts saddle,
> and, leading Paparazzo past three stalls, becomes
> woman-leading-horse-into-daylight. Though the Chu
> army conquered, how long does a victory last?
> The mind sets sliver to sliver to comprehend, spark;
> the mind tessellates to bring into being a new shape.
> When the Blackfoot architect unveiled his master plan
> with a spirit way leading to a center that opened
> to the four directions, I saw the approach to
> the Ming tombs, with pairs of seated then standing
> lions, camels, elephants, horses lining the way.
> I snapped when, through the camera lens,
> I spotted blue sneakers—but not the woman—protruding
> from the sides of a seated horse, and snapped
> a white-haired woman with bound feet munching fry bread.
> Peripheral details brighten like mating fireflies.
> Then Gloria pointed to the east, gasped,
> "Navajos will never set foot here: you've placed
> these buildings in the ceremonial form of a rattlesnake." (29)

The speaker's memory brings the Ming tombs into the building, and when the snapping lens—of camera, eye, and imagination—overlays the two, the woman's presence is fruitfully indeterminable. Is the woman Chinese or Native American? Moreover, is this a single body twice-photographed or two separate women individually captured? The cultural signifiers that would normally solve the problem, bound feet and fry bread, exacerbate the dilemma. The coexistence of what we regularly ascribe to the two is pretty much impossible: it is highly unlikely that one of the few existing pairs of Chinese bound feet could be found at the Native American groundbreaking or that Native American fry bread could be found at the Ming tombs. Bound feet without fry bread would locate the woman in China, and fry bread with unbound feet, in America. However, the coexistence of the two cultural signifiers on the same body reminds us that some Native American cultures probably have a penchant for women wearing overly restrictive footwear and some Chinese cultures eat deep-fried dough. If an optical illusion is nothing but a work intended to subvert and toy with the human impulse to see and to immediately know conclusively, this is an optical illusion of racial recognition.

It is important, however, to note that Sze does not divest the cultural symbols of particularity, history, and, bluntly put, meaning. He is far from a fatalist who views the world as one composed of empty signifiers, a world that easily lends itself to the racist paradigms of conflation and interchangeability which enable the fault we daily see of funneling all things Asian to Chinese (or Japanese), Latin American to Mexican, and threatening to Muslim. One sort of racism insists on the pure interchangeability of the symbolic structures of cultures, but the poem's opening section ends with a turn that bolsters the material efficacy and import of cultural signifiers. This turn is, appropriately, Gloria's words: "Navajos will never set foot here: you've placed / these buildings in the ceremonial form of a rattlesnake." Sze upends racial conflation, not with different cultures from halfway around the world, but rather with different cultures right within our borders and cultures that are formally lumped together under the one label "Native American." Not all indigenous Americans abide by the same traditions; even between tribes signs can have antagonistic, irreconcilable meanings.

Nor does Sze attest to the racist paradigm on the other end of the spectrum, that of insurmountable difference. With the double capacity of the signifiers, fry bread and bound feet, this opening scene from "Spectral Lines" resists an insular philosophy as staunchly as a purely cosmopolitan one. "Do not entrench boundaries," Sze says in a later section, "but work to dissolve them." When describing neo-racism, Balibar observes that culture has displaced biology as the discriminating measure for racism, now that the latter is no longer a feasible premise. This is the common ground Balibar's "Is There a 'Neo-Racism'?" shares with Lévi-Strauss's "Race and Culture," the text with which the later Marxist essay directly engages. Balibar picks his fight by pointing to "Race and Culture" as the harbinger of "differentialist racism," defined as "a racism whose dominant theme is not biological heredity but the insurmountability of cultural differences, a racism which, at first sight, does not postulate the superiority of certain groups or peoples in relation to others but 'only' the harmfulness of abolishing frontiers, the incompatibility of life-styles and traditions" (21). Sze concedes the inevitability of borders with the third section built around an anecdote about neighboring farmers. Moreover, the tessellated poetics ramifies the palpable presence of boundaries. When, a third of the way through "Spectral Lines," Sze exhorts his reader to "not entrench boundaries, but work to dissolve them," the operative word "work" sets his directive apart from the neoliberal utopia's. It is not that borders—these Frostian fences—*can* be dissolved, but we must work to dissolve them nevertheless. Weighted with and driven by the fatalism of a Sisyphean task, Sze works with a mortal's happiness Camus would attribute to wisdom, prudence, and silent joy.

Tessellation uses the borders between its constituent fragments, and the best of these artworks highlight the line where piece butts up against piece. In the opening section for "Spectral Line," tessellation clears the ground for the old lady, who is pictured with fry bread and bound feet. Sze primes the reader for that central optical illusion of racial recognition with a couplet that displays the mind in this act distinctly Sze's: "The mind sets sliver to sliver to comprehend, spark; / the mind tessellates to bring into being a new shape." Sze couples "comprehend" with "tessellate" as transitive verbs with absented objects. By elision Sze implies that the mind comprehends and tessellates nothing, but a palpable nothing that is ever-present in his corpus. The absent object of the mind inaugurates the absent body of snapped sight, and only in the vacuous spaces of object and body is one able to "bring into being a new shape." These absent objects of mind and eye drastically counter those of content-driven collage. With pastiche and collage, an absent object enacts a spotlight searching for an object always just out of reach. Hence the current reemergence of a genre like noir. Since collage is premised on content, it cannot do without a singular line of sight. Tessellation's primary fidelity to form, however, allows the absent object to enact something altogether new.

With its emphasis on structure and pattern rather than content, tessellation disperses a focal point. This dispersion is the product of collusion between tessellation's infinite expanse and its interchangeability. In her review of *The Ginkgo Light*, Dana Levin intuits and then struggles with this dispersed—this truly constellated—effect. With candor, Levin describes her initial bafflement: "I was not a natural reader for the work of Arthur Sze, as . . . there seemed to be no spot-lit singer in Sze's poems." Levin observes, "The 'I' of an Arthur Sze poem was most often an *eye*: poems I read felt nearly documentary in nature, both in form and feeling." I sympathize with Levin when she writes about how anomalous Sze's purely decentralized poems feel in contemporary Anglo-American poetry. With the rich pun, Levin acutely offers Sze's tessellated, "documentary" poetics as a powerful alternative to the confessional tone that has been our tuning fork for a half century now. With the constant evasion of the mind's and eye's objects, this unsettling poetics has the sheer space and segmented framework to achieve, resoundingly, one of Sze's aims, as mentioned in the *Kenyon Review* interview: "demolishing hierarchies . . . to utilize equivocal contrast as a means to heighten the tension between antinomial forces and give shape to the flux." David Baker, the interviewer, agrees with Sze as a reader of his poetry and then classifies this aim, of demolishing hierarchies, as "a primary aesthetic (and probably political) impulse" in Sze's poems, noting that in the "longer poems . . . the effect is even more vividly felt." If Sze's tessellated poetics demolishes hierarchies, proliferates focal points so much so that we have poems without a spotlight, and posits a fundamental interchangeability between any two constituents, these poems can only retain, and exult in, the particularities of each of their fragments with an aesthetic rigor premised on attention to detail. Looking at these poems, I can only say Sze has the gift, the patience, and the parturient doubt to do so. When we see him searching for the perfect word, whether it be a binomial name, a folk name, or a word from a foreigner's mouth, when we see him steer between the Scylla of insurmountable difference and the Charybdis of purely empty cultural signifiers, we witness him discovering that a culture's particularities are lived, social, and historical—that the substance of a culture's talismans, actions, and forms are formed through accumulation, practice, and aesthetic rigor.

In one of American poetry's most important and neglected tracts, *The Life of Poetry*, Muriel Rukeyser wrote that "American poetry has been part of a culture in conflict" (61). "I believe," Arthur Sze declared in a 2004 interview for the *Chicago Review*, "the poetic sequence is the form of our time—mutable, capable of shifting voice as well as location" (202). Looking at these tessellated poems in tandem with Balibar's utterly contemporary essay on neo-racism substantiates the Chinese American poet's claim that this sort of poetic sequence is an extremely fecund form for our historical time and predicament. Any tessellation cannot be a melting pot since it utilizes and pronounces the boundaries made when segment butts up against segment. Tessellation also seems extremely germane as a poetics for current-day America because it retains the expansiveness of manifest destiny, the bedrock for our national ethos, while acknowledging the crowdedness that manifest destiny enables materially but contends with ideologically. When Whitman in the 1855 preface to *Leaves of Grass* speaks of the "greatest poem" as a place of infinite spaciousness, with swaths of virgin nature between any two points of civilization, one cannot help but sense something archaic and nostalgic when he finds himself startled, on a road trip, by a mere three-hour stretch of road uninterrupted by a cluster of big-box stores or an "oasis" of petrol and fast food.

The crowdedness that Sze acknowledges is the very one Lévi-Strauss tries to stave off. "Race and Culture" ends with an isolationist turn: "the great creative eras were those in which communication had become adequate for mutual stimulation by *remote* partners, yet was not so frequent or so rapid as to endanger the indispensable obstacles between individuals and groups or to reduce them to the point where overly facile exchanges might equalize and nullify their diversity" (24; emphasis mine). What started as a speech before UNESCO becomes a call for cultural isolationism, dripping with nostalgia for a hermetic space that would make a utopia, a renaissance. Lévi-Strauss fears an inevitable homogenization when two cultures touch; an Other culture is a sort of contagion from which one should distance oneself. In this way, someone else's culture is as complex and important as one's own only when that other culture is remote. This is the flip side of the neoliberal melting pot stance, one that foregrounds, rather than obfuscates, the fear undergirding what was once—and still is, albeit in a later mutation—our national neoliberal cheer. This fear rears its head all too often, for example when a school vociferously celebrates black history but balks at busing Black American students in from other neighborhoods, or when the blares celebrating Cinco de Mayo mute out the racist under- and overtones driving an immigrant fear made visible by those very same faces we dress ours to liken. Xenophobia, in its various forms, is the primary structure for racism, and Lévi-Strauss's ostensible goodwill is as xenophobic as the ill will that wishes to violently limit immigrant rights and opportunities. This isolationist turn Balibar homes in on to critique anthropology as the exemplary form of academic racism: "If you want to avoid racism, you have to avoid that 'abstract' anti-racism which fails to grasp the psychological and sociological laws of human population movements; you have to respect the 'tolerance thresholds', maintain 'cultural distances' or, in other words, in accordance with the postulate that individuals are the exclusive heirs and bearers of a single culture, segregate collectivities" (22–23). Especially in our day, this cultural seclusion can only be a product of profoundly immaterial delusion, but culture's ostensible immateriality gives one the foothold to mystify oneself if one so wishes. Arthur Sze does not. By the time we reach the trenchant middle section of "Spectral Lines," we know that different indigenous American tribes have different, and possibly irreconcilable, cultural practices. So when that fifth section lists the names of tribes, a line for each, this is an act of honest differentiation. With a tessellated poetics described and brilliantly employed, this section orders the names according to nothing but sound. As Muriel Rukeyser says of writing: "All these words were known, . . . But they were not arranged before the poet seized them and discovered their pattern. This arrangement turns them into a new poem, a new science. Here, as everywhere, the arrangement is the life" (167).

After the American Civil War, "the United States of America" officially became a singular noun, even on the level of grammar. If I were to agree with Whitman's "The United States themselves are essentially the greatest poem" (I hesitate to, but mostly for the superlative), I would do so with Coleridge's banner: unity in multeity. The precarious nature comes from tottering on the threshold between coalescing into monotony and dispersing into utter incoherence. Sze arranges the fragments. He shores them up against each other by locking them into place according to their boundaries as you would puzzle pieces: how a boot-shaped piece could fit under Mississippi or an arm slung westward could hug a panhandle.

BIBLIOGRAPHY

Balibar, Étienne. "Is There a 'Neo-Racism'?" In *Race, Nation, Class: Ambiguous Identities*, by Étienne Balibar and Immanuel Wallerstein, translated by Chris Turner, 17–28. London: Verso Press, 1991.

Bhabha, Homi K. "Interrogating Identity: Frantz Fanon and the Postcolonial Prerogative." In *The Location of Culture*, 40–65. London: Routledge, 1994.

Lévi-Strauss, Claude. "Race and Culture." In *The View from Afar*, translated by Joachim Neugroschel and Phoebe Hoss, 3–24. New York: Basic Books, 1985.

Levin, Dana. "'I am Happiest, Here, Now!': Arthur Sze's Poetry of Witness: *The Ginkgo Light*." *Agni*, April 2010. bu.edu/agni/reviews/online/2010/levin.html.

Rukeyser, Muriel. *The Life of Poetry*. 1949. Williamsburg, Mass.: Paris Press, 1996.

Sze, Arthur. *Archipelago*. Port Townsend, Wash.: Copper Canyon Press, 1995.

———. *The Ginkgo Light*. Port Townsend, Wash.: Copper Canyon Press, 2009.

———. Interview by David Baker. *Kenyon Review*, June 2010. kenyonreview.org/conversation /arthur-sze.

———. Interview by Eric Elshtain. *Chicago Review* 50 (2004): 202–13.

———. Interview by Gerald Maa. *Asian American Literary Review* 2 (2011): 136–61.

———. *Quipu*. Port Townsend, Wash.: Copper Canyon Press, 2005.

———. *The Redshifting Web: New and Selected Poems*. Port Townsend, Wash.: Copper Canyon Press, 1998.

27 ∽ ed roberson and the magic hour

RANDALL HORTON

When dealing with race or racialization in poetry, Ed Roberson, author of several poetry books and recipient of subsequent honors—most notably the Iowa Poetry Prize and the Shelley Memorial Award from the Poetry Society of America—addresses the notion of race and its consequences through a poetic process grounded in *distraction* of language, whether it be through fragmented narrative or the enjambment of a poetic line to present multiple meanings to end-words. The *distraction* incites a spatiotemporal freeze-frame moment, which is merely a suspension of space and time. Within the poetry collection *To See the Earth Before the End of the World*, three of the numbered sections of part III, "Chromatic Sequences," offer an illustration of how Roberson addresses race and the construction of color as he guides the poem's intention via the "magic hour," each section addressing some aspect of coloring and/or light.

It is important to note that Roberson is working within a theoretical concept based on Reginald Shepherd's assertion that "blackness as an identity, assumed or imposed, is a social construct, just as whiteness is. But blackness is the marked construct, while whiteness is the default: it fades into a privileged invisibility" (47). Roberson is acknowledging that race is a construction, and within the construction, identity is based on skin color, and the coloring carries a certain type of history that needs to be forgotten, but only if it is remembered.

The magic hour, especially in cinematography, refers to the quality of the first and last hour of sunlight during the day, when a specific photographic effect is obtained. These moments are captured in the fragmented *distraction*, much like a camera's shudder, and the image is sequestered and then released. The spatiotemporal moments in the three sections i, iii, and 5 offer a complex interrogation of history and the fallacy/poison of skin color propelled by social construction in a language quick but always revealing. Consider section i:

The colors of light
arrived as a time of day
sat in the whites only.   *Formal or not*

the torch of film caught up with changes and American
color   photography was invented with blood.
everything turned golden brown done   in a low sun. The cities
  burnt. (60)

Roberson embraces conceptual photography not only to play with constructed ideologies of black and white but to serve as a chronicler of history as well, and by the time readers gets to "photography was invented with blood," they have already been freeze-framed within "Formal or not." The spatiotemporal moment ("whites only") exposes the image to dispel the image through a sign or symbolism attached to a certain event ("the torch of film"), thereby muddling the concept of beauty having to disassociate itself from the object ("American"). In Roberson's aesthetics, beauty and the object are forever tied, if only for a moment, within the spatiotemporal. Dexterity of language and double-jointed meanings conjure an experience rather than a narrative. One could call the work controlled *distraction* stepping outside that control to challenge notions of what color means in American society.

The spatiotemporal phenomena occurring in "Chromatic Sequences" allow for space, time, and connotative meaning to converge through *distraction* or the rearranging of the narrative based on polemic structures. Looking at how Roberson fragments and double-joints language when dealing with race and the residuals of race, his "poetry forces language to fail, to fall out of itself, to become something other than itself" (Joron 1). What remains interesting in Roberson's *distraction* is the one-on-one relationship with words, with a language that is always against syntactical continuity. Each time we come upon finite meaning within the poem, this could be considered the freeze-frame moment—the moment of connotation and crystallization, the moment that freezes the *self* or *subject* only to be released from the sequestered state.

Throughout the poem history and race are used as polemic grounding stations to incite moments of *distraction*, reflection, and perhaps epiphany through memory. This memory is in direct correlation to Jacques Derrida's *trace*, which "erases itself in presenting itself, muffles itself in resonating" (23). As Roberson frequently but not always focuses on some aspect of the African American experience, trauma often accompanies that memory, or *trace*. By re-creating trauma through syntactical disruption, and sequestering it through a freeze-frame event, Roberson is trying to get to the "reality of the art work in order really to find there the art prevailing within it" (165). In other words, there is an aesthetic beauty enacted through photographic memory, something primal, the scene horrific yet beautiful, perhaps a body hanging from a tree in the glittering sunlight bouncing off the river at high noon.

If we place the poem in historical context, it references the 1960s when race played itself out on the six o'clock news in the homes of contemporary America. More important, the photographic still frames of rioting, violence, and blood graced the covers of major magazines and backdropped most news-casts on television, thereby propelling the image. The images become reified through popular culture, or as Ron Eyerman notes in *Cultural Trauma: Slavery and the Formation of African American Identity*, "The two narrative frames developed through cultural trauma and transmitted across generations in a dis-cursive process of symbolic representation were reformed in the 1960s through the cognitive praxis of the black nationalist and the civil rights movements" (174). Within the freeze-frame Roberson identifies the dominant narrative or the structure in power and those that live underneath that structure in almost kaleidoscope-like fashion—quick and ever changing. These poetic tendencies lend themselves to Charles Olson's concept of "projective verse," which is con-cerned with how the "poet manages to register the acquisitions of his ear and the pressures of his breath" (53). Race and history become a human experience instead of a propagandist and rhetorical approach to an event.

When addressing race, Roberson utilizes not only projective verse but also ghost enjambment, which is the relationship an end-word has to the line that precedes and follows it. Then too, the line may act as a stand-alone entity. What this creates is, perhaps, three possible ways in which one can read a line in a poem that is constantly challenging conventional norms of syntactical structure. This type of poetics allows for investigating the complexity of color given that humans are neither monolithic nor monochromatic. Note in section iii, "Chromatic Spatiality":

> The spaces of color are more than simple
> aerial perspective
>   —those waves layering
> away each color to the blue (64)

"Layering" and "color" are oppositional to each other, while the "waves" con-tinue another realm of possibility in search of aesthetic beauty. The spatiotem-poral phenomenon operates within the scaffolding of history in relationship to race and image. Roberson's freeze-frame produces pockets that not only validate but also alter reality. If, as Kant says, "space is not a conception which has been derived from outward experiences" (40), we can think of space as a set entity through which we experience life. Roberson's poetics seems to be concerned with the idea of the object within space, and how this object is perceived with respect to aesthetic beauty. If the object is influenced by race, then race must be dealt with to dispel race.

Using dark as metaphor for section 5, "Darkly," to link history and negative stereotypes, Roberson again plays with the idea of color by playing with the duality of dark and light within spatiotemporal moments. Given that "light" has been presented as truth earlier in the poem's sequence, "Darkly" builds on color to continue the other part of the polemic. The temporal suspension in this section pushes against light and color:

> Some of the colors tar baby the light
> into not getting away from as color,
> Like the hole that swallows everything
> and never shines   and were never color (67)

"Darkly" pits the stereotypical "tar baby" against the purity of light to conjure a perceived morality. In these two freeze-frames (color/light and hole/shine), Roberson's spatiotemporal balance of light and color with the symbolic "hole" through which all information passes "shines" reflection on the way society willingly accepts the construction of race.

Light only has value when it exposes dark or darkly as a color. The image of light (perceived morality) by virtue of association with the dominant narrative strengthens itself by subjugating the object through traumatic experiences. This is how society advances the idea of color and, consequently, race. When Roberson constructs freeze-frames through the "magic hour," a poetic intent emerges reliant upon *distraction*. If by definition society is unwilling to (un) construct itself, then given the duality of nature, the laws in which humans create culture, perhaps the only way this (un)construction can occur is to operate within coloring's framework. Roberson dismantles color to actualize a collective self, a metaphysical existence where race matters only insomuch as history matters for the advancement of civilization, of humankind.

BIBLIOGRAPHY

Derrida, Jacques. *Margins of Philosophy*. Translated by Alan Bass. Chicago: University of Chicago Press, 1982.

Eyerman, Ron. *Cultural Trauma: Slavery and the Formation of African American Identity*. Cambridge: Cambridge University Press, 2002.

Heidegger, Martin. *Basic Writings*. Edited by David Farrell Krell. Rev. ed. New York: Harper, 1993.

Joron, Andrew. *The Cry at Zero: Selected Prose*. Denver: Counterpath, 2007.

Kant, Immanuel. *Critique of Pure Reason*. Translated by J. M. D. Meiklejohn. 1872. Mineola, N.Y.: Dover, 2003.

Olson, Charles. *Human Universe, and Other Essays*. New York: Grove Press, 1967.

Roberson, Ed. *To See the Earth Before the End of the World*. Middletown, Conn.: Wesleyan University Press, 2010.

Shepherd, Reginald. *Orpheus in the Bronx: Essays on Identity, Politics, and the Freedom of Poetry*. Ann Arbor: University of Michigan Press, 2008.

The Front and Back of the Bus

DAVID MURA

I

In 1989, in my MFA program, I met the African American poet Tim Seibles on the basketball court in a student game. I'm a Sansei, a third-generation Japanese American, and at the time, Tim and I were the only students of color in the program. We became friends and began engaging in discussions concerning race and poetics. One night we were well into one such discussion at a local pub when a white fellow student came up and asked what we'd been talking about. When we told him, his response was "But aren't we all just people?" In other words, race for him wasn't a subject that required further discussion, nor did he really want to hear what Tim and I might have to say on the subject.

When Tim gave his graduation lecture on black aesthetics, a white male poet professor muttered, "That's not aesthetics, that's paranoia." In the next class, this same white poet introduced his lecture on Horace by proclaiming, "Horace didn't write for special interest groups." Though this might have been news to the Roman slaves, the white poet was implying that those who wrote under a black aesthetic were writing for a limited audience. This same professor previously informed Tim that writing that leaves the *g* off "-ing" words didn't last. When Tim won an NEA grant while still a student, another white male poet professor told a white male student, "Us white guys didn't have a chance this year. There were too many minorities on the panel."

One night a famous award-winning white poet read at our MFA program. His poems were short, often depressing, surrealist lyrics; the response was polite golf applause. The next night, when Tim gave his graduation reading, including poems that would go into his first book, the audience responded with laughter, hoots, and waves of loud clapping.

Afterwards I asked myself why I'd been taught to judge the award-winning white poet's work as more literary than Tim's, and why I was ignoring both my own and the audience's responses to the two poets. At the time, I was more able to write a successful imitation of the white poet's surrealist lyrics than some of Tim's poems. Tim's work employed a more colloquial language, humor, an open embrace of sensuality, and a sense of narrative that seemed beyond my ken. Why, I asked myself, did what I understood to be literary standards make me admire a type of poem I could write and devalue a type of poem I wasn't able to write?

I recalled my first encounter with T. S. Eliot's *The Waste Land*: the poem made no sense to me. But then I read Eliot's collected poems, his criticism, criticism about his work, and the works referenced in *The Waste Land*. Gradually Eliot's poem and its value became clearer to me. In contrast, I'd done nothing like this with African American literature (in five years in an English PhD program I'd read five poems by Amiri Baraka and that was it). I knew nothing about the tradition of African American letters, nor had my teachers in literature or creative writing told me that such a study might be a necessity.

In our discussions, sometimes held late at night in the bathroom when other students were asleep, Tim had talked about how some of his poems were meant for the page and some were orally based and used the page to transfer the poem from his mouth to someone else's mouth. Again I knew nothing about this African American oral tradition; given my literary training, my initial reaction was that it could not, by definition, be literary.

After pondering my experiences with Tim and our MFA program, as well as my own personal history, I came to two conclusions: First, the literary standards and practices I had been taught were, in their exclusions, racist. Second, I needed to make my own study of African American literature, its canon, its history, its theoretical and critical contexts.

This epiphany changed the course of my literary development; I would not be the writer I am today without it. Looking back, I realize that while I'd experienced my own issues regarding my identity as an Asian American writer, seeing those same issues reflected in Tim's experiences and the work of other black writers allowed me to perceive *my* racial position with greater clarity.

Certain other Asian American poets of my generation underwent similar experiences in relationship to African American writers and literature. Lawson

Fusao Inada is a jazz musician, and his poetry is influenced both by jazz and by certain orally based practices of African American poetry. Jessica Hagedorn and Janice Mirikitani read their poetry with Thulani Davis and Ntozake Shange in Bay Area bars (the milieu where Shange created *For Colored Girls . . .*). In Los Angeles, Garrett Hongo attended a high school that was a third white, a third Japanese American, and a third black; he understood through his experiences there that race was a central wound and shaping force in American society. At fourteen, Hongo attended the Watts Writers Workshop and a class taught by Quincy Troupe. Troupe introduced Hongo to African American writers such as Ishmael Reed, whose *Mumbo Jumbo*, with its incantatory orality, mesmerized Hongo. Troupe brought Hongo's class to see Derek Walcott's *Dream on Monkey Mountain*. After the performance, Hongo lay down on a bench outside the Taper Forum and tried to absorb how Walcott's creole-inflected language and island vision had entered the soul of a boy who spent his early years in Hawai'i speaking pidgin; though Walcott's language was difficult for the young Hongo to decipher, its spirit entered him, spoke to him of the writer he wanted to become.

In Hongo's recent *Coral Road*, these various influences are present in the poem that opens the book, "An Oral History of Blind-Boy Liliko'i," a poem in the voice of a Hawaiian lap-steel, Dobro, and samisen musician. There's the influence of music and, in particular, the blues; the celebration of an oral tradition; the use of pidgin, a creole language, as in Walcott's plays or his "The Schooner *Flight*"; the connections between people of color; the resurrection of a neglected "minority" history; a celebration of what Henry Louis Gates refers to as "signifyin(g)":

> Ass why me, I like the blues. Hear 'em first time
> from one *kurombo* seaman from New Orleans.
> He come off his ship from Hilo Bay, walking downtown
> in front the S. Hata General Store
> on his way to Manono Street looking for
> one crap game or play cards or something.
> I sitting barber shop, doing nothing but reading book.
> He singing, yeah? sounding good but sad.
> And den he bring his funny guitar from case,
> all steel and silver with plenty *puka* holes all over the box.
> Make the tin-kine sound, good for vibrate.

> Make dakine shake innah bones sound,
> like one engine innah blood. Penetrate.
> He teach me all kine songs. Field hollers, he say,
> dakine slave g'on use for call each oddah
> from field to field. Ju'like cane workers . . .
> Spooky. No can forget. Ass how I learn for sing. (3–4)

II

Given reports from MFA students of color, I would suggest my grad school experiences are still being duplicated. Works by writers of color are still often viewed as secondary rather than necessary. This has a deleterious effect on all students, but with Asian American students it often means they are never presented with an alternative view of literature.

How to think and observe through the lens of race is a knowledge many Asian Americans do not grow up with, certainly not in the same way that a young Hmong or Chinese American learns the culture and traditions of the family. Where African Americans possess a culture that's responded to their racial situation in America for four hundred years, this isn't the case with Asian Americans. The racial history of Asian Americans is something even most Asian Americans are relatively unaware of.

In my second book of poetry, *The Colors of Desire*, I began to deal with the legacy of the Japanese American internment and its effect on myself and my family, and, at the same time, to examine my sexuality through the lens of race. "Photograph of a Lynching," the first section of the title poem, starts by describing one such photograph. It then pictures my father on a day pass leaving his internment camp and getting on a segregated bus in 1942:

> And though directly above them,
> a branch ropes the dead negro in the air,
> the men too focus their blank beam
> on the unseen eye. Which is, at this moment, us.

> Or, more precisely, me. Who cannot but recall
> how my father, as a teenager, clutched his weekend pass,
> passed through the rifle towers and gates
> of the Jerome, Arkansas camp, and, in 1942,
> stepped on a bus to find white riders

motioning, "Sit here, son," and, in the rows beyond,
a half dozen black faces, waving him back,
"Us colored folks got to stick together." (4)

The poem then switches to a scene of myself in a porno movie theater, thirty-five years later, watching *Behind the Green Door*:

On the screen
a woman sprawls on a table, stripped, the same one
on the Ivory Snow soap box, a baby on her shoulder,
smiling her blond, practically pure white smile.
Now, after being prepared and serviced slowly
by a handful of women, as one of them
kneels, buries her face in her crotch,
she is ready: And now he walks in—

Lean, naked, black, streaks of white paint on his chest
and face, a necklace of teeth, it's almost comical,
this fake garb of the jungle, Africa and All-America,
black and blond, almost a joke but for the surge
of what these lynchers urged as the ultimate crime
against nature: the black man kneeling to this kidnapped
body, slipping himself in, the screen showing it all . . .

I left that theater, bolted from a dream into a dream.
I stared at the cars whizzing by, watched the light change,
red, yellow, green, and the haze in my head from the hash,
and the haze in my head from the image, melded together,
    reverberating.
I don't know what I did afterwards. Only, night after night,
I will see those bodies, black and white (and where am I,
the missing third?), like a talisman, a rageful, unrelenting release.
    (4–5)

In this poem I'm trying to unlock the legacy of the Japanese American internment by juxtaposing it with other images concerning race in America. The internment illustrates a racial practice that runs throughout Asian American history, from Angel Island to anti-Asian immigration laws to the internment to Wen Ho Li. The citizenship of Asian Americans is always subject to questioning; this questioning increases as tensions between America and any Asian country increases. Asian Americans are not Americans in the same way white Americans are; our status as Americans can always be revoked.

Part of the poem's inspiration is a brief reference to the segregated South in Bill Hosokawa's history of second-generation Japanese Americans, *Nisei: The Quiet Americans*:

> The evacuees who were sent to Arkansas had been astonished to find they were regarded as white by the whites and colored by the blacks. The whites insisted the Japanese Americans sit in front of the bus, drink from the white man's fountain and use the white man's rest rooms even though suspecting their loyalty to the nation. And the blacks embarrassed many a Nisei when they urged: "Us colored folks has got to stick together."
>
> If there was no middle ground in the South's polarized society of black and white, in the rest of the country after the war, a Nisei could live as a yellow-skinned American without upsetting too many people, and he also discovered it was not particularly difficult to be accepted into the white man's world. (473)

After the war, Hosokawa pictures the Nisei as wanting to be "accepted into the white man's world." In this, he duplicates the gender/racial hierarchy placing white men at the top. Hosokawa voices no desire to be accepted into the black world, despite the racial solidarity blacks on the buses offered Nisei. When I asked my father about his experiences on day passes out of the Jerome internment camp, he said, "We sat where the whites sat on the bus, at the lunch counters, at the movies."

Thus my father's identity wasn't simply involved with his internment because of his own ethnicity and race. No, his identity also involved where he, as a Japanese American, was situated in the matrix of black-white relationships. Once he stepped on that bus, he had to choose. Did he define himself as an "honorary white," or did he sit in the back of the bus, with blacks who saw him as a person of color? Like many Nisei, my father sided with the white world.

"Photograph of a Lynching" then is also about how my father and many Nisei reacted to the camps—with a fervent desire to be "accepted into the white man's world." By achieving economic success, by trying to be "two hundred percent American," by becoming one of the first Asian American families to live in our white Chicago suburb, my father believed he had reached his desired goal. In such reasoning, his son's identity would not involve issues of ethnicity or race.

But that is not how I felt growing up. Confronted with the TV and movies of the fifties and sixties and beyond, my generation viewed images of Asian men either as the World War II enemy or as coolies, cooks, and houseboys, as figures of buffoonery and racial stereotypes. The Japanese American actor Marc Hayashi has summed up these latter tropes: "Every culture needs its eunuchs, and we're it. Asian American men are the eunuchs of America." When I repeated Marc's observation to the black novelist Alexs Pate, he remarked, "And black men are the sexual demons"—a stereotype intimately involved with the lynchings of black men.

Just as my father steps onto a bus in the segregated South and confronts the divide of black and white, so I find myself confronting that divide in the pornographic movie *Behind the Green Door*. But for me it's not as simple as choosing whom I'm going to sit with. Instead, my choices are riddled with complications and contradictions. First, there's the fact that this is a pornographic film and, as such, involves depictions of sexuality through an obviously male lens. But is that lens a *white* male lens? In the stereotypical tropes linking black males with "tribal" Africa and a "primitive" or savage sexuality, the film regurgitates the black man as "sexual demon." But the question of what I, as an Asian American male, am to do with this depiction, or where I fit in, is not part of its white male lens.

When I brought this poem to my MFA workshop, both the white poet instructor and the white students were confused by the line "I will see those bodies, black and white (and where am I / the missing third?)." After class I had a long argument with the instructor, in which I pointed out that how one reads that line depends in part on one's race. Yes, a white reader might not read "the missing third" as referring to an Asian American, I said, but wouldn't an Asian American man think that the "missing third" might be an Asian American man?

Of course, this is what the poem is trying to depict—"the missing third." This "missing third" could be read as Asian American, as Asian American male, and as myself. What's missing is my presence either in the film or as an audience member. What's missing is Asian or Asian American male sexuality.

III

So "where am I, the missing third?" is for me a complicated and perhaps impossible question. At the same time I'm aware that Asian American masculinity is a subject few readers of other races deem of any significance.

"The Affair" is a duet of fictional dramatic monologues (sometimes mistakenly read as autobiographical). In the poem the Japanese American male poet enters an affair with a married white woman photographer:

> We met at this party. Instantly, I hated her, hated
> her husband too, she in a black cocktail dress
> and string of pearls, her eyes blue and furtive,
> that I would catch gazing up at me as she bent down,
> took a sip from her wine, while he stood beside her,
> hand at her back, silver hair slicked back,
> black jacket, shirt, pants, his face a craggy ruddiness,
> the artsy version of say Jack Palance . . .
>
> And yet, not far from
> the lintel of my awareness, there was no getting around
> the fact that they were white, that what captivated and
> enraged me were the compensations they were unaware of
> in their beauty, in their so calmly entering the center
> of my attention, in the correct proportion
> of their presence together. And as each wave
> of compulsion, comparison hit me, I hated them more,
> filled with a *ressentiment* so textbook classic,
> you would have thought it would have toppled me over
> in my tracks, or even turned me around, walked me
> straight back out the door to check the apartment
> number, the address, the building, suddenly certain
> I was in the wrong place (53–54)

In trying to assess his position vis-à-vis this couple, the speaker explores his sense of the couple's social cachet and his own reaction to that perceived cachet. This cachet involves their cultural sophistication which acts as an advertisement for their wealth or class. Though the issues of the woman's class get more complicated later, in the speaker's mind it initially seems "more a class thing than race." The speaker is at a liminal moment in his understanding of race; he's grown up in a white environment and, until recently, has never questioned the assumptions of that environment in any conscious or critical way. But his questioning comes less from any literary or political influence and more from his growing awareness of his own *ressentiment* toward the white world, the automatic presumptions of centrality and value that, for him, the white couple seem to embody. Is this projection on his part? Yes, of course. But what is the source of the projection?

If this speaker had grown up in a solid ethnic enclave—that is, if his first sexual experiences and his family's cultural traditions had decreed his sexual desires be directed toward his own ethnic group—he would be in a different position. But the speaker has grown up in a predominantly white environment; as a result, the social cachet of whites extends to and informs his own sexual desires. His resentment stems from his belief—or awareness—that both members of this couple are automatically situated through their race in a superior position to his as an Asian American male. Certainly he's aware that the racial basis of his resentment and his desire for this woman derive from the same source. Now the reader may decide that everything expressed by this speaker is produced by his own racially twisted mind and his own individual sense of inferiority, and might be caused by reasons other than race. But for me this portrait explores how certain Asian American males contextualize their sexuality and its relationship to the white world.

Beyond the sociological/psychological aspects of race and sexuality, there's another level at which the language is working. Here, to be less subjective, I'll examine a poem on a similar theme by another Asian American poet.

In Garrett Hongo's "Four Chinatown Figures," the poet explores a racial confrontation where race, sexuality, and class intertwine. The poem opens with a white couple, "a Wilshire lawyer and city planner out on the town," walking through Chinatown, the man in a tuxedo, the woman in "a white lamé" dress. After describing their interactions—the couple kiss—the poem introduces two Chinese immigrant dishwashers. Instantly the scene becomes racialized:

> Two dishwashers step from the back door of the Golden Eagle
> arguing about pay, about hours, about trading green cards
> with cousins for sex, setups with white women, for cigarettes
> or a heated hotel room to sleep in on a dry, newspaper bed.
> *Bok-guai*, they curse with their eyes, *Lo-fahn*, as the four nearly
>   collide,
> separate galaxies equal in surprise as they wheel to face each other.
> The lawyer thinks little of these punks in T-shirts and Hong Kong
>   jeans,

but the woman rhapsodizes, for no reason, in suspense/thriller
   prose—
Slender and boylike, the bull's ring curl to their flimsy moustaches;
They must be cold in this dry, winter chill of late December in L.A.
(57)

Bok-guai means "white ghost"; *Lo-fahn* is a more neutral word for white per-
son. Automatically, the Chinese immigrants assume they occupy a position
of racial antagonism with the white couple. This antagonism isn't caused so
much by the couple's actions as by a system of racial hierarchy that determines
the existence and identity of these four people within American society. For
her part, the woman here senses the "otherness" of the Chinese immigrants,
but at this point she, like the white man, seems unaware of the presence of a
racial antagonism.

After the woman's racial rhapsody, the gazes of the two dishwashers lock
with those of the couple, a brief *frisson* of urban racial challenge. The white
woman's warning system goes up:

She tells herself, *Forget it, c'mon*, and, with a hooked finger,
snaps at the man's satin cummerbund. They turn away.
Without a gesture, in the greasy dark, the two Chonks turn away
   too,
back towards each other, and hear, quickening away behind them,
steps receding into the light din of street noise and sidewalk chatter.
The fair one says, audibly, and in English, *Kiss me, white ghost*
(57–58)

As immigrants, the two dishwashers live with other immigrants from their
ethnic group. But they recognize what their Asian faces and ethnicity mean in
regard to the white world; they've also absorbed the prestige that that world
bestows upon white women. Now, this prestige has been created more by
white men than white women. Still, it would be disingenuous to say the white
woman isn't aware of that prestige. It's what allows her to form her little rhap-
sody, to place the Chinese workers within some film noir scene she might be
starring in.

It's here that the issues of racial antagonism intertwine with issues of liter-
ary modes, particularly the question "What is realism?" Although the poem
proffers an ostensibly realistic description of this interracial encounter, the

description drifts to where tropes of the "suspense/thriller" *Chinatown* bubble to the surface. Thus the issue of what is real and what is projected, on either side of this racial divide, becomes ambiguous. In this way, the writing highlights the instability of a realistic aesthetic when it confronts any encounter across the racial divide; such encounters ignite the question of who defines the reality of that encounter, who describes and interprets what is happening. This involves not simply *individual* subjectivities but a contrast in the ways whites and people of color construct their social reality, in how membership in a racial group forms one's subjectivity.

Realism, as David Palumbo-Liu has cogently argued, is an agreement, predicated upon shared assumptions of what the world actually is. It is also an exchange between the reader and the writer where, if what the writer presents is too "other" to the reader, the agreement of realism begins to break down. This, I would submit, is what is happening in Hongo's poem. Starting in a seemingly objective third person, the poem appears to presume the reader can place the white couple, since the culture is rife with portraits of such a couple and what they might feel and think upon visiting Chinatown. But within the white woman's view of the encounter, the poem moves into a more stylized language; the stability of this presumed realism begins to falter. As the poem asserts the reality of the two Chinese immigrant dishwashers, the writing marks a limit to what the white couple can perceive. In certain ways, this limitation is also there for the reader, since an intimate portrayal of the consciousness of two Chinese immigrant dishwashers is rarely presented in American culture.

In other words, the poem provides a glimpse into an alternate or "alien" reality, and this makes its epistemological status uncertain: What are the sources of the knowledge being presented here, of the poem's picture of this encounter? The poem ultimately challenges the white couple's views of the encounter and their limitations, but it also acknowledges its own limitations; it never quite enters the consciousness of the immigrant Chinese workers in the way it does the white woman. It knows her, in the end, better than the workers, though it delineates the outlines of a Chinese immigrant consciousness quite different from hers (and, of course, from the consciousness of the white male, who seems rather oblivious to even the presence of a racial Other).

Thus the poem may start as a realistic description, but that realism becomes unstable *because of the presence of race*. Eventually the poem transforms into an allegory about race (hence the "figures" in the title). One's ability to perceive the complications of this allegory depends on one's understanding of race and a familiarity with the tropes Hongo is working with. With its densely detailed poetic descriptions, the poem's surface doesn't resemble the abstracted language of most allegories, but beneath that surface the four persons involved must be read as positioned by race—that is, as racially designated allegorical figures: the white man, the white woman, the two immigrant Chinese dish-washers. These designations posit a level of abstraction almost always present in a racial reading of poems dealing with the experiences of people of color. And since a racial reading is so often part of the way poems by poets of color must be read, missing this allegorical reading means the reader misses the complexity embodied in the poem's language.

Of course, poems by white poets that ostensibly do not deal with race can also be read through a racial lens—that is, interpreted as an expression of white consciousness. But more often than not, the presence of the racial Other is absented from the universe of the white poet's poem. As a result, the level of racial allegory is (thought to be) absent. Most white poets' existence is racialized only when they acknowledge it consciously. In contrast, many poets of color read their entire existence as racialized, whether race is ostensibly the subject of a poem or not.

IV

In general, when charges of racism or racial bias are brought by people of color, a struggle ensues over the interpretation, or reading, of reality. When whites deny the charges, they are saying to the person of color, "What you apprehend doesn't exist. You're making up what isn't there. Or you're making an incorrect interpretation of what has happened. There is a proper way of reading what has happened, and you're reading into the text of reality a meaning that doesn't exist." The stance here is not so different from a professor chastising a student for an incorrect/illegitimate interpretation of a poem. The white person sees himself as the professor because the white person presumes the position of ultimate judge, the arbitrator of what is a proper or improper interpretation.

But the person of color obviously knows that the white person has a differ-ing interpretation of the events. The person of color also knows what the white person will say in response: that the person of color has misinterpreted certain actions—the text of reality. The person of color also knows that the white person will inevitably have more power to enforce the "white" interpretation.

In other words, the person of color understands the situation as a struggle between two subjectivities, that of the white person and that of the person of color. Both subjectivities exist; both are real. But the person of color alone assumes from the start that both subjectivities exist—and therefore alone must account for the origins and purposes of both subjectivities. For the person of color, the white view of reality makes perfect sense; its function is to allow whites to maintain a disproportionate share of power in our society. There could be no racial hierarchy without a white subjectivity that views white subjectivity as objective and primary.

The assessment by white writers of the works by writers of color concerning race takes place in the same manner. Most writers of color assume we live in a society that practices a racial hierarchy, a society where race is a primary, not a secondary, reality. That hierarchy produces two very different interpretations of the reality in which we live. To establish the existence of their interpretation, writers of color know they are entering into a struggle with white subjectivity. They write against the white view that their subjectivity does not exist or is not a necessity; is secondary or illegitimate, invalid. This struggle cannot be construed as simply an individual struggle; it involves two very different interpretations of the ways our society and our literature function, over who is and is not central to the American experience.

BIBLIOGRAPHY

Hongo, Garrett. "Four Chinatown Figures." In *The River of Heaven*, 57–58. Pittsburgh: Carnegie Mellon University Press, 1988.
———. "An Oral History of Blind Boy Liliko'i." In *Coral Road*, 3–4. New York: Alfred A. Knopf, 2011.
Hosokawa, Bill. *Nisei: The Quiet Americans*. New York: William Morrow, 1969.
Mura, David. "The Affair." In *The Colors of Desire*, 51–54.
———. "The Colors of Desire." In *The Colors of Desire*, 4–5.
———. *The Colors of Desire*. New York: Anchor, 1995.
Palumbo-Liu, David. *The Deliverance of Others: Reading Literature in a Global Age*. Durham, N.C.: Duke University Press, 2012.

29 ～ one migh could heah they voice: conjuring african american dialect poems

CHARLES H. LYNCH

In my creative writing workshop at New Jersey City University I emphasized how concrete diction conveys sensuous experiences. "Since our eyes can dominate our sense perceptions, let's close them for three minutes and imitate your neighborhoods' sounds." Cars zoomed. Trucks honked. Sirens whirred. "Awright. Move it along!" Gruff shouts and shrieks signaled someone was offended or accosted. "Scuse me. Spare some change?" There were calls: hoots, "¡Mira! ¡Mira!" a shrill whistle, "Yo!" "You sho lookin' fine, baby." Dogs barked and snarled. A mother scolded her child: "Told ju gid over here! Shush!" Drug hustlers whispered invitations. Guns popped and clattered.

I was surprised and irritated. In that sonic cull from urbanized Hudson and Essex Counties, danger and confrontation loomed too large. Absent were "See yuh latuh," "*Buenos días*," "Bye-bye," and "Have a blessed day." No kids shouted while at play. No high heels clacked to Sunday services. No convivial chatter, bird chirps, or humming. Perhaps a surfeit of TV, movies, video games, and edgy popular music had attuned students' ears to limited soundtracks of inner city life. A manufactured meta-reality blocked affirming words and gentler noises.

Later I pondered: What sounds and words do I rarely notice—or shut out? In my poetry, especially, who do I hear, and who speaks in it with me? In this essay I excavate questions and conclusions that may interest other black poets. For example, how do social and literary voices we hear, conjure, and transmit shape our cultural and racial identities? How can we honor what Sterling A. Brown in his *Negro Poetry and Drama* and *The Negro in American Fiction* praised: "The wit and beauty possible to folk speech, the folk-shrewdness, the humanity, the stoicism of these people" (42) and "Dialect, or the speech of the people, . . . capable of expressing whatever the people are" (43)? Often it seems those truths are forgotten. We may overlook orderlies, auto mechanics, sales clerks, maids, landscapers, laundry workers, truck drivers, short-order cooks—and people negotiating unemployment and an underground economy.

How can poets of color invite the less "well-spoken" into our poems? What are their competencies and aspirations? Given a platform, how would they define themselves within a complicated, larger society? Above all, how can their humanity and contributions be perceived and acknowledged? In this second decade of the twenty-first century, African American poets should challenge and subvert harmful stereotypes of the working poor, unlettered folks, the unemployed, and the amorphous so-called underclass. Journalists batten on them. National Public Radio's daily programming and Sunday's *New York Times Magazine* feature these sisters and brothers as a burdensome social and economic problem. Ethnographers and sociologists research them, acquiring funds that could be put to better use to alleviate their plights. Too many black entertainers portray them as pathological thugs, mouthy clowns, self-loathing males and females squaring off. Our communities' casual acceptance of rampant vulgarity shows disdain for the self and a discomfort with the body's features and functions. Pervasive cursing *is* a curse, especially "mf" and "nigger," bruiting a false intra-communal voice hard to repudiate, especially by eager consumers of pop culture. "Well, dass jiss how we are!" Yes . . . at times.

A mass media greedy for profits manipulates our speech, creates a fatuous mimicry of cloned voices that erode grammar, drop and swallow consonants, and slur vowels. But what millions may hear rarely captures the magnificent variety of black urban and rural speech. Some presenters "go tuh chutch," clumsily imitating a sermonic style when not trained or ordained within that tradition. Black comedians, radio announcers, and disc jockeys condescendingly "talk country," not with empathy or an insightful identification with small-town or poor inner-city folk. In conjuring "folk speech" they can be snide and dramatize how foolish or bumptious or cruel we can be. For me, those moments harken back to boyhood memories of racist Disney and Lantz cartoons, black lawn jockeys, and the TV sitcom *The Amos 'n' Andy Show*, Uncle Remus stories, and blackfaced Al Jolson's sheepish "Mammy" *baaaa*. That commercial ventriloquism still plagues African American entertainers who pander to stereotypes and emphasize gripes, laments, mockery, petty jealousies, self-pity, and histrionic blaming.

As for contemporary poetry, a major venue for what may be considered African American "folk speech" is hip-hop. Rap has swept the planet as a model to inspire teenagers and young adults to claim Their Word. Its performers can be charismatic, iconoclastic, inventive in creating slang and neologisms, rhythmically enticing, humorous—and endearing in their appeals to our consciences. Nevertheless, extremely profitable gangsta rap is a detrimental, regressive influence on how working-class, poor, and disenfranchised African Americans are portrayed (and may view themselves). Macho minstrels hype an immoral, sybaritic lifestyle and opportunistic mentality. A delimited perspective on "keeping it real" skews realities available to potential leaders, organizers, and thinkers who could uplift black people. For males who lack confidence in intimacy, gangsta rap's lyrics inspire behavior that may become neurotically defensive and aggressive toward other males and females and hostile toward homosexuals. Stripped of its harsh braggadocio and meanness mask, gangsta rap remains a juvenile take on life's complexities. Guys wander the streets, drive by, and stand on the subway blasting and reciting offensive lyrics as proclamations and creeds.

How can black poets pump out antidotes to this poisoned mindset? Incorporating the voices of The People, we need speech acts that redefine our selves and the community. When I taught writing and literature for nine years at the Center for Labor Studies in Manhattan, a branch of Empire State College, I befriended many kinds of workers and heard their life stories. That job was crucial in establishing a positive outlook on how even menial tasks promote the common good. Thus I enjoy coming up with the character and speech of an African American male who left senior high, resides in a lower-income community, and has few prospects of gainful employment—and yet has integrity and a work ethic, is upbeat, and shares a profound trust with his family and peers. My alter ego (or refracted self) is Herald. Well, "Harold" actually, but his illiterate Ma, annunciating his name for the befuddled maternity ward nurse to officially record, clarified it this way: "Lissen Miss. Jiss lak innat Chrismuss carl come raht now ovuh dem hospilull speakuhs? Angjul be sangin bout glowree tuh newboan kang? Dat one!" I trust Herald's script has intricate music, suggestiveness, immediacy of perception, and candid revelations. Heralds are Af-Am brothers who too often are spoken *for* and *about*, although they possess the smarts and word magic to share their own sense of self and worldview. As my projective self, Herald may express my fear or envy, what I feel is too private to reveal, what I might be embarrassed by, and my biases. Yes, I indulge in a contrived, benign mimicry, but becoming Herald deepens my empathy for less privileged people.

To make Herald's speech my own, as I invent, revise, and edit I say lines over and over to smooth their flow. I steal and borrow, reading and eavesdropping (or "easedroppin" as my Dad labeled it) for unusual diction and syntax. In dramatic monologues Herald speaks to his wife Delphine and close friends, or archrival Berneath. My first Herald poem began this way. As a teenager in West Baltimore I heard that Veronica Jiggetts's mother often complained neighbors had no "eelet." The lady refused to explain or spell it. We guessed at meanings and settled on "a lack of courtesy or social graces" and forgot about it. Over forty years later it revivified in "Herald Takes Her Word." Here are the first and sixth (last) stanzas.

> Cord'n tuh Del mothuh onry sistuh Berneath,
> who luh tuh class off since she moo tuh Macon,
> whuh ah ain gah is *eelet*. Now you tell me whuh
> duh hellat spose tuh mean? Evuh heah uh such?

> But Mistuh Samule J. Portee, mah lone tahm barbuh,
> do lots uh studin tuh sef impru. Well, he decide
> it mean thuh reverse uh *crude*, like *polite*,
> *culchuh, famish*, uh *refine*. So, den, okay.

I have had a lifelong fascination with varieties of spoken English but am still self-conscious about how I talk, even after six months of speech improvement lessons with a rigorous coach for actors, voiceover freelancers, and mumbly executives. In the early 1950s when I left "Murlun" to vacation with my aunt and uncle in Cambridge, New Englanders smiled indulgently as they asked me and my younger brother to repeat words because we were UpSouth talk-funnies. "How do you do?" became "Hi do?" or "Hi yuh do." Temperature was "tembuhchuh." Child was "chow." Tiger "tagger," dachshund "dash hound," an eagle "a iggle," a chameleon a "shuh-*may*-lee-un." Aunt Tean "ahrned" shirts and gave us fluffy "tohls" to dry off. My cousin went to "Hahd Universtee" in "Washiton, D.C." Granny Thomas and Daddy said "far" for fire, "lenth" for length, and "awl" for oil. Sounnid fine tuh me, so whah dese Beantown beanhids have a problum?

Decades later, speaking of my poetic voice, I have committed to three distinct vocal styles (sometimes they mingle). A plain, slightly elevated, discursive narrative. Elliptical, alliterative, connotative wordplay. And lines of African American urban and rural vernacular. As a boy I honed in on the talk of men in dark blue work clothes and steel-toed boots, faces glistening with Vaseline in cold weather, dragging home from making steel at Sparrow's Point or pushing and hauling on the waterfront. Junyuh, Esau, Vashie, Queen Esther, Paggy, and Clinzo, kids from Virginia and the Carolinas, mentioned Keesey greens, moon pies, wiping butts with corn cobs, poke chop or onion sandwiches, hoot owls, and summer trips back to "the country" to swim and fish in "the branch." I read and reread our den shelf's battered 1903 edition of *The Life & Works of Paul Laurence Dunbar*, staring at the illustrations of slave life, mouthing English that comforted and amused and yet was estranging in its unfamiliar sounds.

I still rampantly code-switch, glide into "lazy" speech to sound *hamish* and evade mouth strain. Ain gah no problum wiff straigh en narruh, but as a connoisseur of Busted English's fragmints en slides Ah'm fasnated by idiolects' durations, rhythms, intonations, tones, and pronunciations. Black folks dess jiss dis jes duss just have such entrancing options: chilgrin? chilgren? childern? chilin? chirn? chidrid? children? cheeren? chillun? childun? chirren? Ain that suffin? sump'm? sutt'n? suppin? something? suthin? somep'n? sometin? sigh-in? Considering this wealth of alternatives, the perpetuation of vile language and mimicry of cloned, tedious voices does a great injustice to our many African American dialects—and the people who speak them.

Yet, in conjuring black dialect not my own, my memory and imagination endure constraints. As I create poems for Herald, it is tempting to rummage in a psychic kitbag of self-righteous anger, put-downs, gripes, and oh-woe-is-me. At times I have to prime my spirit to celebrate Herald's stalwart nature, pride, accomplishments, and love for his people. Though I indict the gangsta rapper, inventing a poetic alter ego reminds me that my attempts at humor or laments about racial degradation may also trot out stereotypes, neurotic behavior, and sarcastic phrasing. Also, because I cannot determine how Herald may be perceived, I worry that his speech may reinforce a reader's or listener's presumptions about black inferiority. Do I risk patronizing Herald as a caricature? African Americans laugh easily and often; a resilient sheltering has helped us to transcend oppression. However, precise, analytical, affirmative portrayals of "the common folk" are rare in mass media—and too absent from conversations I have and witness.

Another hitch in creating dialect poetry is that craft manuals, handbooks, and workshop leaders may constrain, even dominate, poets' options. Be wary of tin-eared dialect, of betraying the reader's eye, of mockingbird versifying, of jingling exotic speech. Just capture a unique dialect's "flavor." Selectively *approximate*. Attempt to copy verbatim speech and you'll wrench a character's voice or demean your subject. Don't freight your poem with unfamiliar diction, twisted syntax, a bunch of elided vowels and consonants—en, fuh Gawd's sakes, contrived, idiosyncratic spelling. Such practices will interfere with what your audience hears and reads.

I take this counsel lightly. In conjuring Herald's speech what concerns me most is keeping up with its permutations. In the African diaspora social mobility, international migration, and a melding of cultures constantly transform language. I juggle these complexities when channeling black English speakers in Baltimore; New York City; West Cape May, Newark, and Jersey City, New Jersey; South Carolina's Low Country; and Fort Worth, Texas. For example, in "Herald Reflects on Grady Lawrence Suggs" a geographically dispersed chorus may be embedded in the first two stanzas eulogizing a soldier killed in Iraq and identifying his mother:

> Ah recolleck, firs from nis town tuh blow up
> was Elfreda Suggs boy. C'mon. You know. Chain
> speckly glasses tuh neck. Run a herdressin slon
> own Palmetto. Nah, nah. You confusin Cassie Gatewood.
> Much younguh. Cheek mole en nat promnen buss.
>
> Lady Ahm projettin pipe thin. Ugly ornge SUV.
> Two strappy sons. Oldess was stah linebackuh
> at Fannie Hamuh three yers. Ver well mannuh.
> Corral carts en tote sack home fuh Piggy Wiggly.

Some words may be lost on a reader, yet Herald deserves an accurate rendering without my resorting to phonetic symbols. Though the Suggs tribute may not be totally accessible, if read patiently, ALOUD, two or three times, it probably will connect. To lessen dissonance stirred by Herald's rhythms and pronunciation, I regularize the spelling of morphemes and phonemes. To clarify a dense sequence or unfamiliar words, eventually I may offer a paraphrase, a glossary, or explanatory note. When I perform I preface Herald poems with brief explanations to avoid misunderstandings. Some black readers and listeners hear Herald as a very familiar acquaintance. A salient concern is that some folks who speak like Herald may not be literate enough to decipher his printed dialect. Also, whatever U.S. poetry canon continues to load up and boom, folk speech can be marginalized (even though multiculturalism freed poets from Eurocentrism's stranglehold). It is paramount to cultivate alternative voices when social networking and e-mails, byte bites, and tweets flatten African American regional dialects. Our poems can become repositories of the many ways we say and sound.

In fact, Herald is a steward of people I remember, know now, or overhear. Caddy shack repartee at the bluebloods' Green Spring Valley Hunt Club north of Baltimore. Residents' chatter processed when I was on a summer mainte-nance crew in the Cherry Hill housing development south of Baltimore. Jani-tors, porters, and handymen kibitzing in the Schwab House basement's locker room in Manhattan's West 70s, all of us members of the Building Service Employees Union Local #32B. Near the Bronx's Crotona Park I visited clients on welfare. In Harlem's Black New York Action Committee we encouraged cowed tenants to go on rent strikes and to march to protest rising Con Edison gas and electric bills. One morning Floyd Washington, a parking garage atten-dant, greeted me with "Hey-hey! Dare go mah buddy. Where you binat? Ain see you what seem munts." As I brisk-walked along Prospect Park Southwest a passing teen griped to his friends, "Hah. Doan fool me none. Oun nee eh bah know mah bidniss."

African American poets have integrated the Poe Biz, garnered many gradu-ate degrees, and teach in prestigious universities. However, we usually mingle at a great remove from blacks whose voices may go unheard. Today many American poets of African descent are venerated internationally. Unlike Dun-bar and other precursors, no one strains to validate their artistry by having to shield black dialect poetry from the stigma of inferiority. We no longer have to protest to become chancellors of the Academy of American Poets. In 1987 Rita Dove's *Thomas and Beulah* was awarded the Pulitzer Prize; from 1993 to 1995 she was the U.S. Poet Laureate. In 2012 Tracey Smith's *Life on Mars* won the Pulitzer and Natasha Trethewey became the nation's Poet Laureate.

We are in the vanguard of our people's quest for empowering education and articulateness. How will poets of African ancestry address our nation's inhumane disparity in the distribution of opportunities and assets? How can poems pay homage to the complicated lives and perspectives of custodians, day laborers, security guards, sharecroppers, braiders, assembly line workers, mani-curists, home health attendants—and listless souls loitering to make of each day what they can? Transcribe and create poems that make them more visible. Faithfully depict their happiness, pride, meager triumphs, and comprehension of why injustices persist. In solidarity with us, one migh could heah they voice.

BIBLIOGRAPHY

Brown, Sterling A. *Negro Poetry and Drama, and The Negro in American Fiction.* 1937. New York: Atheneum, 1969.

30 ～ what's american about american poetry

KAZIM ALI

On the tenth anniversary of their symposium "What's American about American Poetry?" I was invited by the Poetry Society of America, along with several other poets, to reflect on the question. It never occurred to me to write about anything other than writers from indigenous American communities—their poetry and poetics seeming to me to be the closest literal answer to the question.

I wondered what was meant in the first place by the term "American." It neither really defines national origin, geographical placement ("America" outsourcing itself far beyond its own continental borders to islands across the world), nor linguistic or cultural unity. This country resists itself, has always resisted itself; what it claims to be chafes always against its reality. One of the reasons for this, of course, is that in its founding it delineated a set of defining values for itself that were false; those of different-colored skin and different genders were excluded from the polity. More than two centuries in and we are still defined by gender and heterosexist-based inequality enforced by executive, legislative, and judicial law. This disconnect between thought and deed is part of what must be thought of as "American."

"American" must also mean multiplicities, as we are a nation of countless ethnicities, countless languages, and countless experiences, none of which has a greater or lesser claim to life in the "nation" than any other. And truth be told, in a place where any place has two names or more, we are not "one nation" after all, but many. When we think of a unified or singular American identity, we lose the chance to truly understand our selves and one another. As Bryan Bearhart writes:

Biitan-akiing-enabijig is Ojibwe.
I can't tell you what it means.
  We sit on cuspis.
  A horizon. A margin.
  What makes us "not them."
I only wish I could speak in tongue. (9)

Bearheart makes a breathless grammatical mistake in the last line here, dreaming himself to a monolingual expression he knows he can never nor will ever have. A postmodern aesthetic shows us, on the other hand, the rich possibilities of living in the in-between zones, the horizons, the margins—our chance is to become a pluralistic society, diminishing old class, gender, race, national, and sexual lines that configured most historically hierarchical world societies, and then reconfigure a new "American" society that functions on collective enterprise, cultural and artistic growth, and individual human development and betterment.

The "American dream" has always been not communitarian but individual, based on not only a desire but a need to "get ahead," despite any shortcomings. So, to cite only one example, Malcolm X once criticized our civil rights movement for orienting itself around the individual right to vote or participate in unsegregated arenas of commerce (buses, businesses, restaurants), rather than building class-based solidarity within the United States with labor unions and movements and international solidarity with African nations that were at the same time struggling for independence against European and American powers that controlled mineral interests and thus the political and economic institutions of power on the continent. As Malcolm pointed out, without diamonds for industrial machines, all modern progress would (literally) grind to a halt. These were the types of connections between political theories and organizing communities that both he and, several years later, Martin Luther King Jr. were beginning to build when each was killed.

Is another part of being "American" this self-orientation toward our own concerns and what happens within our own borders, while still requiring the labor, water, land, and mineral resources of every other place in the world? In other words, our material comfort, cultural production, and individual human development and betterment does not rely on any reconfiguration of gender-, race-, class-, or nation-based hierarchies, but actually on an institution of them backed up by American military power (easy when more than

50 cents of every tax dollar goes to support that power), and global political and financial institutions.

We are a long way from the hoped-for definition of "American" we aspired to and still aspire to somewhere in our minds, I believe. So as "American" poets, we do have both versions of America within us, since as citizens of the polity we still do (mostly) benefit from our luck and our willingness to go along, by continuing to elect and support leaders who subscribe to the "American exceptionalism" doctrine and use U.S. financial and military power to support it.

But we have a chance also, with our language, with the form and focus of our art, to begin delineating the truth of our lives as it is and to start imagining on paper and in space the differences we hope to enact.

Sherwin Bitsui in his *Flood Song* writes of a lost connection between language, locality, and lived experience. In speaking of his grandfather, he writes:

Years before, he would have named this season
> by flattening a field where grasshoppers jumped into black smoke. (6)

The season, in this case, like the American landscape itself, is not named for the explorer's imperialist ambitions—as Paul Virilio once claimed, the American imperial object is ever outward: once the Pacific was reached, the incursions continued into the ocean itself; once the hands of empire reached out and around the planet and met each other coming, the direction changed into outer space—or for a romantic idea of the self defined from or manipulated by "nature," but instead for the psychic and kinetic qualities of the land itself.

When the Poetry Society of America convened the poets Sonia Sanchez, Michael Palmer, Louise Glück, Jorie Graham, Kimiko Hahn, and a number of others to discuss the question "What's American about American Poetry?" a consensus emerged tentatively, if affably—a single lively panel kerfuffle between Thylias Moss and John Hollander aside—that the most "American" quality was the quality of constant undefinability. Was it a cop-out?

If the strength of American poetry is its hybrid qualities and leanings, its weakness is also particularly American: its amnesia of history and language. This is not a passive amnesia of forgetting but a brutal and intentional act of erasure: towns and neighborhoods named after plants, animals, and people who no longer exist there. There is a city in Florida called Miami, and more than a thousand miles away in Ohio there is a river called Miami. You have to draw a line that stretches the whole distance between those two places to spell out even the first letter of the word "America." And where are the Miami now? That's the start of the second letter.

In her poem "From the River's Edge," M. L. Smoker writes about the fragmentation inherent in being separated from one's sources by a larger external narrative, and about the ability of poetry to bridge that divide: "Can a poet speak of a / second version of her mother?" She goes on to write:

> The one who lives in a
> silent cave where she allows no visitors, gives no interviews.
> Her memoir is being written there by a shadow seven feet
> tall that can hold no pen or pencil, both hands missing.
> My living mother dreams of new waters that have no
> adequate translation.

So in this historical moment, the possibilities of the various American languages seem twofold: to either homogenize and smooth out all difference (one American urge) or to continue to splinter, refract one another, create dozens of new and glorious forms of creative expression.

And about nations and languages that have disappeared or been suppressed: history isn't just something that happened. As the saying goes, "The past didn't go anywhere." Indigenous and aboriginal populations on the American continent and around the world struggle every day for political self-determination and ownership of their own local land and mineral resources—in other words, liberation from imperialism, whether political, economic, or cultural.

So what we really need, every American poet, is the forms and approaches and languages of poets like Sherwin Bitsui, M. L. Smoker, Bryan Bearhart— and, for example, Dawn Lundy Martin, Gillian Conoley, Mark Nowak, Myung Mi Kim, C. D. Wright—forms that hold within them the voices of alterity and the parallels of experience, lyric and narrative forms that embrace and present new possibilities of understanding America and American experiences.

At the end of his poem "Ars Poetica," Orlando White writes beautifully of the real physical and erotic possibilities when language and experience twist around each other, when the form of the lyric is allowed to fracture and grow anew under the pressure of contemporary realities of alienation, distance, and technology:

> I opened an envelope addressed to me. I pulled out a blank sheet of
> paper,

unfolded it. In the letter: no message, no sender's name, just a
   white space.

"I like that you exist," she said. Like the lowercase i, my body felt
   present on a
page: fitted in a dark suit, white necktie, and inside the black dot,
   a smile.

But it was the way her skin felt as she dressed into a black outfit.
   The way her
body slipped into a long dark dress shaped like a shadow.

He picked up a stone; held it to his ear. Shook it like a broken
   watch. He
opened it, and inside were small gears, shaped like a clock.

I am a skeleton, a sentence, too. Although like you, I am neither a
   meaning
nor a structure, just silence in a complete thought.

Here language itself lives, changes through our actions. The stone has little
gears inside, and why wouldn't it: it is telling time. "In the Lakota language,"
Layli Long Soldier wrote to me, "the word for God or Creator . . . is 'Tunkasila'
which also means grandfather. But the root of Tunkasila is 'Tunkan'—which
means stone, a sacred stone or a stone of great power. What is the connection
between a stone and God/grandfather?" In the case of White, who is Diné
rather than Lakota, it seems that not only the stones speak but every compo-
nent of conceptual and physical meaning-making.

   Besides supporting art like this, art that confronts all dimensions of the
"American" experience, we have to also acknowledge the real military, political,
and economic empire as well as the cultural apparatus that supports that ma-
trix of reality—a reality in which notions of "plurality" and "hybridity" and
"alterity" are just three more convenient ways of organizing a population into
compliant behavior and tokenizing a couple of voices in order to avoid seeing
or seeking out the rest of them.

   After all, our present machine-driven sense of geographical placelessness
isn't real. History and geography *do* still play a role in daily life in America.
Jean Baudrillard in his book *America* painted a stark picture of our current
landscape as a vacant series of sites of consumption (strip malls, some of which

are even *designed* to imitate the small-town-America main streets they brutally replaced), housing developments, and parking lots linked by an interstate system, but it isn't really true. The urban spaces and wildlife, under duress and real political attack (especially by defunding public schools and university systems), still struggle to actualize their possible roles as instruments for a revitalization of real and substantial creative and cultural life.

Our multilingualism and cultural openness have made many spaces in poetry. Kimiko Hahn's writing between poetry and prose, Meena Alexander's innovations in the lyric between sense and sound (especially in her latest book, *Quickly Changing River*), Agha Shahid Ali's transportation (literally) of the ghazal into English (or was it that he transported English-language poetry to the form of the ghazal?) are all examples that seem particularly American to me, as much the benefit of English as a meeting place.

Indian English, I can tell you, is a separate language, both spoken and written, from American English. It has different words, different intonations and pronunciations, different accepted sentence order, different syntax. In my book *Bright Felon* I tried as hard as I could to tell the story of my life the only way I knew how. I did not have the intention of writing "poetry" or "poems" or "memoir" while I was doing it, only sentences. The genre-queerness of that book, called both poetry and prose and prose-poetry, is specifically related to the idea that life-writing should follow the patterns of a by-the-book formula—chapter, structure, sentence, and paragraph. A life might be fundamentally "queer," however, and impossible to tell in any other way. And besides, I'm not the first one to try it: Etel Adnan, Mahmoud Darwish, Alistair McCartney, Sarah Manguso, and so many others, I am sure, have written prose memoirs that dispense with all the usual expectations of what the form ought to do.

Writers like Myung Mi Kim or Sherwin Bitsui or Tracie Morris are actually making new spaces in American poetry, both in terms of what poetry is supposed to look and sound like and also in terms of what its social function as literature actually is. Lucille Clifton wrote, "i was born in babylon / both nonwhite and woman. / i had no models." At least in terms of poetry, for myself, I no longer feel this way: I feel there are so many models for me now.

We have a timeless tradition to draw from. At the original "What's American about American Poetry" symposium in 1999, John Hollander caused a little bit of controversy when he criticized Thylias Moss for citing "the landscape" as her literary forebear. The two had a somewhat testy exchange that ended when Moss leapt up onto her chair and declared to the room, "Some of us don't have people as literary forebears. For some of us whose ancestors lay in holds of slaveships, a crack of blue seen between the planks of wood was our literary forebear."

Dg Nanouk Okpik in her poem cycle "For-the-Spirits-Who-Have-Rounded-the-Bend" in *Corpse Whale* confronts the tradition of the identity poem and the coming-of-age poem in surprising and inventive ways that marry a concern with sound to the more traditional folk images. Rather than being a marrying of opposites, in Okpik's work it feels absolutely contemporary and unified:

> Then as the ligature of Inuit light flux and
> flows like herds of walrus, passing along the coast, Yes then, but maybe this is a seal
>   hook of bear claws clipping
> me to the northern tilt, pinning me to the cycle of night when the day slows, the
>   wind
> shifts to cloud, and the moon shadow grows to sun loops. (70)

Since she is clipped to the "northern tilt" and pinned to movements of night and day, she is able to discover through the process of transformation she undergoes throughout the poem that nothing is lost, that she can live wholly and fully, connected to all her various human and animal sources. There is a danger in it, to be sure, but in the end it is the winged heart that speaks of hope and strength:

> After the border of flesh and church, after the old book is read, when ivory and
> scrimshaw is used with rib tools to create Okvik not Christianity, when the bell tones
> across the sound, until then, I will wash ashore in a dazed white-out, hide flesh to
>   beach
> with my fore-claws hanging limply, my hooded golden
> eyes with concentric circles, lines
> on my chin, with a large backbone for my lungs, and a heart of spotted wings. (74)

I think of something Naomi Shihab Nye wrote in 1999 in her response to the question "What's American about American Poetry?" Nye said:

> When I was working overseas on various occasions, poets in other countries would
> remark that we American poets have a luxury they do not have: we are free to write
> about tiny "insignificances" any time we want to. . . . We write about personal lives,
> minor idiosyncrasies, familial details, tomatoes—not feeling burdened to explore

larger collective issues all the time, which is something writers elsewhere often consider part of their endless responsibility.

There is a way in which all American life, American writing and poetry included, participates in the historical (and geographical!) amnesia inherent in the concept of "America." What is the responsibility of the writer? When you look one place, there is another place you are not looking. We will have to think for a long time to figure out where we are and who we are and what we are doing in this place, thought to be ours from "sea to shining sea," ours by some form of "manifest destiny," some form of "American exceptionalism."

In her essay "Poetics of Generosity," Judith E. Johnson writes, "I am not Alterity: I will not play that role in your mind or in my own. I am not Shakespeare's sister Judith, whose existence Virginia Woolf divined in her prophetic sanity. I am Judith, and Shakespeare is this Judith's brother." She refuses to be defined by her "absence from the center of discourse." She goes on to suggest a new way of thinking about the American poetic landscape:

> Jane Austen, the Bronte sisters, and George Eliot define the 19th century English novel; if that definition does not hold Dickens, Thackeray, and Meredith, they are the deviation from the norm, and their Alterity makes them contingent. Ethel Schwabacher defines Abstract Expressionism; Jackson Pollack is the deviation.
>
> Muriel Rukeyser defines the poetics of energy-transfer; Charles Olson is the deviation . . . you, our illustrious male colleagues and brothers, are the deviation. It will be healthy for you to see yourselves in the full brilliance of your own Alterity for a while, to study our practice as the human norm, and to wonder when and why you strayed from us.

American poets have so much to learn from each other; it has always been precisely those underseen or underheard texts that have provided the greatest influence on the literary landscape at large when they are revealed. Need we any more proof than Dickinson's poems, Nin's uncensored diaries, Melville's late stories? In the case of all three, gender and sexuality were at play in the suppression. Recent attention paid to a younger crop of indigenous writers—a recent weekend of events at Poets House, a feature on Native women writers that Long Soldier edited for *Drunken Boat*, Long Soldier herself being featured by the Academy of American Poets in their magazine, Orlando White being selected for Poetry Society of America's "New American Poets" festival (by me, I will admit)—points to a long-hoped-for shift in attitudes toward indigenous writing, not as "contingent" but as the *real* mainstream of "American literary tradition."

Natalie Diaz is one of the most exciting poets I have read recently. In her poem "Soirée Fantastique" she takes ancient European myth and weaves it together with contemporary American situations and idiom:

> Houdini arrived first, with Antigone on his arm.
> Someone should have told her it was rude
> to chase my brother in circles with such a shiny shovel.
> She only said, *I'm building the man a funeral.*
> But last I measured, my brother was still a boy.

As with most wild parties featuring the dead, things can only get crazier when Jesus shows up:

> There are violins playing. The violins are on fire—
> they are passed around until we're all smoking. Jesus coughs,
> climbs down from the cross of railroad ties above the table.
> He's a regular at these carrion revelries, and it's annoying
> how he turns the bread to fish, especially when we have sandwiches.
>   (66)

Neither the escape artist nor the son of god, two men who specialized in fulfilling destinies, is able to console Antigone and explain to her why she will not be permitted to bury the young brother. Only the speaker of the poem is left to explain it to her, taking away her spade, saying:

> *We aren't here to eat, we are being eaten.*
> *Come, pretty girl. Let us devour our lives.* (67)

Part of our answer is to now start to experience poetry not solely in the mind, nor solely visually, nor solely aurally but through all the senses at once, and it's not enough to say as Americans we have to understand our history. We have to also understand the here and now, the voices we have not heard, couldn't or wouldn't, voices that help to construct and reveal new rooms in the houses of our understanding.

America has gone—militarily, economically, culturally—global. The way I think about it, Mahmoud Darwish was a most "American" poet. He and his family fled his Palestinian home in 1947; returning without papers, he lived in internal exile for most of his young life, and then as an expatriate in Moscow, Tripoli, Beirut, and Paris, before finally returning home in 1997. His poetry constantly engaged with the question of exile, but it wasn't long before he realized that exile is a spiritual and metaphysical condition as well. How much more "American," or true to the American experience, both indigenous and immigrant, can you get?

He came to America just once, for an operation on his heart. Fady Joudah, the Palestinian-American poet who has been translating Darwish, has written a beautiful essay about meeting with Darwish—at a coffee shop in the local supermall. In that peculiarly American locale, poet and translator talked together for the first and only time, sharing stories, talking about poetry.

And that's the key, isn't it? In this life, supported by millions of gallons of oil, this strange life of buildings dropped on top of scoured land, this weird American landscape, this odd reality in which our primary responsibility as flesh-and-bone entities seems to be to consume, to receive and spend money, well, where do you find the poetry, by which I mean any spiritual sustenance at all?

At any rate, I think the "American century" is soon over. Within the next thirty or forty years, when the global food production and distribution system, utterly unsustainable, moves into crisis, when water availability and sustainability reach a crisis point, as fossil fuels begin to evaporate and disappear, only societies that have been able to do more with less will be able to cope. Our society will necessarily be required to start taking real and concrete steps in this direction, exploring free energy, free health care, and free primary, secondary, and higher education for everyone within the borders.

Sometime in the next century we will have to learn, probably quickly and in an atmosphere of duress (whether external or internal or some combination of the two), how to live without many of the things we take very much for granted—to cite three disparate examples: fresh vegetables in the winter, regularly scheduled air travel, and round-the-clock availability of electrical power and tap water. Are we heading back to pioneer days? We will be pioneering in our own hearts the routes of connectedness between us and the earth, us and everyone around us.

Language, modes of communication, and availability to communication media will be critically important in the new world. They will save us, and by "us" I mean all of us. One of the things I think will need to happen is an end to nationalism—not an end to nations, necessarily, but an end to the project of nation-building certainly. We will necessarily see a return to locally based economies, and with it, naturally, we will probably return to locally based languages and forms of cultural expression and a form of multilingualism quite common in the world and in marginal American populations but not yet in the mainstream.

As access to fresh water diminishes, silicon production must necessarily dwindle, so I wonder what the future of electronics will be. We'll find a way to stay in touch with each other, I'm sure of that, but I think a return to the most ancient sources of art, dance, and poetry seems also inevitable.

I think poetry will move back to the oral, back to the musical and back to the mysterious and spiritual and difficult.

From Long Soldier's poem "Edge":

> Large car steady at the curve palest light driest day a field of rocks
> we are not poor sealed in windows. You hum in the back. I do
> not know what to say how far to go the winter near dead as we
> drive you do not understand word for word the word for you
> is little. But you hear how it feels always. The music plays you
> swing your feet. And I see it I Mommy the edge but do not
> point do not say *look* as we pass the heads gold and blowing
> these dry grasses eaten in fear by man and horses.

This draws from her own personal experiences, landscape and physical environment, the sound textures of Stein, and a postmodern linguistic and theoretical sensibility. Visionary work like this, which looks backward and forward at once, encompasses all of the magnificent differences and all the "Americas."

Maybe we will see work like this—Bitsui, White, Diaz, Bearheart, Okpik—as the real American poetry, will see what we think of as the Anglo-American literary tradition as the tradition of alterity, of deviation, will see that this landscape, on this continent, this strange life, needs to be explained in the terms of contemporary Native writers who have been able to fuse the Anglo-American literary tradition with Native languages, poetics, and forms of expression.

As for me, let me wander anywhere and hope Darwish is waiting for me. True, he is buried in Palestine, but he died here, in a hospital in Texas, and perhaps something of his spirit also lingers here, haunting the place, reminding us, as he wrote in his great poem "Speech of the Red Indian":

Oh white man,
of all the dead who are still dying,
both those who live and those
who return to tell the tale.

Let's give the earth enough time to tell
the whole truth about you and us.

The whole truth about us.
The whole truth about you. (144)

BIBLIOGRAPHY

Ali, Kazim. *Bright Felon: Autobiography and Cities*. Middletown, Conn.: Wesleyan University Press, 2009.

Baudrillard, Jean. *America*. Translated by Chris Turner. London: Verso, 1988.

Bearhart, B: William. "Cuspate." In *American Ghost: Poets on Life After Industry*, edited by Lillien Waller, 9–10. Ithaca, N.Y.: Stockport Flats, 2011.

Bitsui, Sherwin. *Flood Song*. Port Townsend, Wash.: Copper Canyon, 2009.

Darwish, Mahmoud. "Speech of the Red Indian." In *The Adam of Two Edens*, 146–47. Syracuse, N.Y.: Syracuse University Press, 2001.

Diaz, Natalie. "Soirée Fantastique." In *When My Brother Was an Aztec*, 66–67. Port Townsend, Wash.: Copper Canyon, 2012.

Johnson, Judith E. "The Poetics of Generosity." Unpublished essay.

Long Soldier, Layli. "The Poetry of Layli Long Soldier." *Talking Stick* 13, no. 2 (April–June 2010). amerinda.org/newsletter/13-2/longsoldier.html.

Nye, Naomi Shihab. Response to "What's American About American Poetry?" survey. Poetry Society of America, 1999. poetrysociety.org/psa/poetry/crossroads/qa_american_poetry /naomi_shihab_nye.

Okpik, Dg Nanouk. *Corpse Whale*. Tucson: University of Arizona Press, 2012.

Smoker, M. L. "From the River's Edge." In *Another Attempt at Rescue*, 17. Brooklyn, N.Y.: Hanging Loose, 2005.

White, Orlando. "Ars Poetica." In *Bone Light*, 54. Los Angeles: Red Hen, 2009.

31 ～ what it means to be an american poet

RAFAEL CAMPO

American poetry owes as much to the incantations of Native Americans and the songs of African slaves as it does to the likes of Whitman, Dickinson, Williams, and Frost. What distinguishes American poetry in my mind's imagination is its inclusiveness, its rich layering of voices and its incessant reworking of traditions. American poetry is a new and a very old thing at once; it has yet to be invented and is as ancient as the sonnet. In what other medium could a gay Cuban American physician like me, the child of non-English-speaking immigrants and the product of a profession at the cutting edge of some of our most powerful, mind-boggling technologies, find such welcome opportunity for full expression? Ultimately, American poetry (like any poetry) is a universal language through which all people—black and white and Latino and Asian, heterosexual and gay, Jewish and Christian and Muslim and agnostic, female and male—can be engaged in the most important discourse known to humankind, that of empathy itself.

I consider myself an American poet precisely because I am a mutt, a mongrel, a kind of happy monster, born in New Jersey but conceived in Cuba and Italy, at once devoutly Catholic and flamingly queer, a Harvard-educated physician who prescribes Nuyorican poetry along with pills, who educates about HIV in Spanish and writes villanelles in English. I am an American poet who reads T. S. Eliot and Gertrude Stein, and Derek Walcott and Eavan Boland and Thom Gunn, with just as much pleasure as Walt Whitman and Emily Dickinson; American poets are at their best when they are questioning, or enlarging, the boundaries and borders that would try to define or contain us too facilely. Sometimes I am downright ungainly, or too sentimental, or too stridently political; I suppose I am like this trying-to-be-free nation that made my very existence possible and now wonders what to do with me. Even as I sit down to write this response to the question "What is American about American poetry?" I must question my own authority: I know the true answer lies in the sum of many answers to the same question, in an unending conversation between Marilyn Hacker and Robert Pinsky, or between Thylias Moss and Richard Howard, or Yusef Komunyakaa and Martín Espada and Hayden Carruth, or Julia Alvarez and Mary Oliver and Louise Glück.

I consider myself fortunate to be an American poet, because despite the efforts to censor me there always exists in this country the ideal of free speech; condom ads on TV and access to clean needles to prevent AIDS, or lifesaving medicines for the afflicted in Cuba or Iraq, such unspeakable possibilities take shape in the poem that cannot be squelched. Despite the efforts to keep out the immigrants, or to exploit the weak, there always exists here in the USA the ideal of freedom; my family's voyage to America, and the struggle for equal rights for gay and lesbian people, begin in the poem I will write tomorrow. I am fortunate because my tradition of American poetry includes undaunted activists like Ginsberg and indefatigable healers like Williams. I only hope that the future of American poetry can live up to their courageous examples, where the politics of poetry itself can be put aside (the small-minded debates around formalism versus free verse, for example, or the entirely fabricated notion of "political correctness") in the new millennium, when *empathy*, as made comprehensible through our great poems, is no longer what we have all been striving for, but joyously already have, writ plain and clear and pure on our pounding hearts.

What's American about American Form?

American poetic form, like America itself, is inclusively democratic and hence full of delicious paradoxes and unresolvable arguments. American form harkens back furthest to the incantations of Native Americans and the songs of African slaves, which have been handed down over the generations and which have expression today in the work of Adrian C. Louis, Joy Harjo, Thylias Moss, Diane Glancy, and Yusef Komunyakaa. Such modes of expression predate, of course, those verse forms received from British and other European poetries that were for so long considered the traditional bedrock of American verse, those iambs and rhymes manifest in the work of early American poets like

Ralph Waldo Emerson, Henry Wadsworth Longfellow, and Anne Bradstreet and later on in the work of Robert Frost, Elizabeth Bishop, and James Merrill, to the current moment, with practitioners such as Marilyn Hacker, Carolyn Kizer, Richard Wilbur, Maxine Kumin, Hayden Carruth, and Rachel Hadas. Despite their different personal and aesthetic histories, no one would suggest that any of those poets is more American than the others. That is because the ends of their work, like their most fundamental origins, are the same. We recognize all as uniquely American because of the universalizing quality of the varied forms they employ, which ultimately makes empathy out of the very act of perceiving, be it in the familiar sound of the heartbeat, in the intoxicating plunge between stanzas, or in the luxuriant discursiveness of narrative.

What is so distinctly American about any of these poets, a quality perhaps most evident in the four quintessential American poets—Emily Dickinson, Walt Whitman, William Carlos Williams, and Allen Ginsberg—is that they all use form and structure to create meaning from language that is not entirely contained in the words themselves. Meaning here springs out of the unsaid, the gesture, the reflected glance, the rhyme, the enjambed line-break, the iamb. It is a connection between poet and reader that is by definition empathic, in that it resists explanation and yet is utterly understood. Dickinson's brilliant reworking of received forms, borrowed from church hymnals as much as from William Shakespeare, stretched space iambs and quatrains into infinite spaces of reflection on themes of mortality, human suffering, and desire; her dashes are the beginning of the empathetic imagination, inviting the reader to be present at the moment of revelation, a participant in the process of creation, as is only possible in America, a country ever in search of its beginnings. Whitman, whose imagining of form more explicitly enacts that same impulse to reach out, in lines long enough to stretch across the same vast and expanding nation, into the consciousness of his far-flung readers, was similarly engaged in the question of empathy, though his poems take shape so differently on the page. Williams, another great innovator in the use of form, laid bare the mysteriousness of perception itself at a moment when American technological know-how seemed capable of explaining everything about us, reducing empathy almost to the level of its physiologic foundations—of seeing, of sensing, of tasting, of feeling. Just when it seemed American form had been pushed to its limits, Ginsberg set it all on fire and left the old building screaming at the top of his lungs. These four poets—all in their own ways mystics, hedonists, healers, activists—give voice to the empathic imagination, a mind that is requisitely American by virtue of our nation's diversity and our resulting demand to comprehend one another's humanity. Only a multiplicity of forms, which together must be considered American, could begin to take on such a daunting task.

It is not surprising that these four poets are also representative in every way of our equally varied identities as Americans. Male and female, queer and straight, Jewish and Christian and atheist, white and nonwhite, mono- and multilingual—they are as diverse as Americans today. The pressures that these identities exert against the chosen forms of these poets are similar to those faced by American poets writing today, and make for an interesting and rich field of investigations. Speaking for myself, I suppose I am present at a number of intersections between form and identity: as a bilingual Latino who writes villanelles, I wonder at my efforts to try to make English sound more like my beloved, inherently musical Spanish, reclaiming the songs of my gypsy minstrel ancestors; as a gay man who writes sonnets, I flex muscles of my own desire against the walls of that heterosexualized "narrow room"; as a physician who incorporates medicalese in blank verse, I thrill to reanimating this language/vernacular with the human heartbeat it too often suppresses. The forms I choose are not themselves a political expression, as some still mired in the tired old debate of "free verse versus form" might contend; rather, I view these structures as opportunities for amplifying what I can say with mere words, for layering my language with possibilities for empathy. Because what is a foreign language but another way to say the things you already knew; or homosexuality, but another joyous expression of human love; or healing itself, but another path toward empathy?

contributors

KAZIM ALI is a poet, essayist, fiction writer, and translator. His volumes of poetry include *The Far Mosque*, winner of Alice James Books' New England/New York Award, *The Fortieth Day*, and the cross-genre text *Bright Felon: Autobiography and Cities*. He has also published a translation of *Water's Footfall* by Sohrab Sepehri. His novels include *Quinn's Passage* and *The Disappearance of Seth*, and his books of essays include *Orange Alert: Essays on Poetry, Art and the Architecture of Silence* and *Fasting for Ramadan*. He is an associate professor of creative writing and comparative literature at Oberlin College and teaches in the Masters of Fine Arts program of the University of Southern Maine.

HADARA BAR-NADAV is the author of three collections of poetry, *Lullaby (with Exit Sign)*, *The Frame Called Ruin*, and *A Glass of Milk to Kiss Goodnight*, and coauthor of the textbook *Writing Poems*, 8th ed. She is an associate professor of English at the University of Missouri–Kansas City.

LUCY BIEDERMAN is a doctoral student in English literature and creative writing at the University of Louisiana in Lafayette. She has written two chapbooks, *The Other World* and *Imitations*.

JASWINDER BOLINA is the author of *Carrier Wave*, recipient of the 2006 Colorado Prize for Poetry, and *Phantom Camera*, awarded the 2012 Green Rose Prize in Poetry from New Issues Press.

RAFAEL CAMPO teaches and practices internal medicine at Harvard Medical School and Beth Israel Deaconess Medical Center in Boston. He is the recipient of many honors and awards, including a Guggenheim Fellowship, two Lambda Literary Awards, and the Nicholas E. Davies Award for outstanding humanism in medicine from the American College of Physicians. His most recent books include *Diva*, a finalist for the National Book Critics Circle Award in poetry, and *The Enemy*, which won the Sheila Motton Award from the New England Poetry Club. *Alternative Medicine* is his new collection of poetry. For more information, please visit www.rafaelcampo.com.

KEN CHEN is the executive director of the Asian American Writers' Workshop and the author of *Juvenilia*, the winner of the Yale Series of Younger Poets. A recipient of fellowships from the NEA, NYFA, and the Bread Loaf Writers' Conference, Ken is a founder of CultureStrike, an artist movement for immigration rights, and of *Arts & Letters Daily*. He successfully represented the asylum claim of a teenager detained by the Department of Homeland Security.

MARTHA COLLINS is the author, most recently, of *White Papers* and the book-length poem *Blue Front*; she has also published four earlier collections of poems and three collections of cotranslated Vietnamese poetry. She is currently editor at large for *FIELD* magazine and an editor for Oberlin College Press.

JOANNA PENN COOPER holds a PhD in American literature from Temple University and an MFA in poetry from New England College. Her chapbooks are *Mesmer* and *Crown*, winner of the Cathlamet Prize. Her full-length collections are *The Itinerant Girl's Guide to Self-Hypnosis* and *What Is a Domicile*.

ADEBE DERANGO-ADEM completed her MA at York University, where she also served as assistant editor for the arts and literature journal *Existere*. Her work has appeared in various North American publications, such as the *Claremont Review*, *Canadian Literature*, *CV2*, and the *Toronto Star*. She is the author of a chapbook of poems, *Sea Change*, and her debut poetry collection, *Ex Nihilo*, was recently published.

Author of *Smith Blue*, *Suck on the Marrow*, and *What to Eat, What to Drink, What to Leave for Poison* and editor of *Black Nature* and the *From the Fishouse* poetry anthology CAMILLE T. DUNGY'S honors include an American Book Award, two Northern California Book Awards, and an NEA. She is a professor at San Francisco State University.

PAULA HAYES holds a doctorate in textual studies and English from the University of Memphis and an MA in religious studies and philosophy from the University of Tennessee, Knoxville. She currently teaches English at Strayer University in Memphis. She is the author of *Robert Lowell and the Confessional Voice*. Her literary articles and poetry have appeared in various journals, including *Hispanic Culture Review*, *Phati'tude*, *Platte Valley Review*, *Black Magnolias*, *The Griot: Journal of African American Studies*, *Dead Mule*, and *Strong Verse*.

Professor at Shandong University, Weihai, TRAVIS HEDGE COKE, MFA, is Tsalagi of mixed descent, born in North Carolina. An alumnus of California Institute of the Arts and graduate of Northern Michigan University and University of California Riverside, Hedge Coke has been a Soul Mountain fellow and Kimmel Harding Nelson resident. He has written for page, screen, and stage, as well as performing readings and displaying visual art in many venues around the world. Author of *Fragments of a Lesser* and *Sweat, Dust, and Light*, he is associate editor of *Sing: Poetry of the Indigenous Americas* and editor of *Future Earth Magazine* and writes a weekly column for *The Comics Cube*.

TONY HOAGLAND's books of poems include *What Narcissism Means to Me* and *Donkey Gospel*. His awards include the Jackson Prize, the O. B. Hardisson Prize, and the James Laughlin Award. He teaches in the creative writing program at the University of Houston, and at Warren Wilson College.

GARRETT HONGO is the author of three books of poetry, including *Coral Road*. He has also edited anthologies, published a book of nonfiction titled *Volcano: A Memoir of Hawai'i*, and been awarded fellowships from the NEA, Rockefeller Foundation, and Guggenheim Foundation and the Lamont Poetry Prize from the Academy of American Poets. He is presently completing a book of nonfiction titled *The Perfect Sound: An Autobiography in Stereo*. He is Distinguished Professor of the College of Arts and Sciences and professor of creative writing at the University of Oregon.

AILISH HOPPER is the author of *Dark-Sky Society* and the chapbook *Bird in the Head*. Individual poems have appeared in *Agni*, *APR*, *The Baffler*, *Ploughshares*, *Poetry*, *Tidal Basin Review*, and many other places. She has received residencies from MacDowell Colony, Vermont Studio Center, and Yaddo and teaches at Goucher College.

RANDALL HORTON is the recipient of the Gwendolyn Brooks Poetry Award, the Bea Gonzalez Poetry Award, and most recently a National Endowment of the Arts Fellowship in Literature. Randall is a Cave Canem fellow and a member of the Affrilachian Poets. His latest collection of poems is *Pitch Dark Anarchy*.

MAJOR JACKSON is the author of three collections of poetry, most recently *Holding Company*. He is the Richard Dennis Green and Gold Professor at University of Vermont and serves as the poetry editor of the *Harvard Review*.

LEIGH JOHNSON is an assistant professor of English at Marymount University, where she teaches American literature, gender studies, and multicultural literature. Her research focuses on counternarratives to established literary voices and identities. She received an American Association of University Women Dissertation Fellowship in 2011.

PATRICK S. LAWRENCE is a PhD candidate in English at the University of Connecticut. His dissertation traces the development of obscenity standards and cultural norms from the Nixon administration through the Culture Wars. His research and teaching also address multiethnic literature, and he is a past assistant editor of *MELUS*.

TIMOTHY LEYRSON received his master's in English from Missouri State University in 2013. His work has appeared in *Midwestern Gothic*, *Atticus Review*, *Hunger Mountain*, and elsewhere.

MATTHEW LIPPMAN is the author of three poetry collections, *American Chew*, which won the Burnside Review Book Prize, *Monkey Bars*, and *The New Year of Yellow*, winner of the Kathryn A. Morton Poetry Prize.

TIM LIU (Liu Ti Mo) is the author of *For Dust Thou Art, Of Thee I Sing, Hard Evidence, Say Goodnight, Burnt Offerings,* and *Vox Angelica* (1992), which won the Poetry Society of America's Norma Farber First Book Award. He has also edited *Word of Mouth: An Anthology of Gay American Poetry.* His poems have been included in many anthologies and have appeared in such magazines and journals as *American Letters & Commentary* and *Bomb.* Liu is currently an associate professor at William Paterson University and on the core faculty at Bennington College's Writing Seminars.

CHARLES H. LYNCH, a Cave Canem fellow, attended Kenyon College and the City College of New York, and his doctoral dissertation at New York University explored the lives and poetry of Robert Hayden and Gwendolyn Brooks. He teaches English at New Jersey City University.

GERALD MAA is an editor in chief of the *Asian American Literary Review.* His translation, poetry, and prose appear in such places as *American Poetry Review, Studies in Romanticism,* and *Common Knowledge.* He currently lives in Los Angeles.

LAURA MCCULLOUGH'S most recent books are *Rigger Death & Hoist Another* and her edited anthology *The Room & the World: Essays on the Poetry of Stephen Dunn.* Her other books are *Panic* (winner of the Kinereth Gensler Award, Alice James Books, and a Foreword BOTYA finalist), *Speech Acts,* and *What Men Want.* She has been awarded scholarships or fellowships from Sewanee Writers' Conference, Bread Loaf Writers' Conference, the Vermont Studio Center, the New Jersey State Council on the Arts, the Nebraska Summer Writers' Conference, and others. Her essays, criticism, poems, creative nonfiction, and short fiction have appeared in *Georgia Review, American Poetry Review, Writer's Chronicle, Painted Bride Quarterly,* and other journals and magazines. She was founding editor of *Mead: The Magazine of Literature and Libations* and currently acts as an editor at large.

PHILIP METRES has written a number of books and chapbooks, most recently *A Concordance of Leaves, Abu Ghraib Arias, To See the Earth,* and *Behind the Lines: War Resistance Poetry on the American Homefront since 1941.* His work has appeared in *Best American Poetry* and *Inclined to Speak: Contemporary Arab American Poetry* and has garnered two NEA fellowships, the Thomas J. Watson Fellowship, four Ohio Arts Council grants, the Anne Halley Prize, the Arab American Book Award, and the Cleveland Arts Prize. He teaches literature and creative writing at John Carroll University in Cleveland. See http://philipmetres.com.

MIHAELA MOSCALIUC is the author of *Father Dirt* and cotranslator of *Death Searches for You a Second Time* by Carmelia Leonte. Her poems, reviews, translations, and articles appear in the *Georgia Review, Prairie Schooner, TriQuarterly, New Letters,*

Poetry International, Pleiades, Arts & Letters, and elsewhere. She teaches at Monmouth University in New Jersey.

DAVID MURA is the author of four books of poetry, *After We Lost Our Way* (National Poetry Series winner), *The Colors of Desire* (Carl Sandburg Literary Award), *Angels for the Burning,* and *The Last Incantations.* He has written two memoirs, *Turning Japanese* and *Where the Body Meets Memory,* and the novel *Famous Suicides of the Japanese Empire.* His book of poetry criticism is *Song for Uncle Tom, Tonto & Mr. Moto: Poetry & Identity.* He teaches in the Stonecoast MFA program and the VONA writers' conference for writers of color. www.davidmura.com.

SARA MARIE ORTIZ is an Acoma Pueblo memoirist, poet, performing artist, scholar, documentary filmmaker, and indigenous peoples advocate. She is a graduate of the Institute of American Indian Arts and holds an MFA in creative writing, with a concentration in creative nonfiction, from Antioch University Los Angeles. Her most recent publications include works of poetry and prose in *Mandala Journal, Ekleksographia, Drunken Boat, Kenyon Review, Yellow Medicine Review, Sentence, American Indian Graduate, Florida Review, New Poets of the American West,* and *Sing: Indigenous Poetry of the Americas.*

JASON SCHNEIDERMAN is the author of two books of poetry, *Striking Surface* and *Sublimation Point.* His essays and poems have appeared in numerous journals and anthologies including *Best American Poetry, Poetry London, Tin House,* and *The Penguin Book of the Sonnet.* He is an assistant professor of English at the Borough of Manhattan Community College.

RAVI SHANKAR is founding editor of *Drunken Boat* and author, publisher, or editor of eight books/chapbooks of poetry, including W. W. Norton's *Language for a New Century: Contemporary Poetry from Asia, the Middle East & Beyond.* He teaches in the MFA program at City University of Hong Kong and at Central Connecticut State University.

TESS TAYLOR was the 2010–11 Amy Clampitt Resident, and reviews books for NPR's *All Things Considered.* Her chapbook is *The Misremembered World.* Her recent book of poems is *The Forage House.*

index